SAFER SURGERY
FOR AFRICA

CHALLENGES AND SOLUTIONS

BRUCE BICCARD

BICCARD
PRESS

Dedication:

This book is dedicated to clinicians across Africa who, despite often dire and difficult circumstances, continue to provide loving care and selfless contributions to the understanding of maternal and surgical outcomes in Africa. Their contributions highlight the need for surgical health equity in Africa.

———

Safer Surgery for Africa: Challenges and Solutions
By Bruce Biccard

ISBN: 978-0-7961-5311-1 (Print)
ISBN: 978-0-7961-5312-8 (Digital)

Design by Gaelen Pinnock / polygram.co.za

Contents

List of abbreviations

APORG	African Perioperative Research Group
ART	antiretroviral therapy
ASOS	African Surgical Outcomes Study
ASOS-2	African Surgical OutcomeS-2 Trial
ASOS-Paeds	African Paediatric Surgical Outcomes Study
CanMEDS	Canadian Medical Education Directives for Specialists
CEMD	Confidential Enquiry into Maternal Deaths
CI	confidence interval
DALY	disability-adjusted life years
DCP3	Disease Control Priorities, 3rd edition
DRC	Democratic Republic of Congo
E8 programme	Malaria Elimination Eight Initiative
ENT	ear, nose and throat
ERAS	enhanced recovery after surgery
EPOCH	Enhanced Peri-Operative Care for High-risk patients study
ESMOE	Essential Steps in Managing Obstetric Emergencies
EuSOS	European Surgical Outcomes Study
ESM-Ketamine	Every Second Matters for Emergency and Essential Surgery-Ketamine
FTR	failure-to-rescue
GBD	global burden of disease
GP	general practitioner
HDI	Human Development Index
IHI	Institute for Healthcare Improvement
ISOS	International Surgical Outcomes Study
NCDI	non-communicable diseases and injuries
NHS	National Health Service
NIHR	National Institute of Health Research
NGO	non-governmental organisation
NSOAP	National Surgical, Obstetric and Anaesthesia Plan
ODA	operating department assistant
RRR	relative risk reduction
SAFE	Safer Anaesthesia From Education

CONTINUED ...

SAPORG	South African Perioperative Research Group
SDGs	Sustainable Development Goals
SSC	Surgical Safety Checklist
SSSA	Safe Surgery South Africa
TAC	Treatment Action Campaign
UCT	University of Cape Town
UNAIDS	Joint United Nations Programme on HIV/AIDS
VISION	Vascular events In noncardiac Surgery patIents cOhort evaluatioN
WFSA	World Federation of Societies of Anaesthesiologists
WHA	World Health Assembly
WHO	World Health Organisation

Preface

Preface

Surgery is required to save lives, cure cancers and improve the quality of one's life. Yet if you have surgery in Africa, these benefits come at a cost. Patients are twice as likely to die following surgery than if they had surgery elsewhere.[1] Sadly, a mother in Africa is 50 times more likely to die following a caesarean delivery than in the United States,[2] and children are 11 times more likely to die following surgery compared to children in high-income countries.[3] Nearly a billion people in Africa either do not get surgery when it is needed, receive surgery too late, or are at increased risk of death following surgery.

To many people in high-income countries, Africa may seem a world away, out of sight. In London in 2019, after I gave a lecture on these poor surgical outcomes, a delegate responded, 'So what?' I had missed an opportunity to clearly communicate this health travesty. The importance and relevance of these poor surgical outcomes in low-resource environments had been lost on some of the audience. This book is my response, as poor surgical outcomes in Africa will ultimately affect everyone, not just Africans.

When people from well-resourced environments venture into Africa, the dangers of the under-resourced healthcare system are superficially kept at arm's length by the potentially false security of medical insurance. Even if one can afford the best healthcare, actually being able to access it, on safari for example, is mired by numerous impediments. While these barriers to quality care may befall the privileged when they least expect it, they are an everyday occurrence for most who live in Africa and other under-resourced environments.

Good health is not dependent on pockets of excellence but on a functional, fully integrated healthcare system. The ability to provide quality surgical care is the backbone of any functional medical system. Surgery provides the building blocks of quality care across medical disciplines by ensuring that the specific skills and resources needed for emergency and critical care are available to all disciplines. The ability to provide quality healthcare for a population is therefore intricately tied to the ability to provide a functional surgical service. This integrative role of surgery and anaesthesia across disciplines is largely unseen for most people. Without a functional surgical system, we experience the poor outcomes evident in Africa. It is time that everyone understands the need for safe surgery and anaesthesia, otherwise we will never achieve health equity in Africa.

This is a story of surgery in Africa. It is a story of mothers, children and adults who die.[1-3] It is a story of poorly resourced and challenging surgical healthcare systems, which are further compromised by the sheer vastness of the continent. It is a story of inadequate funding and foreign aid, which is often inappropriate in allocation, further driving inequitable healthcare.

This is a story of society's blindness to the need for global surgical equity. Africa is neglected, but the continent will shine large in the coming decades. It will be of immense global importance, even to those who sit in beautiful homes miles away, because Africa (together with India) will account for nearly 80% of the global population by 2100, effectively making the two the centre of the universe for future generations. Ensuring the health and productivity of Africa should therefore be of importance to the world at large. Good health contributes tremendously to global productivity and conserves global funds that would otherwise be wasted on the management of poor patient outcomes associated with inadequate access to a holistic healthcare system. These funds could then contribute to other global priorities. Addressing the inequity of surgical health in Africa will thus go a long way to improving global health.

We know what needs to be done to reduce surgical inequity, but figuring out how to do it remains a challenge. There is tremendous learning that can help us overcome this challenge to deliver equitable surgical care, and these principles are discussed in this book. Some of them may be universal, extending beyond mothers and surgery in Africa, to other low- (and high-) resource environments. These lessons may have impact for broader surgical and global health, and therefore contribute to health equity globally.

To this end, *Safer Surgery for Africa* is accompanied by *Earth Cast* season 3, a podcast hosted by Olivia Taylor. I co-hosted the seven-episode season with Olivia, and in it we discussed the final draft of the book. My guests included experts you'll meet in the pages to come: Agya Prempeh, Sue Fawcus, Rupert Pearse, Nicky Kalafatis, Emmanuel

Makasa, John Meara, Lydia Cairncross, Wayne Morriss, Salome Maswime and Tinashe Chandauka. Their work is featured in this book, and their contributions align with our belief that global health is a collective responsibility. This is a story of the responsibilities that governments, funders, clinicians, patients, civil society, and the person in the street all need to simultaneously embrace and own if we truly want global health equity. Until we address the most basic physiological and health needs of our population, we will never be able to fully address the other planetary challenges facing the world.

I tell this story from an African perspective because I am familiar with the environment, but it is likely that a similar narrative is playing out across Asia, Oceania, and other low- and middle-income regions. Finally, this is a story of hope and a new dawn for medicine and surgical health in Africa, and the people who are leading this phenomenal change.

PART 1

Unnecessary surgical deaths

Introduction

Caesarean sections are the cornerstone of safe surgery in Africa – they save two lives, the mother and the child.

Sue Fawcus, *Earth Cast* S3E32

The death of a mother

S ue Fawcus, an emeritus professor of obstetrics and gynaecology at the University of Cape Town (UCT), is a doyen of obstetric outcomes. She was the head of obstetric services at Mowbray Maternity Hospital, a large maternity hospital in Cape Town, and the deputy chairperson of the National Committee for the Confidential Enquiry into Maternal Deaths (CEMD) in South Africa, where she has spent a vast amount of time reviewing and analysing maternal deaths related to caesarean sections. She is quite literally a guru in this field. And a brilliant surgeon. Another eminent anaesthesia colleague tells me that if a mother is bleeding out, you want Sue.

Sue is small in stature, steely in resolve, and extremely compassionate. I think her formidable character was forged by hard clinical exposure in trying conditions early in her career. As a young medical officer in the 1980s, she left the United Kingdom for Zimbabwe to do outreach work in rural district hospitals as part of her obstetric speciality training. She tells me of some of her early work in Masvingo in Zimbabwe. A mother had previously delivered five children safely. She'd been to an antenatal clinic, but considering her impressive obstetric history, it was considered appropriate for her to deliver at the district hospital, some 50 kilometres from a higher care obstetric facility. Her contractions started during the night but she had no transport and was concerned about leaving her children alone, so she decided to stay and deliver her baby at home. Unfortunately, she started to bleed. Her 11-year-old daughter quickly realised that her mother needed help, and left to ask the neighbours to tell the nearby clinic to send an ambulance. When the little girl returned home, her mother lay in a pool of blood surrounded by the younger children. She had succumbed to the bleeding.[4]

Bleeding is the most common cause of maternal mortality.

A mother bleeds out

I stood at Janet's bedside. She was as white as a sheet. In my professional capacity as a specialist anaesthesiologist, I'm comfortable with blood. When a patient starts to bleed out, my training allows me to relax and focus on what needs to be done. This time it was different. I wasn't the doctor, and this patient was a close friend. Janet's blood volume had drained out of her. The result was a cold, living person, so pale that she looked like a ghost. She was freezing despite the blankets pulled up around her neck, and her face had that swollen, puffy look that comes from pouring litres of clear resuscitation fluids into a patient's veins to keep the vessels open and carry the few remaining red blood cells around the body, to provide oxygen to the gasping, hypoxic cells. But thank goodness: Janet had made it.

Janet had been treated in a beautiful, modern private hospital in Durban, South Africa. The hospital was well resourced, with facilities and doctors who pretty much can and do perform every surgical procedure known to man. Private healthcare in South Africa is astoundingly good. As a patient, you can stay in a facility that looks more like a hotel than a hospital. It feels comfortable and smells clean. There is a pervasive air of competence that verges on arrogance. For patients, that's comforting. For me, as Janet's friend, I felt the relief of this palpable excess when I saw her.

I knew it had must have been touch and go. I had been an anaesthesiologist for a few years and I knew how quickly one can bleed out in childbirth, although I'd never expected to know someone who nearly did. Medicine is a small community in most African countries, and it wasn't surprising that I knew the anaesthesiologists who cared for Janet. They were good, undoubtedly on the top of their game. In most operations, a single anaesthesiologist will manage the care of a patient, no matter the severity of the surgical insult. Only in extraordinary situations such as Janet's is a second anaesthesiologist called for help. It is likely that these two exceptionally skilled anaesthesiologists, working in tandem in a well-resourced environment, with a specialist obstetrician and a dedicated theatre team, are what saved Janet's life.

It must have been crazy for the surgical team. Janet had delivered a beautiful baby girl, and in normal circumstances, the placenta would have succumbed to a gentle pull on the umbilical cord, and obediently followed the fetus out of the womb. Instead, the placenta stubbornly stuck, a condition known as placenta accreta. The placenta had grown into the muscle of the womb with no intention of ever letting go. This is rare, and stupid. The presence of the placenta in the womb means that the bleeding will never stop, because the womb cannot contract down, which is necessary to compress and clamp the bleeding vessels that were once the lifeblood of the fetus. The result is that the blood passing through the uterus just pours and pours out of the womb, instead of returning via the mother's veins to her heart for another trip around the body.

At term, about 10% of the mother's blood volume – 500ml per minute – passes through the uterus, providing the fetus with oxygen and nutrients. But if the uterus cannot contract down and clamp the vessels after birth, the result is a torrential flow of blood out of the severed veins of the placenta. At 500ml per minute, the mother will totally bleed out in under 10 minutes. This is postpartum haemorrhage, and it is terrifying. The problem is that we, the fantastic mammalian species of humans, have a fundamental design flaw. If for some reason, the bleeding from the placental bed cannot be stemmed, then the blood accumulates and forms big clots inside the womb. It is not necessarily externally visible, but it is potentially terminal. Clots in the uterus will further hamper it from contracting down completely. The vicious cycle continues as the vessels torn during delivery remain open, and the obedient heart continues to pump blood to the uterus, which continues to leak more blood into its cavity. Without quick medical and surgical intervention, it is a death sentence. With the devastating rapidity and volume of blood lost, the clotting factors that may have stemmed the blood loss from the open vessels also pour into the uterus. The body now does not even have the capacity to form a clot to block the open vessels.

Saving the mother requires skill and the decisiveness to act with conviction. Janet had simply faded out of consciousness, as the decreasing blood volume was simply insufficient to keep her brain alert. The surgeon knew that there were minutes before Janet would die if the uterine arteries were not tied off to stop the perfusion of the uterus and its relentless bleeding. This would be followed by a hysterectomy, as the placenta had no intention of letting go, and the womb itself was now literally a fatigued muscle. The womb had completed a marathon and was exhausted, but now was being asked to give another Herculean effort to clamp down and stop the bleeding. This was never going to happen.

Janet's husband consented to a hysterectomy while one of the anaesthesiologists put a tube into her airway to deliver oxygen. The other secured large-bore cannulae to pour fluids into her veins. It was precarious, but the synchronicity of an experienced team is evident at times like this. Everyone knows their role, and they work at breakneck speed. The surgeon moves decisively toward the offending uterine arteries to clamp them off so that no further blood will be spilled, and the anaesthesiologist provides oxygen, blood, and fluids, while possibly giving a little bit of help to the heart, so that some nutrients can make their way around the body and ensure that the heart, head, kidneys, and other vulnerable organs don't suffer irreversible injury or death before the bleeding is abated.

To save a mother, you need many skilled people, a decisiveness borne of expertise, the support of an experienced team and multiple resources. You need a midwife, a theatre, a surgeon, an anaesthesiologist, a theatre sister, a floor nurse, a paediatrician, equipment, monitors, cannulae, lines, fluids, blood, drugs. And you need to access all of this within minutes, or it will be too late.

My wife and I had just had our first child, a beautiful boy, and mere weeks later a friend of ours had had her first child, a beautiful girl, but had so nearly lost her life. In my privileged social circumstances, where we have access to all the necessary medical resources, I never expected that a friend of mine might die from bleeding following delivery. And she did not. She was saved by being in a well-resourced hospital, with an established team of healthcare professionals. In less-resourced environments, though, it is easy to see why mothers die nearly every two minutes. The fragility of our existence is only too evident in situations like this, but in poorer, less-resourced environments it is literally killing.

Personal experiences of a mother dying

The horrific nature of maternal deaths affects everyone who experiences them. Tinashe Chandauka is a Zimbabwean who studied medicine at UCT, and then went on to Oxford to complete his DPhil. I was fortunate enough to meet Tinashe during his internship, during our first attempt to set up a national surgical plan for South Africa. He is wise beyond his years and has become an inspiration to me. He is committed to improving medical outcomes in Africa, and was convinced that part of this journey involves improving safety practices. The event that set him on this path is recounted in the introduction to his DPhil submission at Oxford, on patient safety factors in the operating theatre:

My interest in safe obstetric surgery in South Africa began with the most humbling of events – a patient's death. As a medical student at the University of Cape Town, I took for granted that the world-class clinical medicine I was learning reflected how medicine functioned everywhere. I knew that severe resource constraints existed, but as a student I ultimately had no responsibility for the outcomes. I had no 'skin in the game'. However, my medical internship that followed in the Eastern Cape was a brutal introduction to medicine in a resource-limited environment marked by unpredictable deficiencies. Sometimes we had everything, then the next day we'd run out of drip needles.

One summer morning, the obstetric surgery team in charge of the elective surgeries started the day with an emergency drill on post-partum haemorrhage. I remember it so well because I was sweating from resuscitating a doll so thoroughly that, for a moment, I swear the pulse oximeter could actually measure some oxygen in its inanimate fingers. The humidity made the air thick and heavy. Our team went through all the steps: calling for help, the ABCs of resuscitation, establishing IV access, attaching monitors for mother and child, taking blood, giving drugs, reviewing progress and moving to increasingly invasive interventions to stop the bleeding. We debriefed and retired to the doctors' room before the first case began. That's when the shouting started. Two paramedics rushed an exhausted woman into the unit in a wheelchair. There was a commotion as they called out for help. Being veterans of the Eastern Cape, our obstetric team knew this could only mean a moribund patient was in urgent need of care. We took our places around her wheelchair, lifting her tired body onto a bed. I remember how she struggled to breathe and how cold and pale her hands were. This sort of thing stays with you, perhaps forever.

While several doctors and nurses put into practice what we had just learnt in the drill, I heard the senior obstetric registrar (chief resident equivalent) ask the paramedics for her notes and clinical handover. They shook their heads. 'Sorry doc,' they said. 'The midwives didn't give us notes. They are bringing them soon. They asked us to just bring her here as soon as possible ... Apparently, she got worse all of a sudden and they called us.'

We were all shocked that they had left her notes behind, but we had to proceed with the resuscitation. Within fifteen minutes our patient, Ms X, had IV access, blood ordered and was delivering her child in the labour ward. Ms X was so fatigued she could not apply any effort to push her baby, and we had to use forceps to assist her. She delivered a floppy child who was rushed to the neonatal ICU next door. But Ms X kept on bleeding. The obstetric registrars and consultant battled to find the source of the bleeding and resorted to using a balloon tamponade to stop the haemorrhage. Oxytocin simply wouldn't work. A decision was made to operate and the team prepared Ms X for theatre. We gave her blood, took blood gases and kept resuscitating her. When she lost consciousness, we intubated her and took her to theatre. We knew we could still save her life by arresting the haemorrhage. An anaesthetic registrar attempted to place an arterial line to measure blood pressure. Minutes turned into tens of minutes until her consultant was called. In the red mist of clinical combat, the trainee had become fixated on the arterial line. Once the consultant arrived, the trainee could focus on the rest of the induction.

Unfortunately, Ms X developed cardiac arrest and despite an hour-long on-table CPR, she died. Our team was devastated and shocked. As we reeled from the shock, a nurse from the community delivery facility that had referred her arrived with her notes. A diligent night shift student nurse had charted her prolonged labour and even marked with red ink on the partogram the points where Ms X crossed the alarm lines. It was not clear why no action was taken. Ms X was overweight, but other than that she had no underlying condition. The loss of her life was acutely felt by the district service. The maternal morbidity and mortality audit concluded that her death was preventable, and that it was the result of several system and human factor errors lining up. I went to bed that night knowing that I needed to use my doctoral degree at Oxford to do something about this.[5]

Sadly, death after childbirth is not uncommon. Compared to the nearly 13 000 people who died in Africa from Ebola since 1976,[6] between 2014 and 2017 there were in excess of 190 000 maternal deaths in Africa annually, or 778 000 deaths over those four years.[7] Globally, about 300 000 women died every year during this period, or a total of nearly 1.25 million deaths over the four-year period. A mother died following childbirth every 1.75 minutes, 24 hours a day, 365 days a year during this period.

Why did these mothers die? And what was different that my friend survived massive haemorrhage? Are these post-caesarean deaths symptomatic of a larger societal health problem related to surgical care? Can we save mothers with simple healthcare strategies?

I hope to answer these questions in this book by introducing you to the work of colleagues who have been touched by these personal experiences of death and have worked towards providing surgical equity – and health equity – for all.

Mothers dying

Maternal deaths over time

To start to answer these questions, one must go back to the historical origins of tracking deaths. It was the Swedish clergy who started recording all the births and deaths within their parishes as far back as 1749, which very quickly led to the registration of the entire Swedish population.[8] This morphed into a national database or *Tabellverket*, where the registrar general started tracking national mortality statistics.[9] As early as 1751, maternal deaths in Sweden were being recorded accurately, reliably, and without interruption, and have been ever since.[8]

Counting maternal deaths has demonstrated our tremendous progress in maternal health. In Sweden, in the 230 years between 1750 and 1980, maternal mortality fell 150-fold, with two-thirds of the improvement seen in the eighteenth and nineteenth centuries. Death registrations started later in England (1837),[8] and maternal mortality statistics were included from 1857 onwards,[9] although the UK's improvement was not quite as impressive as Sweden's.

Part of the success in maternal outcomes reflects an improving social status over time, as social status confers a survival advantage and is a clear determinant of health.[10] It has resulted in tumbling infant and maternal mortality. The real benefit of social status is seen within the aristocracy, the beneficiaries of the ultimate social status. It certainly was not a 'misfortune to be a great ladie', as fewer than 5% of all aristocratic mothers died in childbirth between 1558 and 1959.[11] Indeed, it was more dangerous to be married to Henry VIII than to bear his child. It is incredible to think that Queen Victoria had nine children and survived.

Tracking the maternal mortality in England and Wales showed the improvement in the rate as society progressed through the 1800s, but then it started to slow, plateauing between 1880 and 1930.[8,12] Maternal mortality was still running at a horrifying 500 deaths per 100 000 births during this period.[12] Although improvements in quality of care had reduced the number of haemorrhagic maternal deaths in England and Wales, with a 56% reduction in haemorrhagic deaths between 1874 and 1926, there was no real reduction in overall maternal mortality. This was because of the increasing problem of sepsis associated with delivery, driven by a lack of antibiotics at the time.[13]

Tracking maternal deaths nationally resulted in some pivotal moments in improving maternal outcomes. At the simplest level, counting deaths made it possible to identify poorly performing areas. By the early 1930s, the maternal mortality rate ran at 460 per 100 000 in the UK,[8] although it varied tremendously across the country. Rochdale, an industrial town in the greater Manchester area of northwest England, stuck out like a sore thumb. It was a textile powerhouse with navigable canals that ensured access to the sea trade routes, but this industrial star also had the highest maternal mortality in England, with 900 deaths per 100 000 births, nearly double the national average.[14] The social deprivation of most women in Rochdale was not enough to explain the poor maternal outcomes. Andrew Topping, the newly appointed Medical Officer of Health in Rochdale, was clearly unhappy with the status quo, and described the obstetric management of some general practitioners as 'a little short of murder'.[14] He was well aware that Rochdale was a slight to medicine and obstetrics in England, and that this reflected negatively on his position. He responded with an obstetric quality improvement project, which became known as the 'Rochdale experiment'. This included establishing antenatal clinics and a puerperal sepsis ward, ensuring that midwives and general practitioners met to discuss patients, and that the programme was supported by a specialist obstetrician together with educational and public meetings. Between 1930 and 1935, the impact of his project to improve the standard of obstetric care was a resounding success, as demonstrated by the maternal mortality rate falling from 900 to 170 per 100 000, and then holding steady.[14] While improving social status is often a factor in better health outcomes over time (famously demonstrated by Sir Michael Marmot),[10] the brilliance of Andrew Topping's experiment was that the social status did not really change in Rochdale during this period, thus demonstrating the massive beneficial effect of improving the quality of obstetric care on maternal mortality, even in a socially deprived environment. Indeed, these were not fancy interventions, but simply 'an ordinary standard of good obstetric practice, not necessarily at the level of the hospital specialist', and this was shown 'to have a *profoundly* beneficial effect in societies that still suffer high maternal mortality'.[14] The Rochdale experiment produced an 80% relative risk reduction (RRR) in maternal mortality in a five-year period. Such an impact on maternal mortality can only be dreamt of today. The intervention delivered in the Rochdale experiment had focused on improving the quality of maternal care provided by birth attendants.[12] Andrew Topping's simple yet appropriate view of health was later recognised when, in 1950, he went on to became dean of the London School of Hygiene and Tropical Medicine, famous for its global public health initiatives and leadership.

The RRR provides data on the efficacy of an intervention, and Andrew Topping's intervention and RRR of 80% is simply remarkable. It's closer to the realm of primary prevention interventions, such as vaccine immunisation programmes. The RRR for mortality in these interventions is huge, and often well over 90%. It means we can almost certainly prevent death. And this is what we saw with the roll-out of vaccinations for Covid-19. Essentially, most vaccines are absolute lifesavers. However, once you get into the messy world of clinical medicine, the number of factors impacting a patient's outcome are many. A mother who is bleeding after surgery, for example, could die for a number of reasons. A delay in treating the bleeding may result in irreversible changes to coagulation that cause torrential bleeding. The mother may die because blood or the blood products needed to treat her were not available, or the surgeon was busy with another operation, or she got to surgery but died on induction of anaesthesia because she had already bled out too much. She could have a great operation but continue to bleed slowly into the abdomen, eventually drifting out of consciousness and dying in her sleep. A myriad of factors can result in a mother dying, and for this reason, most interventions nowadays have a much lower chance of decreasing maternal mortality on their own. The result is that in clinical medicine, the RRR associated with an intervention for mortality is much lower, as there are so many processes that may ultimately kill a patient. Realistically, in clinical medicine, when managing complications on the ward, we now get excited when an intervention has an RRR of 30%. That means an effective intervention is likely to only save about one in three from death, because in the other two cases our attempts will be thwarted by unrelated contributors on the pathway to mortality.

It is possible for interventions in quality improvement to achieve a higher RRR, if they simultaneously and successfully address more than one potential pathway to mortality as shown in the Rochdale experiment, which targeted clinics and wards, clinicians, and education. This is appropriately demonstrated in the World Maternal Antifibrinolytic (WOMAN) Trial, a large trial in women who bled following delivery. Here, a drug known as tranexamic acid was used to prevent the breakdown of early clots, thereby preventing ongoing bleeding. Death due to bleeding was significantly reduced in the patients who received the tranexamic acid, falling from 1.9% to 1.5%, or a 19% RRR, with a 95% confidence interval (CI) of zero (no benefit) to a 35% RRR reduction in bleeding.[15] While the study shows a 19% RRR, the CI demonstrates the spread of certainty for the actual efficacy of the intervention. Basically, the absolute best efficacy for this intervention is a RRR of 35%, and the best estimate of efficacy (which is the trial result) is just under 20%. Although most would agree that administering tranexamic acid is essential for a woman who is bleeding post-delivery, this is not a panacea. The impact of any single intervention is potentially far more limited than effecting a number of quality improvement initiatives addressing various factors associated with mortality, as in the Rochdale experiment. A woman who is bleeding after a caesarean delivery needs a functional healthcare system to ensure that she gets timeous and appropriate care to stem the flow of blood. In low-quality healthcare systems, we are likely to get a better return on improving outcomes when we have many interventions that work across many parts of a dysfunctional system. Giving tranexamic acid alone may save a bleeding mother, but if one is unable to provide the supporting surgical care necessary to remove any clots or remaining placental products from the cavity of the uterus so that it can contract down, or even to remove the uterus to halt bleeding if the uterus is too tired to contract, many more mothers will die because of these limitations. In high-quality healthcare systems, where the many parts of the system are functional, people spend more time looking for new single interventions to nudge towards further improved patient outcomes. In contrast, in low-quality healthcare systems we need to pay attention to the entire healthcare system if we want to improve patient outcomes.

Another famous example of the impact of improving quality of care through multiple interventions, is Florence Nightingale's work in the Crimean War, between 1854 and 1856. This, too, resulted in an unbelievably high RRR for mortality in a complex environment. Nightingale was a nursing pioneer, a data tracker and statistician of note. The British soldiers from the Crimean front travelled across the Black Sea to Scutari Hospital, near Constantinople in Turkey, where Florence was working with a team of about 40 other voluntary nurses. In February of 1855, 43% of the arriving soldiers died in the hospital. Florence was convinced that there were five factors contributing to these deaths: overcrowding; poor ventilation; sewerage; and a lack of cleanliness and hospital comforts. From her previous nursing experience in London, she calculated that the patients in Scutari had about a quarter of the space of patients in London hospitals. She could not change the overcrowding, so she and her team set about addressing the other four factors in March 1855: they opened the windows, removed the rubbish, buried the dead animals, flushed the sewers, washed the clothing, and provided eating utensils. By June, a mere three months later, the mortality had fallen to 2%.[16] That's a *95% RRR* for mortality.

A massive reduction, produced by the power of simple, generalisable interventions that tackled multiple quality-of-care issues head on. These interventions simultaneously affected multiple potential pathways to death.

The army's principal medical officer could not accept that such a massive swing in mortality could have been effected by Florence and her team of nurses, and he claimed that it was due to the condition in which the soldiers had arrived. But Florence was both a genius and a force to be reckoned with. To rebut the principal medical officer, she compared Scutari's improved mortality rate to two groups in worst- and best-case medical scenarios. In the worst-case-scenario group were soldiers who were too sick or injured to be moved from the battlefront to Scutari. At the front, they faced a mortality rate of 27%. But when Scutari was at its worst, before Florence's interventions, the hospital had a mortality rate of 43%. In other words, the soldiers at the battlefront who were considered too far gone to survive the boat trip to Scutari, were actually *less likely to die* than soldiers who went to the hospital. This meant that the massively reduced mortality rate was not due to soldiers arriving at the hospital in a better physical condition than those left at the battlefront. Florence then compared Scutari's best outcomes, seen by June 1855, with the outcomes in the desirable London hospitals. Astonishingly, the mortality in these London hospitals was higher than that in Scutari after the nursing team made improvements in care.

Florence Nightingale had used numbers to support her case, just like the Swedish clergy had used numbers to track their parishioners.[17] She showed a link between her sanitary interventions and mortality in the languishing soldiers. She had decreased exposure to many pathogens causing sepsis on various surfaces across the ward. She tracked the outcomes in circular pie charts that she had developed, known as Coxcomb charts. Florence was providing real time feedback on the success of the interventions to her team. She had her finger on the pulse of mortality in Scutari Hospital, and she could respond timeously as a result. Her leadership inspired her team to continue its impressive work.

Getting on top of sepsis was to result in another period of reducing maternal mortality across England and Wales between 1932 and 1952. Between 1880 and 1930, sepsis had been limiting the reduction in maternal mortality. However, the success in managing sepsis between 1932 and 1952 resulted in a swing from sepsis been the main driver of maternal mortality[13] to bleeding becoming the bigger problem. This was despite the gains made in decreasing haemorrhagic deaths between 1932 and 1952 with the introduction of drugs to contract the uterus down, and blood transfusions. The introduction of the Confidential Enquiry into Maternal Deaths (CEMD) in the 1950s in the UK, identified the retained placenta after delivery as one of the main drivers of haemorrhagic deaths.[13]

While Florence Nightingale had started to improve mortality by improving the quality of care delivered in her wards, a nurse across the Atlantic was making her mark by taking care to the patient and demonstrating that early access to care could decrease mortality. Clara Barton's initiative was to take horse-drawn 'ambulances' to soldiers in the battlefield during the American Civil War in the 1860s. Later she went on to establish the American Red Cross.

In the early 1950s in Cape Town, South Africa, mothers were still receiving care too late and were dying at home. So, care was taken to the mothers with the introduction of the 'flying squads' in September 1953. Just as Clara Barton had improved the outcomes for soldiers at the battlefront by getting care to them early, the obstetric flying squads also decreased maternal mortality by taking timeous obstetric care to mothers in their homes.[18] The squads included young obstetric doctors, nurses or midwives, and medical students, who travelled by road to mothers in distress. Just as the UK CEMD had identified the retained placenta as a major driver of maternal mortality in early 1950, so too in the Western Cape there was an appreciation that 'the beds available for routine and emergency obstetric care [were] grossly [insufficient in number] and a large proportion of the mothers [were] not aware of the advantages of competent ante-partum and intra-partum care, which, moreover, [was] not always attainable'.[19] The reasons given for the flying squads are as relevant today in low-resource environments as they were in Cape Town 70 years ago.

If you want to get a feel for what it was like to be part of the 1950s flying squad at that time, the District Six Museum has an excellent photographic display. Proud midwives wearing starched uniforms stand next to their shiny, green, short-wheelbase Land Rovers. My mother was a midwife in one of the obstetric flying squads, and she's told me of how she would arrive with a doctor and enter a dark, smoked-filled room with walls covered in soot, to find a mother lying on a kitchen table in a pool of blood. If that was the situation at home, we can understand why mothers had little chance of survival if they still needed to travel to the hospital for treatment. It is unsurprising, then, that the impact of the flying squads was huge. In the first 33 months following their introduction, there were 192 calls, of which 165 (86%) were for postpartum haemorrhage (classic retained placenta stuff, the same killer as in the 1952 UK CEMD), with six deaths (3.1%) in total.[19] All the mothers that died, had died from haemorrhage. Three were dead when the squad arrived, and the other three died within 15 minutes of their arrival.[19] Those six mothers had no chance, as most of their blood volume had already been lost through the open vessels of the uterus, just like the woman who died at home in Masvingo, Zimbabwe. The success of the flying squad was tangible, as shown by Cape Town's amazing fall in maternal mortality, with a nearly 80% RRR in maternal mortality between 1953 and 1959.

YEAR	MATERNAL MORTALITY RATE PER 100 000 DELIVERIES
1953	301
1954-1956	199
1957-1959	66

Table 1. Maternal mortality in Cape Town following the introduction of flying squads in 1953 [20]

Increasing access to care by taking midwifery to the mother had a massive impact on maternal outcomes. The increase in access decreased failure-to-rescue cases, and the good midwifery services improved the quality of care given.

Sadly, the maternal mortality in Cape Town in the 1950s and in Rochdale in 1937 is lower than the present-day maternal mortality in sub-Saharan Africa, which currently runs at 546 deaths per 100 000 live births.[21]

This is equivalent to the UK in 1900, or Sweden in 1880. Increasing both access to care and the quality of care is likely to have a massive impact on maternal mortality in sub-Saharan Africa.

Caesarean deliveries and the inverse care law

Sue Fawcus' first caesarean section was in a district hospital in Zimbabwe, for a case of cephalopelvic disproportion – basically the baby was not going to make it out of the pelvis vaginally, as the head was too big for the pelvic outlet. At about midnight, after the porter had fetched the patient, he waded across the river to turn on the generator to power up the operating theatre for the procedure. A final-year medical student administered the spinal anaesthetic, and then donated some of her own O-positive blood, as the mother's haemoglobin was already low. The medical student was not only the anaesthetist and the blood donor, but also the paediatrician, quickly moving round to 'catch' the baby after Sue delivered it, so that she could dry, warm, and stimulate the newborn to breathe. This mother and child had faced many hazards, but fortunately both made it through unscathed. This despite having no dedicated anaesthesia or paediatric care, amongst numerous other risk factors that included potential blood reactions and a relatively inexperienced medical team. In most district hospitals at the time, the same doctor administered the spinal anaesthetic and then went on to perform the surgery, with an experienced nurse monitoring the patient's vital signs and anaesthesia.

In resource-limited environments, healthcare workers at the coalface are continually balancing risks. Here, Sue had a mother needing a caesarean section. An unnecessary delay could have resulted in the deaths of both mother and child, so the procedure had to be done in circumstances that were far from ideal: an anaemic patient, a young doctor in training for obstetric specialisation, a medical student conducting the anaesthetic and the neonatal resuscitation, and no back-up expertise for either. The alternative was an unforgiving trip to the hospital in Harare, predominantly on a dirt road with only a little bit of tar towards the end of the journey. Easily five hours of difficult travelling. Five hours was too long. Sue was battling the perennial problem in resource-poor environments: limited and difficult access to an appropriate level of care, at a time when the patient's needs were most acute.[22]

We have seen that increasing access to and quality of care improves outcomes. Tudor Hart wrote 50 years ago that 'the availability of good medical care tends to vary with the need for it in the population served'.[23] Stated another way, 'disadvantaged populations need more healthcare than advantaged populations, but receive less'.[24] This is the inverse care law. This is the dilemma that Sue faced in her early days as a young doctor in Zimbabwe and a scenario that she has subsequently seen play out countless times when reviewing maternal mortality in confidential enquiries across her career. When one now asks Sue to explain her understanding of maternal outcomes, she states it clearly around the principles of the inverse care law:

> skilled personnel are concentrated in urban areas doing unnecessary caesarean sections in low-risk women, whereas poor women in rural settings have necessary caesarean sections performed too late, by less skilled personnel, because of poverty and barriers to access, and

patients die. Reading through cases of women who die from bleeding at caesarean section is tear jerking because the majority need not have died.

The inverse care law is primarily about the inequity (and injustice) in healthcare that results in the unfair social inequalities in health.[24] Those with the least means, get the least care. A graph of the inverse care law is shown in Figure 1, and you'll see that, as social status and available resources improve, so does the care, until it plateaus at a high level. Then, in extreme circumstances of over-servicing, an excess of care actually results in unnecessary harm, seen on the right of the graph.

This phenomenon was already prevalent in maternal health in the 1930s in the UK and Sweden. The over-servicing of 'high society' was so excessive that one would have expected the maternal mortality to continue to fall, but it didn't. Although over-servicing did at least realise some of the benefits of better obstetric management, with plummeting haemorrhagic deaths in the UK,[13] the increased access to maternal care among the wealthy also resulted in many inappropriate and unnecessary obstetric interventions, causing septic complications at a time when effective antibiotic treatment was not yet available.[8]

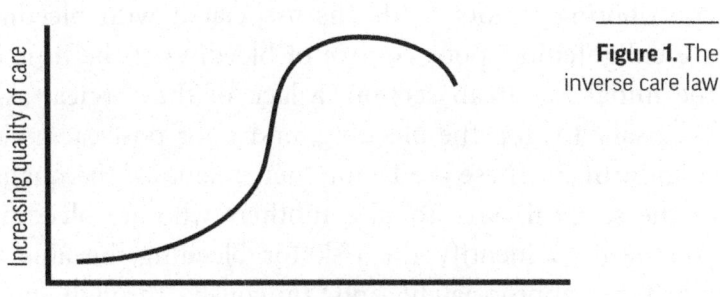

Figure 1. The inverse care law

One may expect to see the same with unnecessary caesarean sections in the 'too posh to push' society of today.

Nowadays, aseptic techniques in labour, along with the prevention of prolonged labour and antibiotics, have decreased septic deaths following caesarean sections, leaving haemorrhage as the leading cause of maternal mortality globally, with nearly 45 000 deaths in 2013,[25] or one woman dying every 12 minutes from maternal haemorrhage. While haemorrhage is only one of the leading causes of death in high-income countries, it is *the* leading cause of death in low-resource environments,[26] and it is also the leading cause of post-caesarean mortality in Africa, contributing to nearly half of all maternal deaths.[2]

Surgery not only needs to be available to stop ongoing haemorrhage following caesarean section, but may also be needed to stop bleeding following vaginal delivery, when hysterectomy is required as a therapeutic intervention. When one considers the proportional contribution of vaginal and operative deliveries to haemorrhagic deaths in mothers, the South African Saving Mothers report for 2008–2010 states that bleeding associated with vaginal delivery was responsible for nearly three quarters of the haemorrhagic maternal deaths,[26] because of an inability to provide access to surgical care in these patients.

For the mothers who had caesarean deliveries, the contributing factors to deaths associated with bleeding are enlightening: poor control of bleeding at the time of the initial caesarean section, a lack of the surgical skill necessary to stop the bleeding, and poor post-caesarean monitoring.[26] These are factors dependent on the quality of the surgical care. To save mothers who are bleeding, you need to identify the risk for bleeding, be able to intervene appropriately and timeously through non-surgical interventions (such as removal of the placenta, or providing drugs, uterine massage, and blood) and you need the ability to provide surgical control of the bleeding if necessary. Surgical interventions may include removal of remaining placental parts from the uterus, ligation of the uterine arteries feeding the uterus, and hysterectomy. The poor control of bleeding at the time of the caesarean section, and the lack of surgical skills, suggest limited training and practical surgical experience.

Tracking the volume of caesarean sections performed in a population provides an important insight into the twin requirements of the minimum practical experience necessary for quality care, and the appropriate access to surgical obstetric care necessary for safe maternal care. The sweet spot is about 19 caesarean sections per 100 live deliveries. If one cannot provide at least this number of caesarean sections, then maternal mortality increases (Figure 2).[27] In Africa, we cannot provide this number of caesarean sections per 100 live deliveries. In fact, we only provide about a quarter of that, at five caesarean sections per 100 live deliveries. This low number of caesarean

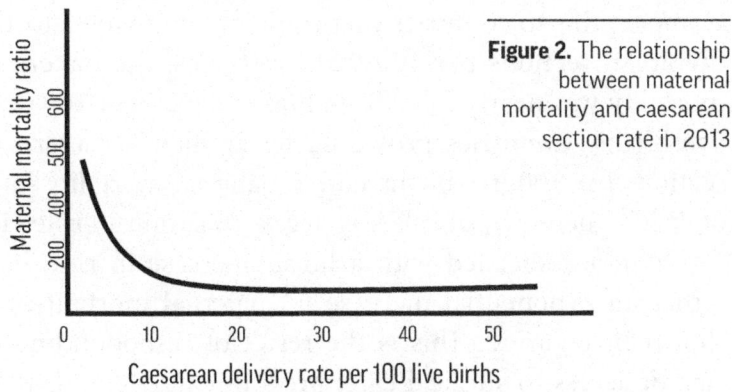

Figure 2. The relationship between maternal mortality and caesarean section rate in 2013

sections reflects the combined problems of insufficient access to surgical maternal care, insufficient resources to provide surgery and insufficient skills necessary to deliver quality surgical care. And just as maternal mortality increases with decreasing access to caesarean sections, so too does neonatal mortality increase. This is the situation for most of Africa.[28]

Limited access to caesarean sections results in women dying unnecessarily at home, as happened to the mother in Masvingo, or women being operated upon by teams with limited skills and insufficient practical exposure, such as Sue's first caesarean section outside Harare. Literally every operation is a risk, with unnecessary deaths on the table. And it shouldn't have to be like this. Surgery is a key component of maternal health. If at least 19 caesarean deliveries are required per 100 live births to maximise maternal and neonatal health, then it is reasonable to suggest that surgery accounts for at least 19% of maternal obstetric health. Unfortunately, poor maternal outcomes increase exponentially as access to surgery is curtailed. For example, in 2013, countries that were able to provide between 19 and 27 caesarean sections per 100 live births had a maternal mortality rate of 36 per 100 000 live births. Compare this to countries that could only provide 7 to 19 caesarean sections per 100 000 live births: the maternal mortality was nearly four times higher at 137 per 100 000 live births. Countries providing fewer than 7 caesarean sections per 100 live births had a maternal mortality rate of 463.[27] Therefore, decreasing access to surgical obstetric care is not associated with a linear increase in risk, but rather an exponential increase in maternal mortality, as shown in Figure 2. This is the result of compounding a lack of access to surgical care: predominantly emergency caesarean deliveries are provided by surgical teams with inadequate surgical exposure and/or insufficient resources necessary to deliver quality surgical care. And these simple demonstrations of lost lives do not even consider the massive impact of losing a mother and young adult within a family, the broader community and a country.[29] Indeed, the proportional contribution of surgery to maternal health probably far exceeds 19%.

Although tracking maternal mortality is grim, it has the power to identify areas of need, and the impact of access and quality of care on outcomes. It has allowed us to understand the non-surgical and surgical contributions to maternal and neonatal health. Tracking maternal mortality allowed Andrew Topping to demonstrate the powerful effect of quality of care on maternal outcomes in Rochdale, and it allowed the Cape Town flying squad to improve maternal outcomes by increasing access to early care. Tracking maternal mortality has also allowed us to understand the need for a minimum number of surgical deliveries to ensure that the entire obstetric package of care is sufficient to keep mothers safe and optimise the outcomes for both mother and child.

Surgery in Africa

The excess deaths following surgery in Africa

Surgery, of course, includes far more than caesarean deliveries. It is about comprehensive care across medical disciplines. But all surgeries are about balancing risk and benefit. Surgery is indicated when the net benefit exceeds the risk to the patient, and that risk includes death. The worst-case scenario would be 100% mortality associated with surgery. That is, every patient that has surgery dies. Unbelievably, in the history of surgery, there is an English surgeon with an infamous 300% mortality, for an operation performed in the 1840s. John Liston amputated a leg with such haste (as anaesthesia and analgesia were yet to feature in surgical care) that he cut through his surgical assistant's fingers at the same time. Both the patient and the assistant died from surgical site sepsis (which, incidentally, remains the leading killer following non-obstetric surgeries to this day), and a spectator collapsed and died after witnessing the ordeal.[30] Fortunately, surgery is now extremely safe. Over the last century, perioperative mortality has decreased over a hundredfold. In Europe, in-hospital mortality runs at an average of 3% following all elective surgeries.[31] This may sound high, but it includes all the really big cancer surgeries, where the majority of patients would almost certainly die without surgery. Unfortunately, these surgical benefits are not available to all.

Rupert Pearse is the lead intensivist at Queen Mary University of London. He shot to fame in 2012 after leading the European Surgical Outcomes Study (EuSOS), a snapshot study of in-hospital mortality following surgery across Europe.[31] It led to some controversy because, after risk adjustment, it appeared that when compared to the UK, patients were more than twice as likely to die following surgery in Ireland and about five times more likely to die in Latvia. It is unlikely that this is actually the case, but that is another issue, based on numbers and sampling. The important point was that surgical outcomes varied across countries, and your surgical destiny (and mortality) could be determined merely by your place of residence. I had the good fortune of hearing Rupert present the results in London in 2012 and was struck by the study's simplicity. Being a nerd, I wanted to replicate the study in South Africa to understand our surgical outcomes. Rupert willingly shared all his study materials and resources, and we conducted the study successfully.[32]

Almost at the same time that our work was published in 2015, the Lancet Commission for Global Surgery released its Global Surgery 2030 report.[33] It was a clarion call for increasing safe surgical and anaesthesia care necessary to support global health equity. The report proposed global indicators of surgical performance to ensure that 80% of the world's population would have access to safe and affordable surgery by 2030. These included access to surgery, volume of operations, the workforce constitution, tracking mortality (naturally!), and the financial burden of accessing surgical care. We knew from Rupert's work in Europe and ours in South Africa that these indicators were not readily available in all environments, so it was difficult to know what surgery was happening, and what the surgical outcomes were across the globe, but we were primed to respond to Lancet's call. We established the African Surgical Outcomes Study (ASOS), a continental study to document the current state of surgery in Africa. We adopted the study model that Rupert had developed to document global surgical outcomes,[34] which would allow for global comparisons with the African data.

The ASOS data were distressing to say the least. From the nearly 250 hospitals in 25 countries across Africa, each hospital conducted on average only 29 operations per week, yet each hospital was serving a population of nearly a million people, with less than one specialist per 100 000 population delivering this service. With such a limited surgical system in Africa to support such a vast population, it was unsurprising that post-surgery mortality in Africa was twice the global average.[1] The ASOS findings challenge us to address the drivers behind the deaths of all surgical patients in Africa.

The lack of health equity in Africa

Global health is well documented on the 'Our world in data' website (https://ourworldindata. org/health-meta), and from their findings we see that life expectancy is increasing, and child and maternal mortality are falling across all countries. The relative difference in health outcomes between countries is also falling, which means that society is moving towards greater health equality. The clarity of the progress made in health is well described in Steven Pinker's book *Enlightenment Now* (2018).[35] However, we must not be fooled. Although all graphs show decreasing gaps between income groups, we are still a long way from population health equality, especially if you consider that the mortality following caesarean delivery in Africa is 50 times higher than that of high-income countries.[2]

The real issue about health is not about equality, but equity. Equality speaks to all individuals or groups of people having access to the best treatment. We could consider the increase in life expectancy and fall in mortality as markers of increasing equality. However, this is not equity. Health equity, if achieved, means that each person, despite their different circumstances, has access to the resources and opportunities needed to receive the best treatment necessary to good outcomes.[36] So while equality is increasing, equity is certainly not. In Africa, for example, not all patients can access the treatment needed; it is the region with the lowest global health workforce at the nursing and midwifery level, and at a physician level, with 12.4 and 2.7 per 10 000 population respectively.[37] Compare this to the global nursing and midwifery ratio of 28.6, and physician ratio at 13.9.[37] Africa has less than half of the global average of nurses and midwives, and less than a fifth of the average number of physicians. This means that it is impossible for the workforce to adequately treat all patients. In addition, the resources available to these healthcare professionals are also insufficient to treat all the patients, while some resources are completely absent, negating some surgical therapeutic options completely. This is inequity.

While mortality and life expectancy numbers may demonstrate increasing equality, I will demonstrate, with surgical examples, how they hide the inequity in health and, in particular, how they hide the inequity in surgical care that is compromising the health of the entire population in less-resourced environments. This is because surgery is required to ensure complete health coverage across all disease categories: maternal and child health, noncommunicable and communicable diseases, and trauma. I will demonstrate why there is a need for more and better surgical care in Africa (and other low- and middle-income countries) if we are to advance towards health equity. The foundations are to be found in the Lancet Commission for Global Surgery recommendations for safe surgery, which include:

1. access to timely surgery, in a facility that can conduct a caesarean section, a laparotomy and manage an open fracture within two hours
2. a specialist workforce of at least 20 specialists per 100 000 population
3. the ability to conduct at least 5000 surgical procedures per 100 000 population, and
4. protection against impoverishing and catastrophic expenditure through out-of-pocket expenditure necessary for surgical care.[33]

Too little surgery

I t was only through the Covid-19 pandemic that the problem of too little surgery was felt by patients and families in high-income countries. With the overwhelming hospital admissions, and the critical care expansion necessary to accommodate the critically ill Covid-19 patients, outpatient visits were curtailed and elective surgery came to a grinding halt. Many of us now have personal experiences of people whose cancers progressed to the point that they were incurable, and palliative care was all that could be offered. This is the result of a health system that could not cope, and a surgical system under duress. The time to full surgical recovery following Covid-19 is years away, and the potential impact on cancers and patient prognoses is now globally devastating.[38]

The problem in Africa and other low-resource environments is that cancers progressing due to a lack of surgical capacity is a norm, not just a Covid-19 phenomenon as it was in high-income countries. It can be agony for the surgeon, and my most visceral experience of this was watching a colleague become visibly distressed at the sight of the emergency surgical board. This electronic board shows bookings for the operating theatre, and highlights the urgency of the emergency cases in the triage colours from red, to orange, to yellow, to green. My colleague's patient had been on the board for days, waiting to get treated for a hernia – a defect in the abdominal wall with bowel pushing through the defect. It's a potentially benign pathology that can be easily managed with surgery, but for that reason the patient got repeatedly bumped down the priority list by red and orange cases throughout the day and night. This is inevitable when there are more patients than operating theatres. In the meantime, the hernia became obstructed, and the extravasated bowel had begun to swell, so that the bowel could not reduce and return into the abdomen. The rising pressure was decreasing the perfusion of the herniated bowel, and it was dying. My colleague had made a last attempt to get her patient into theatre, but it was not to be. The theatres were full with higher priority cases. What had started as a simple hernia was ultimately going to kill him, as he was now too sick to survive surgery. The realisation of this lost opportunity was too much for my colleague, and she broke down in tears next to the board. Her only option now was to give the patient morphine and keep him comfortable. Abdominal sepsis of the bowel has a devastating outcome, but it is not an uncommon scenario in a low-resource environment.

The 11-year-old child who sat next to her dead

mother lying in a pool of blood is another example of a bigger problem in healthcare in Africa. Limited access to surgery has devastating implications. People die at home for predominantly two reasons: either they can't get to hospital for surgical care, or they are unaware that many home deaths are unacceptable and unwarranted. When people frequently die at home due to limited access to surgical care, it essentially normalises inadequate access and poor outcomes within the community. Some patients may also delay their presentation to the hospital out of a fear of surgery and anaesthesia. These prevailing belief systems may be compounded by observations that people die after surgery, especially in environments where there is a high case-fatality rate. This is likely to exist in Africa, where mortality following caesarean section is 50 times higher than in high-income countries, and mortality following adult surgery is twice the global average.[1,2] These observations can be incorrectly interpreted as 'surgery kills', but they are the result of patients presenting too late for surgery, and surgery being performed in a low-quality environment due to limited resources.

It is estimated that a functional healthcare system needs to be able to provide 5000 surgical procedures in an operating room per 100 000 population.[33] Based on data from large observational studies,[1,31,34,39,40] one can get a fairly good picture of surgical volume delivered across Africa, and more broadly in countries across the range of the Human Development Index (HDI), as shown in Table 2.[41] This is thanks to the great work by the UK's NIHR Unit on Global Surgery, and Dmitri Nepogodiev, who curated and analysed these data. The number of surgical procedures performed across Africa is nearly equivalent to the average seen across all low-income countries globally.

The number of operations performed is low, really low. It's at least 10 times lower than the minimum for acceptable surgical provision. Lower-middle-income countries don't do much better, only achieving a fifth of the minimum acceptable volume of surgery for the population, while in upper-middle-income countries, a fifth of the population *do not* receive the minimum acceptable volume of surgery.

REGION	SURGICAL CASES	SHORTFALL	RELATIVE INCREASE TO REACH TARGET
AFRICA	482	4518 (90.4%)	10 x
LOW-INCOME COUNTRIES	356	4644 (92.9%)	14 x
LOW-MIDDLE INCOME	1096	3904 (78.1%)	5 x
UPPER-MIDDLE INCOME	4028	972 (19.4%)	1.2 x
HIGH-INCOME COUNTRIES	11 150	0	0

Table 2. Surgery conducted per 100 000 population according to the HDI*[41]

*Target: 5000 surgical operations per 100 000 population

The volume of surgery in Africa leaves a lot to be desired. Countries like Chad require 50 times more surgery than currently delivered, and even the relatively affluent African countries such as Mauritius and Namibia still need twice as many surgeries to reach 5000 surgeries per 100 000 population annually.[41] Access to surgery is wholly inadequate across all income categories, with the exception of the generally over-serviced high-income countries.

What are the implications if you cannot provide enough surgery in Africa and low-resource environments? Appendicitis is a surgical disease from which one should almost never die. It is a core surgical procedure for which every surgeon is trained. Thus, even the worst presentation of appendicitis in high-income countries has an expected mortality of approximately 0.1%, or one in 1000 cases. In contrast, in low- and middle-income countries the mortality is at least six times higher, at 0.6%. And once surgery is unavailable, then the mortality rockets: 10% in moderate cases, and 19% in severe cases at 30 days. The excess mortality impact of this unmet surgical need is devastating. It is highest in Africa – between 6500 and 8300 excess deaths per 100 000 patients with appendicitis – followed by South-East Asia at 6300 to 7300 excess deaths per 100 000.The economic burden of not providing surgery to local standards for appendicitis in Africa is estimated to be between $4.5 and $6.3 billion (or 0.13 and 0.19% of total GDP). Globally, the economic burden of not providing surgery for appendicitis balloons to $73–92 billion per annum.[42] In contrast, the economic burden of providing the best surgical care for treating appendicitis is small: it would cost about $0.1 billion per annum in Africa, and $2–3 billion globally. This is only a 2–3% increase in the economic burden to ensure that everyone can receive surgical care for appendicitis if it is needed. Not providing surgery for appendicitis when it is needed is more expensive than ensuring the best surgical care for all. It is imperative that we do all that we can to improve access to surgery. Table 2 shows the extent of the challenge.

How do we get patients to surgery? Social circumstance is a major determinant of access to surgical care. It is tied up with physical and financial access, and patient acceptability. Maria-Lisa Odland and Professor Justine Davies, researchers in public health from the University of Birmingham, sum up the delays in access to surgical care succinctly as delays in 'seeking', 'reaching', 'receiving' and 'remaining' in care. Health is fundamentally a human condition, and it falls prey to the vagaries of the human psyche and the communities in which people live when considering whether to seek care. The factors that may prevent people from seeking care include (amongst others): fear of a lack of privacy; fear of the community's knowledge of illness; fear of dying; patriarchal structures within which women are not allowed to make decisions about surgery; distrust in the healthcare system; and the unaffordable cost of accessing healthcare. Reaching care is dependent on the physical distance to travel, the conditions of the roads, the travel costs, the potential loss of earnings in leaving work to get medical care, and the dysfunctional, complex and disjointed health systems that result in numerous redundant pathways for the patient.[43] Receiving care is dependent on funding and on the training and knowledge of the healthcare providers to make an early diagnosis. It also entails: the need to communicate and refer across sites and disciplines within the health system; to have and maintain the necessary equipment and skilled staff; and access to an operating theatre without unacceptably long surgical waiting times such that the benefits of surgery are lost.[43] To remain in care, patients need the ability to travel, as well as the time and money for surgery. Even if these exist, individuals may be hampered by the fear of community stigma, the extraordinary waiting times, and possibly by a lack of follow-up protocols, which result in patients been discharged out of the healthcare system before the necessary care is complete. It makes one despair. Frankly, getting surgery in this environment is nothing short of a miracle.

Any number of factors can contribute to a surgical patient's death. Physical barriers to access could include the distance and quality of roads (which was what led Sue and the medical student needing to do a caesarean section, despite limited experience), or financial factors such as cost of access and loss of earnings. In some countries, if you cannot pay for the 'surgical pack' of disposables and instruments needed for the operation, you will not get to surgery.[44] A complex and disjointed health system can further raise the physical and financial barriers to access. Healthcare workers may lack the training and knowledge necessary for an early diagnosis, and poor communication within the health system results in a slow and convoluted path to definitive care. Equipment shortages hampered by poor maintenance further limit access. Having insufficient resources means limited theatre time, long waiting times, and long operations with slow turnover due to a lack of supervision for junior doctors, amongst numerous other problems. All these barriers to access are interconnected, and together they demonstrate how accessing care is much more than a medical issue – it's also a social issue.

Once, when flying home from a meeting, I picked up a paper in the airport lounge to read with my coffee, and a small photo caught my eye. It showed an elderly man pushing a wheelbarrow along a sandy footpath through the veld. In the wheelbarrow was an even older man, probably in his seventies, with a wizened face and grey hair. The caption stated that this was a patient being taken to hospital in the Eastern Cape in South Africa. The irony could not have been starker. Here I was in the same country, about to board a plane home, while someone else had to be pushed, probably for days, in a wheelbarrow, to be seen at an under-resourced hospital.

It's obviously an extreme case, but it highlights how long it could take to get to a hospital. South Africa has a comparatively good healthcare system when compared across Africa, but there are still parts of this relatively advantaged environment where getting to care is unbelievably challenging and disheartening. Here are some figures to mull over from the Western Cape, which arguably provides the best public-sector healthcare in South Africa. At Groote Schuur Hospital, one of the tertiary centres in Cape Town, the estimated average time for a patient to arrive at the colorectal cancer service is about a year after their initial symptoms.[45] Breast cancer is the most common cancer among women in South Africa, yet patient awareness is lacking, and the ability to present to a secondary level hospital breast clinic in the Western Cape takes 67 days (or 10 weeks) on average.[46] The European Society of Breast Cancer Specialists accepts up to a six-week delay to present to a diagnostic breast clinic, while the South African guidelines suggest that a woman with a breast lump should be seen within three weeks. The problem is that to achieve the three-week consult and the six-week diagnostic recommendation, a potential breast cancer patient must navigate multiple delays between the first symptoms and presentation to a healthcare provider. These include her own initial denial of a potential cancer, a lack of education of first symptoms of possible cancer, and the difficulty in getting to a healthcare provider. Then there is the provider delay: the delay before referral to a dedicated breast centre, the subsequent diagnostic delay, and finally the treatment delay.[46]

What is the consequence of delayed access and inadequate volumes of surgery? We see the following three consequences in Africa, all of which contribute to an increase in morbidity and mortality for the patient. Firstly, a late presentation means that the disease will have progressed. The longer it takes to get to surgery, the worse the patient's surgical outcome. A surgery that should have been elective becomes urgent and emergent. The proportion of emergent surgeries is a marker of a lack of access to surgery. The majority of surgery should be elective (or planned) to realise the full benefits, but in Africa the majority of surgery is urgent or emergent.[1] Late presentation results in patients presenting with advanced surgical pathologies, and often the opportunity for cure has been obviated by the passing of time. In our collaborative African work, it is not uncommon to see a picture on a regional WhatsApp group of a massive fungating mass covering the breast and thorax of a patient in a remote, resource-limited environment, from a clinician asking for help with the diagnosis and guidance on the management. A patient like this is often going to die with or without surgery. In Soweto, at the Chris Hani Baragwanath Academic Hospital, the risk of patient presenting with a later stage at breast cancer diagnosis is 1.25-fold higher for every 30 kilometres that the patient is further away from the hospital.[47] A simple 30 kilometres substantially increases the delay in making it to the breast clinic, thereby increasing the risk of a late-stage cancer diagnosis, which ultimately increases the risk of death. It is mind-blowing that at 60 kilometres, one in three patients will therefore have a late-stage breast cancer diagnosis. A systematic review of seven cancer types (bladder, breast, colon, rectum, lung, cervix, and head and neck) showed that for each four-week delay to surgery there is a significant increase in mortality, with 10 additional deaths per 1000 women with breast cancer with a four-week delay, 20 deaths at eight weeks and 31 deaths at 12 weeks delay.[48] Based on the Western Cape data,[46] we should expect between 20 and 30 additional deaths due to the delay in accessing a breast clinic.

The second consequence of a limited surgical service is that it will only have the capacity to address urgent or emergent surgery, as is evident across Africa.[1] This means that the majority of surgeries that should be elective (or planned) are not seen timeously, due to the demand of urgent and emergent surgeries, and the opportunity for cure associated with planned elective surgery is compromised by the time lost awaiting elective surgery once in the healthcare system.

The third consequence of limited access to surgical care in Africa presents a bizarre phenomenon. The Lancet Commission's proposed benchmark for accessing emergency surgical care is two hours of travel time.[33] In sub-Saharan Africa, only 16 of 48 countries (33%) reached the international benchmark of more than 80% of their populations living within a two hours of the nearest hospital.[49] We tried to determine the impact of distance and time on surgical outcomes in Africa, using the data from the ASOS study.[50] We controlled for patient and surgical risk factors known to be associated with mortality, and then looked at the effect of 'geographical or travel remoteness' on patient outcomes. Interestingly, whether you defined 'remoteness' by either distance or projected travel time, the outcomes improved as the distance or time increased. In other words, the more remote the hospital, the more likely that the patient was predicted to survive surgery. These data are unpublished, because we found it hard to make head or tail of the signal, but I now feel that I may understand this counter-intuitive result. There are several factors at play here. Firstly, when the distances are large, only the fittest patients will make it to the hospital. There is undoubtedly a Darwinian survival element to accessing necessary healthcare in low-resource environments. Essentially, the harder it is to access care, the more likely it is that weaker patients will be 'selected' to die before they even get to a hospital. That elderly patient being pushed to a hospital in a wheelbarrow in the Eastern Cape, will clearly be more likely to die before getting care. This means that the patients arriving at remote hospitals may be the fitter, and therefore better, surgical candidates than the weaker patients who have already been 'selected out'.

Secondly, those who make it to the hospital, are essentially strong and 'prehabilitated' for surgery. In high-income countries, patients are given preoperative prehabilitation programmes to make them fitter and stronger before surgery. This is very common with big cancer surgeries, and the patients end up doing better. For a low-resource environment, accessing a hospital far away may entail a long physical struggle, making for a natural prehabilitation programme.

Finally, we do not know much about patient selection for surgery at remote hospitals. From the hospital perspective, it could be that the team develops a skillset to manage specific surgical problems, or they stick to a clearly defined set of competencies, and either way there are certain surgical cases upon which they will never embark. Hence, although the surgical outcomes look good for the surgeries conducted, the broader outcomes for all surgical pathologies (operated and not operated) are worse, as some patients are just never offered surgery because the procedures they need are simply not available. Do remote surgical teams only select the patients that they are confident that they can treat adequately, and triage the higher risk patients to no surgical intervention? Sure, it is possible that some remote hospitals provide excellent care, but this cannot be considered the norm. Indeed, the norm is poorer outcomes in more remote sites, given that a low volume of surgery is associated with worse surgical outcomes.[51] In a study in Liberia where the surgical volume was estimated at 462 cases per 100 000 population (less than 10% of the suggested minimum), the determinants of surgical volume were unsurprisingly associated with infrastructure and the availability of human resources.[51] Until these two key factors of resources and infrastructure are addressed, the odds are stacked against any surgical team and patient in these remote hospitals.

The in-hospital surgical outcomes are awful in Africa. An adult patient is twice as likely to die after surgery,[1] a child is 11 times more likely to die,[3] and a mother is 50 times as likely to die following a caesarean section,[2] when compared to global averages or high-income countries. Yet the total number of deaths we see in hospitals are only the tip of the iceberg of surgical deaths. There are numerous uncounted surgical deaths in the community, of patients with surgical pathologies who never get the opportunity to have curative or life-improving surgery. From Table 2, we can expect that there are 14 times as many patients in African communities with surgical pathologies who never get surgery, resulting in many unnecessary (and unseen) deaths. In lower-middle-income countries, there are at least five times as many surgical diseases resulting in unnecessary deaths in the community than what we see in the hospital. There is an unacceptable excess mortality in the community as a result of the failure to provide surgical care. It is estimated that increasing surgical services to meet the Universal Coverage of Essential Surgery could decrease all deaths or disability by nearly a third.[52] Let me say that again. Increasing *only surgical services*, just to provide essential surgical universal health coverage, can decrease *all deaths* by a third, and increase the quality of life for a third of the population.

As we have seen in the data from the Cape Town flying squad intervention, delays in accessing obstetric care also affect maternal outcomes. The barriers to timely surgical obstetric care are numerous,[53] and are similar to the barriers limiting access to surgical care. The barriers to maternal care may be further compounded by factors associated with gender inequality in accessing care.[53] These delays stack up, and besides the risk to the mother, there are also dire consequences for the fetus. In Nigeria, doubling the time to provide care to the mother increases the risk of a stillbirth. Here, the minutes count between good and bad fetal outcomes, with travel times of 15 minutes for live births compared to 26 minutes for stillbirths.[54]

An ectopic pregnancy is a pregnancy in the fallopian tube and not the uterus. This can progress to devasting haemorrhage if not treated surgically even if it was diagnosed correctly. Recently while I was on call, a patient with an ectopic pregnancy was wheeled into casualty after arresting from hypovolaemia due to massive internal bleeding. I was driving frantically to the hospital when my distressed colleague called to tell me that despite their ongoing resuscitative attempts, she had arrested a second time, with a prolonged period of resuscitation. I arrived to a patient unresponsive on the gurney, cold as ice, with an endotracheal tube in situ and adrenaline running at an obscenely high rate. She'd been given all the O-negative emergency blood available in the casualty ward but was still as pale as a sheet, and we would have to wait for more blood and other blood products to arrive from the blood bank across the city. Despite her terrible condition, we had to get her to surgery to stop the bleeding. We were fortunate to have two senior obstetricians with us, and we quickly made the dangerous trip along corridors and in lifts to the operating theatre. In the more controlled environment of the operating room, I was joined by a third anaesthetist, and between us we divided tasks and quickly established more intravenous lines and beat-to-beat monitoring lines, and got her off to sleep. The surgeons were incredible, and in minutes they had gone into the abdomen, which had been grotesquely distended by blood, and clamped off the uterine arteries. With the bleeding stemmed, we had time to resuscitate her. But it appeared futile. Her temperature was 33 degrees Celsius, and her pH was 6.9. If only she could have presented earlier to the hospital, maybe we could have made a difference. The surgeons carefully closed the abdomen after the operation, ensured that there were no obvious bleeders and we continued to resuscitate her after the surgery. We were relieved when more blood and clotting factors arrived. Now that lifesaving surgery was over, we removed the cold, bloody sheets, dried the patient, covered her with clean, dry sheets, and continued to warm her. Despite the ongoing care, progress was slow. Eventually we left the operating theatre for the intensive care unit, but she remained outrageously cold with a severe metabolic acidosis. Against all the odds, she recovered, and we extubated the next day. She made it home. This would never have happened without the expert surgical care that she received. However, it need not have been this close. How could she arrive so late in casualty in the city of Cape Town, with its well-connected infrastructure?

Many patients in South Africa are not nearly this lucky. In the 2017 to 2019 South African CEMD, there were 119 ectopic pregnancy deaths. These deaths occurred predominantly in district hospitals, and in some the initial diagnosis was missed. As expected, four out of five of these women died from hypovolaemic shock from bleeding. Every one of these deaths should be considered totally preventable. Instead, for 20% of the patients that presented there was no attempt at resuscitation, and another 40% did not even get to theatre. This is what happens when you do not have access to surgery: young women with conditions that are totally amenable to surgery, die unnecessarily in early pregnancy.[55]

For those patients who make it to surgery and survive, we still have the challenge of ensuring that they remain within the healthcare system, to ensure appropriate surgical follow-up. Sadly, the same barriers that stop people from accessing surgical care are likely to result in patients leaving care after surgery: transport, cost, and social stigma.

A final and extremely worrying consideration is that it is possible that the estimate that 5000 surgical procedures are needed per 100 000 population annually, may be an underestimate of the need in limited-resource environments. This is certainly possible, because with limited (or an inadequate provision) of surgery, the number of patients requiring surgery will continue to increase in the community. Some early work in Ethiopia suggests that the country may need as many as 16 000 procedures per 100 000 patients – three times higher than the recommended surgical capacity made by the Lancet Commission for Global Surgery.[33,56] The Lancet Commission, commenting on the future of health in sub-Saharan Africa, has stated that the current pace of healthcare improvement is unacceptably slow to provide the same health opportunities by 2030 as other countries.[37] Slavishly following the Lancet Commission for Global Surgery's indicator guidelines may further perpetuate this scenario when one doesn't consider the associated backlog of care needed. Although 5000 surgical operations per 100 000 population should be considered the absolute minimum, it should be individualised to the needs of low-resource countries, where the demand may be a lot higher than expected.

The missing surgeries

Dolly Munlemvo, an anaesthetist from the Democratic Republic of the Congo (DRC) tells me a story of a young pregnant woman who fell from a tree while collecting wood, sustaining a chest injury. In the DRC, there are few thoracic surgeons and very few general surgeons who would accept a patient with a thoracic injury in a remote hospital. The patient was in Bandundu, a village over six hours from Kinshasa by car, according to Google Maps. She was short of breath and had punctured her lung, requiring a chest tube insertion. The only thoracic surgery in the DRC was in the capital, so she was taken to Kinshasa on the back of a motorbike.

Dolly's story illustrates the importance of being able to provide a range of essential surgeries at district hospitals. The World Bank identified 44 procedures that one should be able to do at a district (or first-level) hospital,[57,58] and among these are essential trauma services that require expeditious diagnosis and treatment, including the management of a pneumothorax or haemothorax (air or blood outside the lung, but in the chest cavity, which squashes the lung down). This essential procedure is what the woman from Bandundu needed and it's relatively simple, yet it was nearly six hours away. For some, that is too long. Fortunately for this young pregnant patient, it wasn't, and she survived.

The Lancet Commission for Global Surgery identified three bellwether (or indicator) surgical procedures that should be readily available at a hospital within two hours' travel time: a caesarean section, a laparotomy (an open abdominal operation), and a reduction of an open fracture.[33] To get an idea how far away we are from realising these targets in Africa consider the following. In the UK, only 2.4% of all surgeries are for caesarean sections.[59] In Africa, as measured via ASOS, a *third* of all surgeries were caesarean sections.[1] Caesarean sections basically drowned out all the other bellwether procedures in district hospitals.

Table 3 (right). Surgical case-mix by Human Development Index quintile[41]

* The demand for cancer surgery has been corrected by the proportion of deaths attributable to cancer according to the WHO 2016 data,[61] as there is a lower proportion of cancers in low- and middle-income countries, due to the younger patient profile.[62] In high-income countries, cancer-attributable deaths are approximately 27%, while in LIC it is 7.1%, LMIC it is 9.3% and UMIC it is 20.7%.[61]

TYPE OF SURGERY	PROPORTION PERFORMED	QUINTILE 1	QUINTILE 2	QUINTILE 3	QUINTILE 4	QUINTILE 5
EMERGENCY SURGERY	Proportion of total surgical volume	25.6%	21.6%	32.3%	58.5%	56.9%
OBSTETRICS & GYNAE-COLOGY	Proportion of elective surgery	11.8%	13.1%	12.7%	26.4%	36.7%
OBSTETRICS	Proportion of overall obstetrics & gynaecology	20.0%	40.0%	40.0%	45.0%	47.5%
COLORECTAL SURGERY	Proportion performed for cancer*	65.0%	60.0%	35.0%	30.0%	20.0%
HEAD & NECK	Proportion performed for cancer*	17.5%	20.0%	15.0%	10.0%	12.5%
PLASTIC SURGERY	Proportion performed for cancer*	40.0%	40.0%	20.0%	20.0%	17.5%
UPPER GASTRO-INTESTINAL & HEPATO-BILIARY	Proportion performed for cancer*	30.0%	40.0%	30.0%	20.0%	15.0%
UROLOGY	Proportion performed for cancer*	33.8%	30.0%	25.0%	10.0%	10.0%
OTHER SURGERY	Proportion of elective surgery	20.7%	21.0%	22.0%	20.5%	10.4%

For example, in the district hospitals in KwaZulu-Natal, South Africa in 2015, 96% of the bellwether procedures were caesarean sections, 2% were laparotomies and 2% were open reductions of fractures.[60] The laparotomies and open reductions are just not being delivered at the district level within the accepted travel time for treatment.

An insufficient volume of surgery (as shown in Table 3) results in surgical procedures being driven by surgical urgency as opposed to population need. As the resources to deliver surgery decrease (reflected by the decreasing Human Development Index), the proportion of emergency and obstetric surgeries increases, while the proportion of cancer surgeries and 'other' surgeries (subspeciality surgeries that individually contribute less than 5% of all surgeries performed) decreases.

In summary, if surgery is not readily available, the proportion of emergency surgeries increases, as a large proportion of surgical diseases convert from needing elective to emergency procedures as the surgical pathology progresses or complicates without timely treatment. The result is an increase in morbidity and mortality. The proportion of obstetric procedures increases[1] at the expense of cancer and specialised surgeries (which are effectively 'removed' in low-resource environments). If you have a cancer in Africa, the odds are heavily stacked against you.

How much more surgery do we need?

To understand the surgical volume and surgical case-mix requirements for Africa, and across all low- and middle-income countries more broadly, it is instructive to use the United Kingdom as a benchmark for a high-income country, as the UK provides just over

5000 surgical procedures per 100 000 population per annum, or just over the recommended minimum number of surgeries necessary for safe surgery.[41] If we assume that the proportions of surgeries delivered in the UK are representative of need, then we can compare the surgical volumes provided for cancers, benign surgical conditions, obstetrics, and the surgical subspecialities termed 'other', which individually contribute less than 5% of all surgeries performed across Human Development Index groups. The 'other' category is important, as it includes subspecialities such as breast surgery, cardiac surgery, neurosurgery, thoracic surgery, and vascular surgery.[41] The dramatically low volume of surgeries performed across the board are clearly seen in Table 4, and the proportional increase in surgical volume per category is also shown.

In Africa and other low-resource environments, subspeciality surgeries and cancer surgeries should be considered 'neglected surgeries'. That is why the woman in Bandundu, DRC had to travel nearly six hours for a chest drain, and this is why in Soweto, South Africa, your odds for a late-stage breast cancer diagnosis increase by 1.25 for every 30 kilometres from the hospital.

What we have not considered are children. Although the global surgical case-mix of children is not yet well documented, it is unlikely that this picture of unmet surgical need is any different. Indeed, it is probably worse in the paediatric population due to the higher proportion of young people constituting country demographics in low- and middle-income countries. In sub-Saharan Africa, children under the age of 15 years account for 42% of the population.[64] A large study of surgery in children in South Africa estimated that we are only meeting between one third to one fifth of the predicted surgical need in

HDI	CANCER†	INCREASE NEEDED	BENIGN	INCREASE NEEDED	OBSTETRICS	INCREASE NEEDED	OTHER	INCREASE NEEDED
Africa	53 (10.9%)	4x	304 (63.2%)	10x	78 (16.2%)	2-3x‡	47 (9.7%)	22x
Low-income countries	22 (11.1%)	10x	122 (61.3%)	24x	37 (18.6%)	2-3x‡	18 (9.0%)	58x
Low-middle-income	71 (11.7%)	4x	356 (58.5%)	8x	56 (9.2%)	2-3x‡	126 (20.7%)	8x
Upper-middle-income	519 (14.2%)	1.2x	2150 (58.7%)	1.4x	182 (5.0%)		811 (22.1%)	1.3x
United Kingdom	860 (17.2%)		2975 (59.5%)		120 (2.4%)		1045 (20.9%)	

children.[65] This is an important observation, as South Africa is an upper-middle-income country, and these countries achieve approximately 80% of the surgical volume needed. The paediatric surgical volume is between 20% and 33% of the need in South Africa, but it is likely to be far worse across Africa, which is predominated by the more poorly resourced low- and lower-middle-income countries. Paediatric surgery should therefore also be considered a neglected subspeciality surgery. Paediatric surgery and anaesthesia require additional skills, and therefore it is understandable that it is proportionally under-represented.

The Lancet Commission for Global Surgery has estimated that approximately 5 billion people lack access to safe and affordable surgery, of which about 1.7 billion are children.[33,66] Surgical disease is estimated to account for 28% to 32% of the disease burden in low- and middle-income countries, with the disability-adjusted life years (DALYs, the years of full health lost), being double that of malaria, tuberculosis, and HIV combined (or 214 million DALYs lost for surgical disease).[52] Increasing surgical services to provide the Universal Coverage of Essential Surgery could prevent 32% of deaths and decrease DALYs by 35% in low- and middle-income countries.[52]

Table 4 (left). Surgery conducted per 100 000 population according to surgical category*

*Target is 5000 surgical operations per 100 000 population
†The demand for cancer surgery has been corrected by the proportion of deaths attributable to cancer according to the WHO 2016 data,[61] as there is a lower proportion of cancers in low- and middle-income countries, due to the younger patient profile.[62] In high-income countries, cancer-attributable deaths are approximately 27%, while in LIC it is 7.1%, LMIC it is 9.3% and UMIC it is 20.7%.[61] For Africa a conservative estimate of 7.1% for cancer attributable deaths was used.
‡Estimates for African countries[63]

Death and dying in low-resource environments

When and where do surgical patients die?

Surgery is getting safer. Gaisford Harrison, a giant in anaesthesia and head of the Department of Anaesthesia at the University of Cape Town and Groote Schuur Hospital in the 1970s, tracked anaesthesia-related deaths at the hospital over a 30-year period from 1956 to 1987. What he showed was a sixfold fall in anaesthesia-related mortality from 43 deaths per 100 000 (between 1956 and 1966) to 7 per 100 000 (between 1977 and 1987).[67] The data showed that, before the 1970s, global anaesthesia-related mortality was about 65 per 100 000, and between the 1990s and 2000, it had fallen to about 14 per 100 000.[68]

Canadian cardiologist PJ Devereaux subsequently took this outcome work further. PJ is a giant in perioperative clinical trials. He is currently the lead cardiologist at McMaster University. McMaster is essentially the global epicentre of large clinical trial research, cardiovascular medicine and evidence-based medicine. PJ was mentored by David Sackett as a medical student, and then worked with Gordon Guyatt, the two pioneers of evidence-based medicine. As a cardiologist he worked with Salim Yusuf, who became the father of large cardiovascular clinical trials, starting with his DPhil in Oxford in the 1980s.[69] After working with giants in these fields, PJ, too, is now a giant, and he's taken his immense understanding of evidence and clinical trials into the surgical space, conducting large research projects and clinical trials in perioperative care globally. It is unsurprising that PJ is a real stickler for evidence, both in its generation through robust clinical trials, and in the delivery of therapies with robust evidence. He is forthright in a very North American way. He will be clear in his objectives and will not stand down if he believes you are wrong or misguided, emphasising your mistakes with his index finger. He has really driven the evidence for the care of surgical patients forward with his leadership and large clinical trials. PJ led a global project known as VISION – the Vascular events In noncardiac Surgery patIents cOhort evaluation – which has provided tremendous insight into when, where, and why surgical patients are dying. With data from over 40 000 patients globally, we know the following about deaths following surgery. Globally, less than 1% of patients die in the operating theatre. Instead, most patients die on the ward before discharge (see Table 5).[70] In Africa, the proportion of patients who die on the day of surgery is slightly higher, probably due to resource constraints, but nearly 95% of surgical patients are still dying on the ward postoperatively.[1]

What are the big complications killing these patients? When controlling for patient risk factors, PJ has shown that 45% of mortality can be attributed to three groups of complications: bleeding, sepsis, and cardiovascular complications.[70] When talking about the findings of VISION, PJ speaks passionately about how safe surgery and anaesthesia have become. He is convinced that it is the continuous presence of an anaesthesiologist, aided with beat-to-beat monitoring, that has led to the sixfold decrease in mortality that Gaisford Harrison documented. The one-on-one care from the anaesthesiologist in an operating theatre is designed to provide quality care. PJ is correct.

REGION	DEATHS IN OPERATING ROOM	IN-HOSPITAL DEATHS AFTER SURGERY	DEATHS AFTER HOSPITAL DISCHARGE
NORTH AMERICA, EUROPE, AUSTRALIA	1%	70%	29%
ASIA	1%	62%	37%
SOUTH AMERICA	0%	73%	27%
AFRICA	1%	80%	19%
WORLDWIDE	1%	70%	29%

Table 5: Time and location of deaths following surgery[70]

As a result, however, surgical deaths have moved from the operating room to the postoperative ward. This is because you take a patient who has one-on-one care in the operating theatre, and then suddenly de-escalate their care once they arrive in a ward of 30 or 40 patients with limited nursing. Patient observations go from the continuous monitoring in the theatre, to intermittent monitoring on the ward, which can be as infrequent as observations every few hours. What are the implications of this change in the frequency of care?

Most patients die due to a failure-to-rescue

For the surgical patients who dodged the Darwinian bullet by making it to the hospital, a new struggle to survive begins. They must still navigate the period where most deaths occur in surgical patients – the surgical ward.[1]

Agya Prempeh, a Ghanian colleague, met one such patient early in his internship. Agya had just finished six years of medical training. As a keen young doctor on the ward round, his attention was caught by an elderly gentleman with sepsis of the urinary tract. The man looked awful. Most of team on the ward round had seen this picture before. To them, he was a 'goner'. So they swiftly moved on; there were others to see, and even though this elderly patient had had the strength to make it to the hospital, he was certainly going to die before the next morning's ward round.

But Agya didn't agree. Perhaps because he'd not seen this scenario play out before, or maybe he saw something that made him believe the patient still had some life in him. As the sun set and his colleagues made their way home on foot, Agya turned his attention to the patient. He got one of the few blood pressure machines in the hospital and wrapped the cuff around the man's clammy arm. He set the blood pressure to cycle every five minutes. He had the drip running, and as the blood pressure sagged, he upped the drop rate. Agya scrambled for some adrenaline. He had to give the vessels an adrenaline squeeze to keep the blood pressure up and the heart a little boost. The blood pressure started to respond. The patient drifted in and out of consciousness.

The patient's temperature sored. He was feverish and

needed antibiotics. Antibiotics were difficult to come by, especially to treat a savage infection like this. Agya had heard about an antibiotic clinical trial running in the hospital. It was over now, but some of the antibiotics could still be lying around. He called a colleague who had been involved in the trial. The antibiotic arrived. Quickly, Agya mixed it and injected it into the drip. The infection was rampant, and despite the adrenaline boost, Agya had his work cut out to ensure that the patient could hold on long enough for the antibiotics to start kicking in. Time was of the essence, and the patient looked like his time was about to run out. It was a relentless lonely night for Agya, opening and closing the drip clamp, fighting sleep, and responding to the patient's physiological needs. Eventually the sun slowly rose, the ward warmed up, and his colleagues arrived. They could not believe what they saw: the goner looked good. Agya had done a sterling all-night job. After the ward round, he went home and to bed for a well-earned sleep.

There was a certain spring in his step when he returned to work, but the elderly patient was dead. If you turn your back, patients slip away. With a limited workforce, no one could continue with the one-on-one care Agya had provided, and the patient deteriorated and died as soon as Agya's colleagues turned to the others in need.

The rate of surgical complications is generally consistent across the globe following adult surgery,[1,34] and across cancer surgeries.[71] But surgery is precarious. No matter how shiny your hospital, the global complication rate following elective surgery is about *one in five*.[34] Yes, elective surgery – that is, planned and scheduled surgery. It is accepted that most complications will be minor, and most patients would accept them as par for the course, but there remains a 5% (or one in 20) incidence of severe complications following all elective surgical procedures globally.[34]

In Africa, with limited resources, limited running water, and other challenges, one would expect the complication rate following surgery to be higher, but in fact, it is not much different from the global average.[1] This sounds unlikely, but there are reasons that may explain this scenario. Probably the main reason is that this comparison is purely numerical. It is not risk-adjusted for other patient and surgical factors associated with complications. In reality, the classic inverted-funnel shape of the African population graph reminds us that surgery in Africa is conducted predominantly on younger, healthier patients than that seen in a global average.[1] So, if risk-adjusted, complications would in reality be worse in Africa than reported elsewhere.[72] But let's forget that for the time being, and accept that, proportionally, the complication rate in Africa is similar to the global average.

Most complications get better. However, a complication that progresses and results in death is known as failure-to-rescue (FTR) .[1] FTR could be considered a performance benchmark. It tells us a lot about the medical system at large, and its ability to respond to the patient in need. In Africa, FTR following surgery is twice the global average.[1] Agya's patient is a typical example of FTR.

Let's put that into context. Elective surgery patients in Africa are younger and fitter than the global average. But despite being young and fit, when patients in Africa complicate (and patients complicate often), they are twice as likely to die.[1]

Most people would not accept this postoperative surgical risk. Unfortunately, it doesn't end there. Mothers are a totally different story. Complications following caesarean section in Africa are about 2.5 times more likely than in high-income countries, and the mortality following caesarean deliveries is 50 times that of high-income countries. FTR following caesarean section in Africa is 20 times that of high-income countries.[2] I will repeat that: mothers in Africa are 2.5 times more likely to complicate following surgery, but 20 times more likely to die if they complicate!

How can all adult surgeries in Africa have an FTR of twice the global average, but caesarean sections run at 20 times the global average? Ten times higher than the average surgical FTR rate? What is it that sets caesarean sections apart from other surgeries?[19]

The answer lies in the types of complications that kill mothers, compared to other adult surgical patients, and the rapidity of the complications that kill them. Following caesarean section, one in five mothers who complicate will complicate with a significant bleed. Of the mothers that die, one in four will die following a bleed.[2] We know from the earlier discussion, that the high uterine perfusion rate means that a mother could bleed out in under 10 minutes if the bleeding is not stopped. The other major contributor to maternal deaths is anaesthesia complications.[2] Like bleeding, these complications move rapidly if not adequately dealt with. When the airway is compromised, death is only minutes away.

And how does massive haemorrhage present? Death is not as loud and violent as it is often portrayed in movies. Mostly, it is quiet and solitary. Mothers may slip away, with unrecognised bleeding at home or in understaffed wards at night. As the blood drains out, the perfusion of the brain falls, the mother gets drowsy, drifts into unconsciousness, and then she is gone. Often without a murmur. Alone, in a bed in a cold surgical ward. No one notices, as the blankets are thick and pulled up to keep her warm, but under the sheets, the mattress is soaked in the blood that has been pouring out of the uterus. It is easy to miss this untimely death. This is failure-to-rescue at the coalface.

Why are these mothers missed? Is it because they are generally young and fit, and no one really expects them to die? Is it because there are louder, sicker patients dragging our attention away from the routine observations that are necessary to make sure everything is fine? Is it that the resources are insufficient to keep track of all the patients, especially those who are so vibrant and young? Or is it a symptom of a larger societal problem, where women do not have a voice?[73]

There are several large studies that document surgical outcomes globally. These allow for an interpretation of surgical outcomes in lower-resourced environments, such as Africa (see Table 6). Mortality is twice as probable in Africa following adult surgery,[1] 50 times higher following caesarean section,[2] and 11 times as likely following paediatric surgery[3] when compared to high-income countries.

The frequency and type of complications also differs in Africa. In a larger international cohort, the VISION study showed that the most common complications were major bleeding (15.6%), myocardial injury (13%), and infection (8.9%).[70] These complications explained nearly half of all deaths. In Africa it is slightly different: the complications that dominate mortality are mostly infections following adult surgery, and haemorrhage in mothers.[2,77]

If we want to improve surgical outcomes on the wards in Africa, we need to understand which complications are killing patients, and when and where these complications occur. Then we will be able to develop strategies to

COHORT	REGION	DATE	MORTALITY TIME FRAME	MORTALITY OUTCOME
ADULTS				
VISION (all surgeries)[74]	Global	2007–2011	30-day	1.9% 95% CI 1.7%-2.1%
ISOS (elective surgery)[34]	Global	2014	In-hospital	0.46% 95% CI 0.4-0.52
ASOS (elective surgery)[1]	Africa	2016	In-hospital	1.1% 95% CI 0.8%-1.4%
ASOS (all surgeries)[1]	Africa	2016	In-hospital	2.1% 95% CI 1.9-2.4%
PAEDIATRICS				
APRICOT[75]	Europe	2014–2015	30-day in-hospital	0.1% 95% CI 0.07%-0.14%
ASOS-Paeds[3]	Africa	2022	In-hospital	2.3% 95% CI 2.0%-2.6%
CAESAREAN SECTION				
NSQIP[76]	USA	2006–2012	In-hospital	0.01% 95% CI 0.01-0.02%
ASOS[2]	Africa	2016	In-hospital	0.5% 95% CI 0.3%-0.8%

Table 6: Mortality and global surgical outcomes.
CI: confidence interval

improve surgical outcomes. We know that patients die predominantly on the postoperative ward and, on average, at least five days after surgery. This suggests that there is time to save these patients,[1] and prevent FTR.[34]

How poor-quality care further compromises outcomes

'Jenny, Jenny!' I screamed as I ran out of my operating theatre and down the theatre 'street'. 'Jenny, where are you?' I was frantic. I ran into one theatre; she wasn't there. Out and into the next theatre. The same. Out and into the next theatre – there she was.

'Bruce what's wrong?'

'Jenny, I have put a spinal anaesthetic in, and the patient has no blood pressure. What do I do?'

'Give some ephedrine,' she responded calmly. 'The patient will be fine.'

I bolted without thanking her. Back in my theatre, the mother lay still. I fumbled in the anaesthetic cart, found the ephedrine and drew it up. Ephedrine squeezes the blood vessels, much like adrenaline, and that would get my patient's blood pressure up. But how much was I supposed to give?

I placed the syringe in the injection port, but something felt wrong. The dose? Seemed massive to give 50mg. I looked at the pale patient. I figured I could get to Jenny and back before she died.

I sprinted out again. 'Jenny!'

'Give her 5mg Bruce, then repeat if necessary.'

'Flip!'

I sprinted back. Gave a little bit.

'You okay?' I shook the patient. 'Hello!' I gave her bit

more. Opened the drip full. 'Hello!' Not too responsive. Breathing though. A bit more ephedrine. The blood pressure machine cycled again. Thank goodness. At last, little bit of blood pressure. Systolic pressures in the fifties. 'Hello!' I gave the patient another shake and another dose of ephedrine.

She looked up at me quizzically. Thank goodness, a response. The blood pressure machine started cycling again.

'Doctor, I feel sick.' Systolic pressure 90. No surprise that she felt nauseous with such a low blood pressure.

I really thought the patient was going to die on the end of my spinal needle that day. Without Jenny, she probably would have, or it would have been close. I was lucky to have had a mentor working with me, allowing me to provide safe-*ish* care, albeit a bit late. Jenny had been helping someone else, but she got me on track, and got me to give a safe dose too. It was fortunate that I'd decided on one more sprint across the theatres to Jenny, otherwise I would have administered a dangerously large dose of ephedrine. It is incredible how quickly things can go wrong, and a patient could die right in front of you.

I was working in Edendale Hospital at the time, a large regional hospital in KwaZulu-Natal, South Africa. It had a fantastic anaesthesia diploma training programme led by Dr Jenny King. She was diminutive Scots woman, fiery and strong (as you would expect), but at the same time a mother figure to us all. Because of her strong leadership and fantastic programme for aspiring young anaesthesiologists, we flocked to Edendale from across the country. I was one of the lucky few who made it into her department. Jenny would later be recognised by the World Federation of the Societies of Anaesthesiologists (WFSA) for her contribution to anaesthesia education. She had the highest conversion rate to subsequent specialist anaesthesiologists out of all the of non-specialist anaesthesia training programmes in South Africa at the time. She was that good. Through her passion for anaesthesia she created a love of the profession.

But how could the wheels have come off my own operation so quickly? This is the stark reality for many who provide anaesthesia care for caesarean sections in low-resource environments. Fortunately, my patient was fine, but many women in similar scenarios in Africa die. Why? The first clear issue was my complete lack of knowledge of how to handle the situation. I was lucky to have an experienced supervisor, but for many providing anaesthesia in low-resource environments, there is no supervisor, and a poor situation can result in a catastrophic outcome. We did not have one-on-one supervision at Edendale, but we did have Jenny, who undoubtedly stopped many complications from progressing to death.

Spinal anaesthesia is an easy way to start anaesthetics. You are given a beautiful, fine needle, and if the patient has a thin back, you can easily feel the spaces between the vertebral spinal processes and gently insert the needle through the interspinous ligament and into the dural sac. A small pop, and the cerebrospinal fluid starts to flow out into the needle. With as little as 2 millilitres of local anaesthetic, a patient quickly loses sensation and muscle function, allowing for surgery on the lower legs and into the abdomen. This is how most caesarean sections are done. This is also how I got into trouble at the start of my anaesthetic career. I was at the 'do one' stage of the 'see one, do one, teach one' training philosophy characteristic of most resource-limited medical environments. I had just done my first spinal anaesthetic when the patient's blood pressure plummeted, and she became drowsy and less responsive. I felt that she was going to die in front of me, and that may well have happened without Jenny.

The risk of mortality is associated with the available resources and the quality of care it allows one to deliver. But quality of care is not only dependent on resources. From the Donabedian perspective, quality of care is also dependent on the relationship between structures (e.g. adequate staffing) and processes (e.g. adequate ward routines for monitoring patients) that determine outcome.[78] I could have done better at Edendale if the processes for managing a falling blood pressure were available, either through better education or memory aides in the operating theatre, and if I'd had ephedrine drawn up and ready as a matter of standard practice. This would have saved valuable time in responding to the complication. Now imagine if I had this experience in a hospital with even less resources than mine. There'd be no supervision, or no supply of the simple drug necessary to respond to the fall in blood pressure, and a relatively common and easily managed side effect would quickly convert into a life-threatening complication.

Social inequality is intricately tied to the challenge of delivering of quality care in low-resource environments. Social inequality results in patients being unable to pay for healthcare, access subsidised health, or co-invest in health. From a non-financial perspective, providers and resources are more likely to be present in advantaged communities. Poor social circumstance is certainly associated with low quantity and quality of surgical provision, and the associated poor outcomes.[79]

My friend and colleague Zane Farina is an anaesthesiologist in KwaZulu-Natal, South Africa, and he's worked extensively in maternal outcomes and community obstetrics and anaesthesia. Caesarean sections are the most common procedure in Africa, constituting a third of all surgical procedures.[2] Zane reviews reports of confidential enquiries into maternal deaths in South Africa, and says that many attending clinicians describe a scenario that goes something like this:

> The fetal heart rate was falling. We got the spinal anaesthetic into the mother quickly, and the spinal was going well and then the patient suddenly died. We don't know why she died so it must have been a pulmonary embolism or amniotic fluid embolus. [80]

These are seen as sudden and mostly unavoidable deaths. However, it is possible that in many cases the cause of death is different to what the clinicians suggested. Caesarean sections need to be promptly available to manage fetal distress, but it may be a spinal anaesthetic by an inexperienced provider that kills the mother. Without Jenny, I may well have written a similar report to the confidential enquiry.

Four out of five mothers who die following caesarean sections in South Africa, die after a spinal anaesthetic.[80] The real problem, though, is that a spinal anaesthetic is decidedly simple. In a resource-limited environment, this results in the anaesthesia for the caesarean section being delegated to less and less competent individuals – often healthcare workers who wouldn't dream of doing a simple general anaesthetic. They lack the skills to identify the physiological warning signs of distress in their patients, which a skilled anaesthetist well-versed in human physiology would spot a mile off. For the unfortunate junior anaesthesia provider, the first sign they notice may the patient's heart stopping. The first warning to the surgeon may be the darker, deoxygenated blood, or the decrease in bleeding at the surgical site. These are the things that could have happened to me, if Jenny was not around to help, or we didn't have the drugs to manage the complication. The problem with the confidential enquiry reports are that the reporters only speak about the classic sudden-death events, such as pulmonary or amniotic embolus, but the much more common scenario of poorly managed hypotension with a spinal anaesthetic is frequently unappreciated by junior anaesthesia providers, and may well be the real cause of death in many cases.

I suspect that this scenario is common throughout Africa. Nearly a quarter of all caesarean deliveries are administered by non-physician anaesthesia providers,[2] so human and other resources are certainly a contributing factor. However, as Avedis Donabedian predicted, even if you control for the resources available at a hospital, the processes will still determine differences in patient outcomes. A study that assessed the outcomes of patients in hospitals with similar levels of birth attendants (i.e. resource characteristics) demonstrated that maternal mortality varied between six and twelvefold across the middle-income countries studied, and neonatal mortality between three and fourfold.[81] I had no structure to support the processes necessary for safe anaesthesia when I gave my spinal anaesthetic, and that nearly led to a catastrophe. Ideally, I would have had things like printed management guides in the theatre or specific training on managing spinal anaesthesia complications, either in the classroom or in a simulation environment. I am not alone. Clinicians across Africa have asked for similar support for ensuring the delivery of safe, quality surgical care. The challenge of delivering the processes necessary to provide quality care are evident in a study of research priorities for Africa. The training and monitoring of patients in Africa were considered the two most important priorities.[82] Clearly, there is discomfort with the level of training offered to provide safe perioperative care (the processes), and the level and availability of monitors (the resources) to track the progress of surgical patients.

Surgical health matters

In a world with limited resources, should we really focus on surgery, as opposed to other areas of medical need? Yes, we should. It matters that there is too little surgery, that surgical outcomes are poor, and that the quality varies across hospitals and countries with similar resources in low-resource environments and Africa. Until people are healthy, their ability to provide for themselves and their families is compromised, and so too, is their ability to contribute to society.

Surgery matters for five clear principles.

1. **Surgery is conducted on (mostly) well-defined risk–benefit considerations, to ensure either improved survival or quality of life.** However, despite these clear benefits, if surgery was considered as a disease category on its own, it would be associated with the third highest mortality globally, only trailing coronary heart disease and stroke, and accounting for nearly 8% of all global deaths.[83] That's 4.2 million postoperative deaths annually, of which half occur in low- and middle-income countries. The number of postoperative deaths exceeds the deaths from HIV, tuberculosis and

malaria combined.[83] Despite the clear benefit of surgery based on the accepted indications, we cannot continue to accept the excess mortality seen in low-resource environments due to limited access and poor quality surgery. Addressing these factors would have a massive impact on the global deaths.

2. **The distribution of the global population is moving towards low- and middle-income countries.** It is projected that by 2100, the world population will be just over 10 billion, with approximately 4 billion people living in Africa and a further 4 billion in Asia. That's 40% of the world population living in Africa, and 80% living in regions which are currently poorly resourced. If we do not intervene to improve surgical care in these environments now, the proportion of excess morbidity associated with necessary surgical procedures will increase in the foreseeable future with these rapidly increasing populations, due to the higher mortality associated with surgery in low-resource environments. This will have a profound effect on the health of the global population.

3. **Access to surgery needs to be dramatically increased in low-resource environments if we are to provide the necessary surgery for all.** Increasing surgery as much as 14-fold in low-income countries and fivefold in lower-middle-income countries will catapult surgery-associated deaths above stroke and coronary artery disease, making it the leading cause of death globally. Sadly, the increase in surgical volumes will be in countries with limited resources, where there is already excess mortality associated with surgery, and limited resources and processes limiting an acceptable quality of care. We have to intervene now.

4. **The ability to provide surgery requires the skills of surgeons and anaesthetists, which cut across disciplines.** For example, besides making surgery safer, the ability to provide safe anaesthesia ensures that there are providers who have the skills to manage airways (whose importance was so acutely experienced during the Covid-19 pandemic), manage massive bleeding, provide intravenous access (which is important in difficult patients such as children, who are particularly vulnerable to fluid losses with diarrhoea and at risk of death from dehydration), and the organ support necessary for the critical care patients. Zane Farina refers to these transferable skills as 'cross-training', because they increase the resilience of the medical system and improve the quality of care. Cross-cutting skills make a health system more resilient by providing a backbone of emergency and critical skills across medical disciplines, which will prevent deaths in other fields. The inability to provide adequate anaesthesia support results in an erosion of the emergency and airway skills that are developed and maintained by the ability to provide general anaesthesia. These skills also have the potential to save mothers and bring lifesaving skills to other parts of the hospitals and the health system.

5. **The provision of surgery can go a long way to addressing the UN's Sustainable Development Goals (SDGs).**[84] Through the ability to improve health and quality of life, surgery contributes towards ending poverty by: promoting health, wellbeing and a healthy workforce; promoting decent work and economic growth; supporting industry, innovation and infrastructure; reducing inequalities; and surgery can promote peace and justice, and strengthen partnerships for goals.[84]

Based on these five principles, the current surgical inequity could result in one of the biggest global health crises if we do not urgently address it now. Health equity will never be achieved until we increase the surgical volume, ensure that neglected surgeries are available to all patients, make the postoperative ward a safer space, and ensure that quality of care is amply supported by resources and processes. The challenge to deliver safe surgery is enormous. If safe surgery is defined by the whole package of timeliness, surgical capacity, safety, and affordability, then approximately 5 billion people globally do not have access to safe surgery. However, the proportion of populations without safe surgery varies across regions, maxing out at a distressing 95% of the population in South Asia and sub-Saharan Africa, compared to an impressive 5% or less in Australasia, North America, and Western Europe.[85]

To put the impact of a lack of safe surgery in context in Africa, we could compare it to the totally unacceptable current maternal mortality rate for caesarean sections of 543 per 100 000 operations.[2] The adult surgery in-hospital mortality rate in Africa is 2100 deaths per 100 000 population.[1] The excess mortality (anything above what we would expect following adult surgery) accounts for about half the deaths following surgery in Africa (or 1050 deaths per 100 000 population). Excess mortality after adult surgery in Africa is double the maternal mortality rate. And the current maternal mortality rate is similar to that of the UK in 1900! We have such a long way to go to make caesarean deliveries and other surgeries safe in Africa.

The African Surgical OutcomeS-2 Trial

To improve the outcomes of surgical diseases and realise the benefits of surgery, we need to do the following:

1. Increase access to surgery (i.e. get more patients into hospitals).
2. Increase the scope and volume of surgery offered in low-resource environments.
3. Decrease mortality by decreasing instances of FTR.
4. Ensure quality surgical care.

Of these four drivers, the one we can address immediately is FTR. Potentially, it does not require any extra resources, as it can theoretically be addressed by process changes within the health system. As clinicians in Africa, we thought that if we could address FTR, we would then improve the quality of care across Africa and decrease mortality.

When we analysed the results of ASOS we were horrified. Twice as many people die in Africa compared to the rest of the world, just because they needed surgery. How could this be? And then when we saw that a third of all surgeries in Africa were for caesarean section, we were mortified that their mortality was 50 times that of high-income countries. It felt like women were literally dying across Africa just because they were carrying children. And these deaths appeared to be due to a failure to adequately identify and treat deteriorating patients after surgery. Our hypothesis was that the lack of human resources (at 20 to 50 times less than what was recommended to deliver safe surgical care) meant that there were not enough healthcare providers to identify all the patients who were deteriorating postoperatively, and intervene timeously to save them. There was a genuine desire to rise to the challenge across Africa, to rapidly reverse these excess deaths following surgery.

It is difficult to explain the urgency for positive change that the African Perioperative Research Group (APORG) felt after seeing ASOS the findings. I've been a nerd most of my life and had been involved in traditional global clinical trials, which usually take upwards of six years from conception to publication of the results. We felt that this was just too long. It was unacceptable to think that we could allow surgical patients to continue to die at this rate following surgery across Africa, and that 1 in 200 mothers could continue to die following caesarean section. The group were desperate to do something. We felt that if we could increase postoperative surveillance of high-risk surgical patients, we could identify the ones who were developing complications earlier, and then escalate their therapy early and decrease the number of complications leading to mortality. If we could do this quickly, within a year or so, then we could show a generalised intervention that could be deployed across Africa, and hopefully post-surgical mortality would plummet.

We quickly set about establishing a large trial across Africa to demonstrate that increased postoperative surveillance for high-risk patients would improve the quality of care through early identification and management of patients who developed complications following surgery. This resulted in the African Surgical OutcomeS-2 (ASOS-2) trial. It was designed as a large cluster randomised trial across Africa, which would randomise about 300 hospitals to providing normal care, and another 300 hospitals to providing increased postoperative surveillance to the patients at highest risk of postoperative complications and death. These high-risk patients would be identified by a risk stratification tool we had developed during ASOS – the ASOS Surgical Risk Calculator.[86] The idea was to focus the limited available care on these high-risk surgical patients by providing increased postoperative surveillance in an attempt to decrease FTR. The interventions were simple and included the following:

- admission to a higher care ward than planned (if it was possible)
- increased nursing observations
- ensuring the patient could be seen from the nursing station
- allowing family members to stay with the patient in the ward
- placing a 'high-risk patient guide' at the bedside.

The teams were advised to offer as many of these interventions to the high-risk patients for as long as possible postoperatively.

We recruited 332 hospitals from 28 African countries between May 2019 and July 2020 with 160 hospitals (13 275 patients) randomised to increased postoperative surveillance and 172 hospitals (15 617 patients) to standard care. The trial was stopped before we reached our required patient recruitment number, due the immense pressure of the Covid-19 pandemic on the hospitals and clinicians across Africa. Fortunately, we had recruited enough patients to understand whether increasing postoperative surveillance in Africa was efficacious. What we found was distressing. Despite clinicians being able to identify high-risk patients using the Surgical Risk Calculator, the intervention of the healthcare workers did not result in a decrease in hospital mortality or severe complications with increased postoperative surveillance.[87] So our trial had made no difference at all to the patient outcomes. Why? How could this happen? It made no sense.

We'd spent thousands of hours running ASOS-2. I was convinced that we could get the trial done in a year, and that we would provide a definitive answer on how to improve outcomes for surgical patients across Africa. I am an optimist and I pushed hard. We developed and wrote the ASOS-2 protocol fast. I was continuously badgering my colleagues in tutorials we ran in the early mornings before surgery, looking for evidence on managing FTR to include in the protocol. We were consuming papers on early warning scores, quality improvement, teamwork, and the like. As we pushed through to ethics approval, the University of Cape Town baulked at the concept of a trial of 60 000 patients across Africa where the one group was clearly going to get more care than the standard care control group (which wasn't even the case, in the end), because they would have to cover the insurance, which, for a trial like this is prohibitively expensive. Insurance for mortality or morbidity related to a trial costs millions, and the university was terrified to be the sponsor. We met with the head of finance, and the ethics chair supported me when I made the case that this was a low-risk intervention. We were going to do clinical care better. If we didn't win with the finance department, the trial would have been shelved before it got out of Cape Town. Fortunately, and to the credit of the university, they eventually agreed that this trial could run without insurance. It was a calculated risk for which I am immensely grateful, and a necessary step towards improving quality care through simple pragmatic trials. Then I spent the next two years cajoling, calling, and messaging colleagues on WhatsApp, Viber, and Telegram to build the network to get the massive number of patients we needed to answer the question. I had country WhatsApp groups, hospital WhatsApp groups, leader groups, strategy groups, you name it, I had it. I upgraded my phone during the trial, and the sales assistant who transferred my data asked if I wanted WhatsApp backed up.

'Of course,' I said.

She paused. 'All ten thousand plus of your messages?'

A colleague used to jibe me about my thumbs bleeding from incessant messaging. We had to navigate ethics boards across the continent, meet them virtually to explain why we were doing this, why it was important, and why we could not afford $500 for every ethics board review. We had sites deep in the DRC with little internet where the trial case report forms would move across the country in trucks to Kinshasa for uploading. We used Google Translate day in and day out to answer questions in French and Portuguese and Arabic. And then the pandemic hit. New challenges. Clinicians were terrified about this new virus ravaging populations. Some friends across the continent had little or no personal protective equipment to provide care. The trial was now a risk. In some circumstances, it could result in the unnecessary exposure of clinicians to patients and vice versa, thereby increasing the risk of infection. So, the trial came to an end.

It felt like a relief. It had consumed two full years of my life, and that of many others. Night and day. We were about to change the world. But little could prepare me for the first blind analysis results from the biostatistician. No difference in outcome! No difference. It couldn't be correct. While I was reeling through Elisabeth Kubler Ross's five stages of grief, I kept thinking that one of the sensitivity analyses was going to show that increasing postoperative surveillance improves outcomes at least for *some* patients. Surely high-risk surgeries, and the very high-risk patients would benefit? But when these results came through, they were the same. No matter how you looked at it, there was no benefit associated with our interventions for increased postoperative surveillance. I had failed all these colleagues across the continent. How were we going to explain this? How would people accept our work? What did it mean for the challenge of improving surgical outcomes in Africa and other low-resource environments?

I have failed often, but not quite as spectacularly as this. But I have also learnt that failure is a greater teacher than success. This experience was probably the biggest learning curve for me, and it led to the rest of this book, driven by two insights that taught me to look beyond the numerical results of clinical trials to the healthcare workers in their working environment. I got the first insight sitting with Rupert Pearse in his kitchen in London, back when ASOS-2 was about to start.

He said, 'Bruce, you really need a process evaluation.'

'What is a process evaluation?' I asked. I was so naïve.

'At the end of the trial, you need to understand what really happened on the ground when you were trying to implement these simple interventions for postoperative surveillance.'

I took Rupert's advice, and learnt more from him and Tim Stephens, an improvement scientist from Queen Mary University. Both of them had already had a tough learning experience in a large quality-improvement project across the UK National Health Service (NHS) that failed to show benefit.[88] Rupert clearly realised how difficult our task was. He built a safety net for us with the process evaluation and opened a door to understanding care in Africa in ASOS-2. What we found was that implementing the trial intervention package in these resource-limited environments was difficult, and it actually outstripped the limited resources at the test sites. We learnt that for an intervention to be successfully implemented, it required leadership (surgical staff enthusiasm and nursing management support), teamwork across the surgical team, and ensuring that the intervention was context-appropriate for the setting where it was to be used. We will never know if the failure to improve outcomes in ASOS-2 was because we failed to increase postoperative surveillance, or if there weren't enough resources to respond adequately to deteriorating patients, or if the interventions to improve outcomes were not initiated.[89] It is likely that it was a bit of all of these. What was clear, however, was that the soft skills of leadership and teamwork are key to improving quality of care, and that any quality improvement interventions need to be tailored to the specific setting in which they are to be implemented.

The second big lesson came from the clinician investigators across the continent. Before the results of ASOS-2 came out, we asked them about their thoughts and experiences of the trial and implementing the intervention. The overwhelming response was that they believed that increased postoperative surveillance would decrease both FTR and mortality.[89]

So, I wasn't the only optimist. I wasn't the only one who believed we could improve care in Africa. I wasn't the only one who believed that giving postoperative attention to high-risk surgical patients on the ward would make a huge difference. The clinicians across Africa were astounded that we failed to show increased survival, but even after the negative finding the group still believed that increasing postoperative surveillance would decrease death postoperatively. This has led to a lot of soul-searching, reading and discussion as we tried to work out what issues prevented us from being unable to show any benefit for the patients. What would we have to do to decrease FTR and improve the quality of surgical care in Africa, to advance health equity?

PART 2

The inside-out quality surgical care model

Introduction

To share the learning in quality improvement, we must understand the different factors that determine great healthcare across countries.

– Rupert Pearse, *Earth Cast* S3E33

When it comes to improving the quality of surgical care in Africa and other low-resource environments, ASOS and ASOS-2 have provided much learning. The anguish following the results of ASOS-2 trial led to hundreds of hours spent discussing the results and the implications for improving surgical care with my colleagues Rupert Pearse, Pierre Barker, Rowan Duys and others. The process evaluation provided amazing insight into the mistakes we made in ASOS-2 and has given fantastic signals on what needs to be done to improve surgical care in Africa.

There are six generally accepted core challenges facing healthcare systems, originally described by Bate et al.[90] (2008) and then adapted by Vincent et al. (2010),[91] which we need to address if we want to improve the quality of surgery in low-resource environments and make surgery safer.

- **Cultural challenges:** problems related to ensuring a shared collective meaning, value, and significance for quality within an organisation
- **Educational challenges:** problems related to training and learning
- **Physical and technological challenges:** problems related to designing physical and technological structures that support quality improvement and the delivery of safe, high-quality care
- **Emotional challenges:** problems related to motivation
- **Political challenges:** problems related to engaging the relevant parties, managing conflict and relationships, and socio-economic challenges
- **Structural challenges:** problems related to co-ordinating stakeholders and planning and structuring systems with adequate resources (finance, infrastructure, equipment, and workforce)

To overcome these challenges, I propose that we need three complementary approaches to improve care. All three are needed if we are to make surgery safer in Africa.

The first approach centres around optimising our delivery of care in the workspace, and this includes addressing the emotional, cultural, and educational components associated with care. The aim is to provide the best care possible within the current work environment. This strategy centres around the people, relationships, and processes within a hospital. The second approach deals with creating an enabling work environment by addressing the structural challenges (or, rather, the environment in which surgery is delivered). These structural challenges are around resources, both physical (infrastructural and technological) and human (in terms of numbers, skill sets, and education). We want to capacitate hospitals so that surgical teams can provide the necessary procedures required to ensure safe surgery for all. The third and final approach addresses the societal challenges (which includes politics, the community, and advocacy).

A model to improve surgical health in low-resource environments

For the first approach I propose a healthcare provider model for quality surgical care based on the work of Schein,[92] Chandauka[5] and the findings of ASOS-2. This model focuses on the guiding principles of individual excellence, system excellence and communication, using the following steps:

1. Align the **beliefs and values** of the individuals with the organisation.
2. Ensure that the team has the **knowledge and education** to improve care.
3. Bring the team to agreement upon a **deliverable intervention**
4. Reflect on **process** and provide **feedback**
5. Remove the limits on **resources** for delivering quality care

This is an 'inside-out' stepwise model, where we start at the core and work our way outwards, with each step dependent on the delivery of the previous one. A graphic depiction can be found in Figure 3. If we do not address the steps sequentially, the subsequent steps will be compromised, and the ability to provide quality surgical care is likely to fail. This whole model is cradled by communication, as each step is dependent on effective and clear communication.

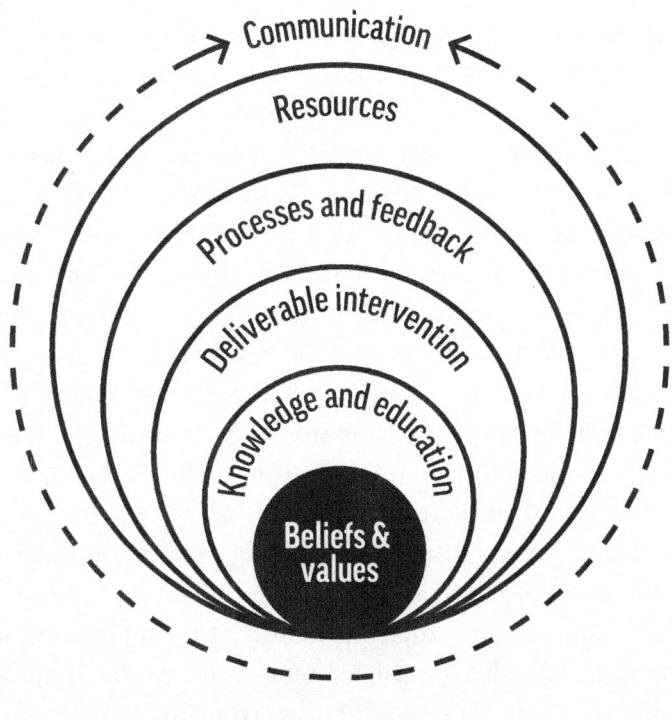

Figure 3. The 'inside-out' quality surgical care model

At the centre of the model are the beliefs and values of the individuals and the organisation. The organisation represents the surgical team. It can be a small group, such as the surgical ward, or the bigger organisation, such as the hospital. The beliefs and values of the organisation must be aligned with the vision of improving the quality of surgical care. If the individual's beliefs and values are inconsistent with the espoused values of the organisation,[92] then there will be no chance of improving the quality of care.

Once the beliefs and values of the individuals and the organisation are sufficiently aligned to improving the quality of care, then it is essential to ensure that the team has the knowledge and education to understand why the chosen evidence-based interventions are needed to improve care. At times, this knowledge and education step may also support the understanding necessary to galvanise the values and beliefs of the team consistent with the broader vision. Only once these two steps have been navigated will the team understand why we plan to do what we want to do, and how it could improve patient outcomes.

Then it is time to provide a deliverable intervention. A deliverable intervention has three components. Firstly, it needs to be simple. Too many steps would decrease the ability to deliver the intervention with enough fidelity for successful implementation and set us up for failure. We must resist interventions that are dependent on many components. Secondly, the healthcare providers need support in their practice, to implement the intervention. Ideally, this should include training and group problem-solving. Finally, frontline workers and more junior colleagues need the autonomy to ensure that implementation of care starts early, rather than being made to wait for more senior clinicians to come and treat patients. Time saves lives. This is the 'golden hour' concept of early intervention to save lives.

The next stage is to develop the processes needed to support the proposed care interventions. Once the team has the knowledge and understanding to provide the intervention, then the processes need to be co-developed within the surgical team on the ground. Co-development requires the input of both the doctors and the nurses of the surgical team, as the entire team needs ownership to buy into the delivery of the intervention. Everyone needs a voice to explain why some interventions won't work, or why they need to be reworked to fit in the local care pathway. This is an iterative process of trial and error, with check-ins and feedback. To ensure compliance with the processes, auditing and feedback on adherence is needed. Process adherence must be supported by regular feedback on both the processes and the outcome of interest. The knowledge and educational base of the care intervention needs to be current, to ensure that the processes supporting implementation remain appropriate. Each team member needs to understand how the processes affect the implementation of the care intervention. Only then will the team be able to refine and improve the processes necessary to support the intervention.

Regular feedback sessions need to be part of the clinical culture, to track the quality outcomes, the adherence to processes, and the implementation of the intervention. It is important to embed effective processes in the team and organisational culture by auditing the processes. This can be supported by policies that embed the processes in clinical care.

However, there will be a ceiling effect to the quality of care attainable, and this is determined by the resources available. This ceiling is dependent on the organisational infrastructure and the healthcare providers available. To break through the ceiling, it is essential to strategically improve resources and continuously move towards (at the very least) the international minimum standards of care.

Communication is an overarching factor across all these levels of care. Even if the values and beliefs, knowledge and education, processes, and resources are aligned, it is essential that communication is appropriate, informative, kind, and compassionate. Poor communication can break down the best attempts at improving the quality of care, even in a system that appears to have a functional organisational model. This was seen in the ASOS-2 process evaluation results, where a steep hierarchical team structure resulted in little teamwork, and subsequently poor implementation of the quality improvement intervention.[89] Quality care is not built by senior staff barking orders, but with collaborative care.

The Institute for Healthcare Improvement (IHI) has a white paper on the 'IHI Framework for Improving Joy in Work'. It begins with what matters to individuals, and the identification and removal of impediments to joy.[93] This strategy is similar to the beliefs and values approach in my model. If individuals and teams find value in their work, then there will be hope for quality clinical care. Helping people find value in their work is an important early component of ensuring that a team will commit to making an intervention work.

This is the inside-out surgical model of quality care. It starts at the inside with a core of belief and value systems that affect surgical treatment, and then moves outwards until the individuals and the organisation hit a ceiling of attainable quality of care, and cannot make more improvements to care until their available resources are increased.

Rowan Duys is a colleague in Cape Town, an anaesthesiologist and implementation scientist, and he views the beliefs and values core as a Trojan horse. He believes that if we can inculcate common beliefs and values, consistent with quality improvement within our workspace then 'a health system will ultimately heal itself'. I agree that this is possible, especially in Africa, as the espoused values of the clinicians in these difficult settings are consistent with a caring, self-improving healthcare environment.[94,95] This is evident in their positive response to the distressing findings of the ASOS study that patients were twice as likely to die following surgery in Africa, and women were 50 times as likely to die following caesarean deliveries. They rapidly established and executed the ASOS-2 trial – a massive undertaking, especially considering that it was essentially unfunded and conducted without any additional support. Instead of being overwhelmed by the enormity of delivering the clinical trial, the response across Africa was to get the trial done as fast as possible in the hope that the proposed intervention would ultimately save thousands of lives.[96] The subsequent failure of the ASOS-2 trial to decrease mortality following surgery led the African clinicians to a pivot, I believe, from seeing the problem as a challenge to treating it as a *cause* to enable a quality surgical healthcare system in Africa.

Beliefs and values

Beliefs and values in healthcare

I was at a meeting of clinical trialists in Prato, an Italian city near Florence. As a nerd, I considered it a highlight of my year, and on this occasion I was also presenting our plans for the proposed ASOS-2 trial. We were determined to ensure that any postoperative complications would be identified early, and catastrophic outcomes averted.

Shortly after my presentation, PJ Devereaux walked over. PJ has always been a fantastic mentor to me, and he simply said, 'Bruce, just make sure that the clinicians *do* the intervention.'

I have been fortunate to work with PJ as a collaborator on some of his global projects. He'd been mentored by the giants of evidence-based medicine, and like them he was informally mentoring me on that balmy July afternoon in Prato. Research in the perioperative space is not easy, especially in low-resource environments. To generate good evidence on whether an intervention works or not, one must ensure that the clinical trial itself is well conducted and delivers the proposed intervention in the trial. Failure to deliver the intervention makes it difficult to interpret the evidence and can produce a false negative result. A false negative would mean that the results showed no benefit from the intervention, but that the intervention was beneficial in reality. A false negative would be a disaster for the trial, because patients will be denied the beneficial treatment in future based on the misleading results.

In hindsight, it was unsurprising that PJ had walked up to me after my presentation and reminded me to 'make sure that the clinicians do the intervention'. But it took me thousands of hours to register the importance of this statement.

ASOS-2 failed to decrease mortality and so our vision of a simple intervention to change a surgical healthcare system never came to fruition. Instead, ASOS-2 was a massive learning curve about the many factors that need to be addressed to improve surgical outcomes in low-resource environments. The successful implementation of an intervention at a local site begins with inspirational leaders who can articulate their belief in the intervention and inspire a team to follow them. These leaders need to be locally present and respected.

When working within an organisation, one needs to determine whether the true beliefs and values of the group are consistent with the proposed management for improving the quality of care. In Schein's original model of organisational culture, he suggests that an organisation's culture consists of three core components. At the most superficial level, from the outside, we can see the artefacts of the organisation, predominated by the physical appearance of the workspace and the individuals who work there. However, at the centre are the 'ultimate, non-debatable, taken-for-granted values' of the group. These are the true beliefs, which we do not see. As outsiders, the values that we see are the 'espoused values' – the ones that are declared publicly through mission and vision statements. This is how the group would like to be seen by others. The espoused values of the group are the rationalisation for their behaviour, and their subsequent visible behaviours and materials, which become the face of the values and assumptions of the group (see Figure 4).[92] So what you see does not necessarily reflect what the true values are.

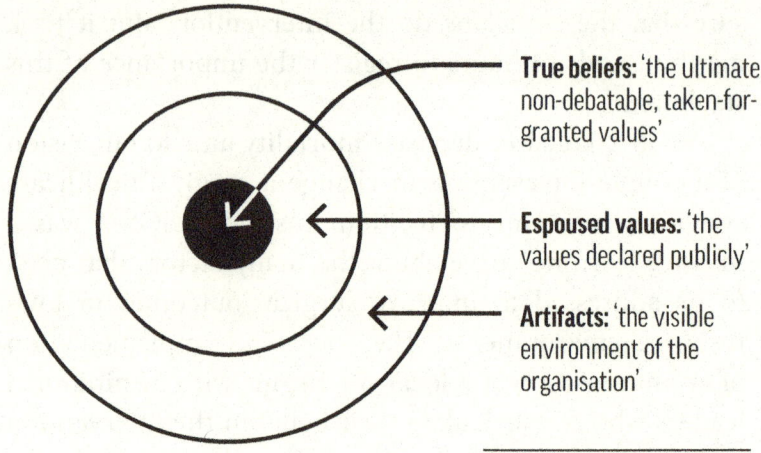

True beliefs: 'the ultimate, non-debatable, taken-for-granted values'

Espoused values: 'the values declared publicly'

Artifacts: 'the visible environment of the organisation'

Figure 4. Schein's three core components of beliefs and values (modified) [92]

To effect change, the primary objective is to ensure that the true beliefs and values of the individuals within a group or larger organisation are consistent with achieving the objective of the proposed intervention. People can say they will do something, but if they inherently do not want to do it, or have reservations about its value, or it conflicts with another internal value, it will never be done. Most parents are used to this. You ask your child to do something, and they say yes. This is the child presenting an espoused value to the parent. But any of the three reasons (reservations, compromising oneself or conflict with another priority) will result in the child dragging their feet, as it is not part of their true belief, so it will not be done. To improve the quality of clinical care in a health system, the first step is to understand the basic, true core beliefs and values of each member in the team.

So where did we fail with beliefs and values in the ASOS-2 trial? One big mistake was to assume that giving more care to high-risk patients, and spending less time on the care for low-risk patients, would not change the workloads of the nursing staff. This assumption was flawed. The nurses believed that increasing postoperative surveillance of high-risk patients would also increase their workload,[89] and they were already working in a very resource-limited environment. In some situations, nurses were working alone or with one or two others in large surgical words. It didn't matter if individual nurses believed that the intervention would improve care; they couldn't or wouldn't do it. Clearly, the 'true belief' about how increased postoperative surveillance of high-risk patients would affect workload contributed to the failure of the trial. Until this fundamental personal value conflict is resolved, it will be impossible to successfully implement the care intervention. So, the place to start when planning to implement a potential healthcare intervention is to openly discuss the true beliefs of the individuals within the team, and the values of the organisation, to ensure that they are consistent with delivering the proposed intervention. If one cannot reconcile individual true beliefs that diverge from the greater cause, then the quality care intervention will fail.

You may wonder how, in low-resource environments, it will ever be possible for healthcare providers to have personal beliefs and values consistent with providing better care, when there are so many other issues to consider. You might expect that Maslow's hierarchy of needs would play out here, and the work of caring for others would be of a lower priority than the more basic, personal needs of food and clothing, safety and job security, love, belonging and friendship, esteem, and self-actualisation. Indeed, healthcare workers in some environments have come to be perceived as uncaring. Is it possible to provide more care for others when one's own environment is so challenging?

I believe that there are many good reasons to conclude that, despite challenging circumstances, healthcare workers in low-resource environments not only genuinely care about their patients but that their true beliefs are consistent with their espoused values of caring. People in need understand need. Here are some examples.

After the publication of ASOS, we surveyed the opinions of the participating clinician investigators from across Africa.[94] The results, coming from across 27 countries, strongly supported an espoused value of continuing to do similar research across Africa, even if it was unfunded and added to the workload of the clinicians. More than 90% of the respondents considered the research valuable. It is likely that their true beliefs were consistent with values they espoused, as this same group conducted the ASOS-2 trial with no funding, and took on the substantially increased workload of a clinical trial while still providing their normal clinical work and care. This bodes well for improving healthcare in Africa, as it suggests that the overriding true beliefs of most clinicians is consistent with a desire to improve outcomes. Could this selfless contribution of healthcare workers providing surgical care extend to other resource-limited environments? I believe it can. On 12 February 2021, a peer-reviewed surgical care paper was published with 15 025 clinician collaborators from 116 countries. Most of these collaborators were from low- and middle-income countries, and they were also unfunded.[95] The Guinness World Records recognised this research paper as having the most authors on a peer reviewed paper. I would suggest that the true values of most healthcare providers in low-resource environments are consistent with improving surgical outcomes immaterial of the resources available. I know this is a generalisation, but in most cases I believe it to be true.

One may be astounded by this overwhelming value base for good when considering the adversity in which so many African clinicians operate. The work by Nicky Kalafatis, a South African anaesthesiology colleague, provides an insight into one of the dominant reasons, which is 'humaneness' or the quality of compassion or consideration for others.[97] Humaneness is best illustrated by what happened the day before the publication of the ASOS obstetrics outcomes paper.[2] A news video of Dr Azza Mashumba, the head of paediatrics at Parirenyatwa General Hospital in Harare, had just gone viral. She was standing in a patient reception area, clearly distressed, with tears streaming down her cheeks as she described the futility and despair of working in a dysfunctional, ill-resourced environment:

> *A mother presents, the baby is distressed, I can hear a fetal heart, we come here to main theatre, the fetal heart is dwindling, it's going. We get into theatre, I'm ready to receive the baby, and I am given a stillbirth. There is just no urgency. We are trying so hard, we are making a plan, come up with contingency plans … I come to work, I do my very best, but my output are stillbirths, my output are disabled babies. Elective lists are not being done, we wait for it to become an emergency. When it becomes an emergency, I am given a baby with a hypoxic brain injury. This child now has permanent disability. This is not acceptable …*

It was essentially a prophetic summary of the findings of our study. She concludes:

> *I am here because I am desperate. I have tried, we have tried, but I feel that we are not getting heard. We need to move. I am so sorry, but this is really heartbreaking for me ... but we are struggling with the work we are doing ... we are not helping patients.*

In her doctoral thesis, Nicky studied the characteristics of 'fitness for purpose' in the medical training of South African anaesthesiologists. She confirmed the appropriateness of the Canadian model of medical education known as the Canadian Medical Education Directives for Specialists (CanMEDS) in the South African environment. But she found two striking differences: the addition of humaneness and context awareness. In the centre or core of Nicky's revised CanMEDS educational structure for South African anaesthesiologists was humaneness, and the whole model was encapsulated in context awareness (Figure 5).[98]

When we conducted the survey on barriers and facilitators to collaborative surgical research across Africa,[94] the same messages supporting humaneness kept coming through in the responses from our collaborators, from reflecting a desire to improve clinical practices and the quality of care provided, to broader overarching themes of 'making things better in Africa' and trying to 'help humanity'. It appears that despite limited resources and overwhelming adversity that compromise the ability to provide care, there remains a genuine compassion and sense of care from those involved in healthcare delivery in these environments.

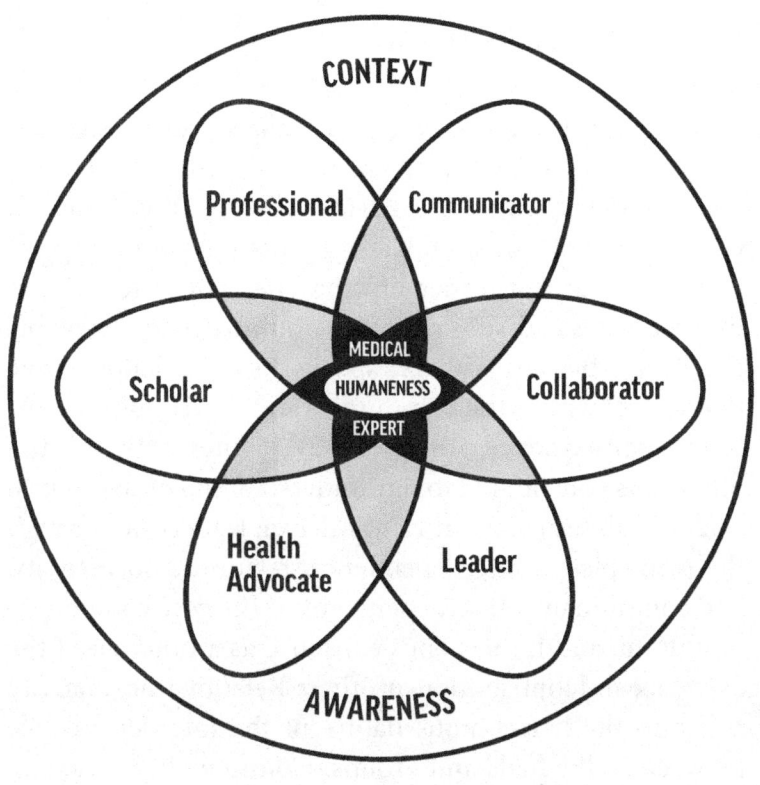

Figure 5. Nicky Kalafatis' CanMEDS model
of South African anaesthesiologists[98]

I would suggest that the challenge in low-resourced environments of marrying true beliefs and values with espoused values may be easier than we think, so that what you see becomes what you get.

Values-driven leadership

The consistency between true beliefs and the espoused values displayed by Azza, the ASOS network (which is now known as the African Perioperative Research Group (APORG)), and Nicky's doctoral work suggest that values-driven leadership may be central to African perioperative and surgical care. Ubuntu, or the principle that 'I am because we are', speaks to the relational role that others within the community and society play in our individual existence. The work by Painter-Morland and others has contributed to our understanding of the central role that ubuntu plays in values-driven leadership through the principles of interdependence, relational normativity, and communality. Interdependence is the core component of ubuntu, and frames one's existence as a function of the existence and contributions of others. Relational normativity refers to the harmonious nature of the interdependence between individuals and groups. Communality speaks to the individual's service and care, and that the organisation is a 'potential agent of transformation'.[99] This contributes to a pursuit for common good. Tinashe Chandauka's doctoral studies were of the patient safety culture in South African obstetric theatres[5] under the mentorship of Peter McCulloch, an Oxford surgeon passionate about global health. In comparison to Tinashe and Peter, I was once again so naïve at the beginning of our work. Soon after ASOS was published, Peter pushed me hard on processes and safety, yet at that time I was fixated on evidence-based medicine alone and establishing evidence for simple therapeutic interventions. However, it was the learning of ASOS-2 that provided the springboard for understanding this complex environment and the relationship between values, communication, education, and resources in determining the ultimate outcomes of patients during and after care. Tinashe observed that 'South African surgical teams … are transitioning from a culture where individual excellence is seen as the main bulwark against patient harm toward a systems approach to patient safety.'[5] This observation is consistent with ubuntu and its effect on values-driven leadership in Africa. Most of my generation were educated in the old medical system of surgical tyrants who put the fear of God into you. This system of yesteryear is now dead. Surgical care is not about the skill of a single surgeon with a knife, but rather the dexterity of the team.

The values-driven leadership has iteratively developed a 'ME-WE-WORLD' framework in its African work.[99] Individuals (ME) are connected through a mesh of relationships (WE), and more broadly to the WORLD. We cannot disconnect one from the other. We all have shared values, contexts, and perspectives, which has been demonstrated across the African perioperative surgical work discussed here. We are fortunate to have a dominant philosophy of collectiveness in Africa, which results in humaneness and compassion despite the challenging environment. The previous examples of ubuntu where true beliefs and values are consistent with espoused values and the humaneness of the carers would suggest that other factors contributed to the failure of ASOS-2. ASOS-2 showed that some of these challenges centred around communication and teamwork.[89] When there is a failure to escalate care for sick patients, there are also barriers to communication created by hierarchy, the fear of criticism, and a desire to work independently. These are key lessons for leaders and team members if one is to realise the vision of ubuntu.[100] Certainly, some sites in ASOS-2 were hampered by hierarchical structures and poor leadership that compromised the WE in values-driven leadership. Discussing this with a colleague involved in nurse education related the following: 'When you use the word "*you*", I know that we are not a team. I know we are a team when you say "*we*".' Words matter.

So where did we fail in values-based leadership in ASOS-2? In trying to get the clinical trial completed quickly, we probably cut important corners in the preparation before the study. Corners that possibly should never be cut. You need everyone in the group to openly discuss their true beliefs and values. What we need from the group are for people to get comfortable discussing their true beliefs and values, and to be willing to be challenged on them. They must understand also that if the team is to respond to the needs of a quality care project, there have to be people within the group facilitating and owning these difficult but important discussions. A hierarchical approach will not cut it, as the values and solutions must come from within. Ultimately the team must work to a point where their true core beliefs are consistent with the espoused values necessary to sustain the quality improvement intervention.

Failure to implement interventions is often due to the ongoing competing priorities of each staff member. These competing priorities may dominate decisions and actions that compromise leadership and intervention delivery. Without sufficient personal priority for the intervention, it is impossible to create a vision or purpose for the group to improve care. Without a common purpose, the underlying challenge remains the same: overcoming the conflicting priorities that team members may have, which hinder the implementation of quality care. This is clear in the ASOS-2 trial where the following comment was made: 'Nurses are generally overburdened, too many patients etc. ... Generally when I handed over [the ASOS-2 interventions] it was seen as extra work and the response often was ... [that] they didn't appreciate the addition to their work.'[89] If nurses are already overburdened, then they will not support an intervention implementation if they believe it amounts to additional work. Furthermore, if a personal priority is, for example, to get home as soon as possible after work because they are concerned about their children, then an intervention that potentially impedes their ability to complete their work is doomed to failure. Clearly, balancing personal priorities against team priorities is the key initial step to ensuring intervention implementation. Only once the true beliefs and values of each person in the team is consistent with that of the vision of the organisation, can an intervention be implemented. Until we address the basic needs of frontline staff, we will fail to improve the quality of care through intervention initiatives.

Success of the first step is dependent on the team working through their true beliefs and values, until such time as it allows each individual to support the implementation of the quality improvement intervention.

Knowledge and education

The hypothesis and the programme theory

O nce you are certain that the true beliefs and values of the team members are aligned with the quality improvement project, it is important that the hypothesis behind the project and the programme theory are clearly understood. Figure 6 shows an example of the programme theory for decreasing FTR in ASOS-2.

Figure 6. The programme theory for decreasing failure-to-rescue in ASOS-2[89]

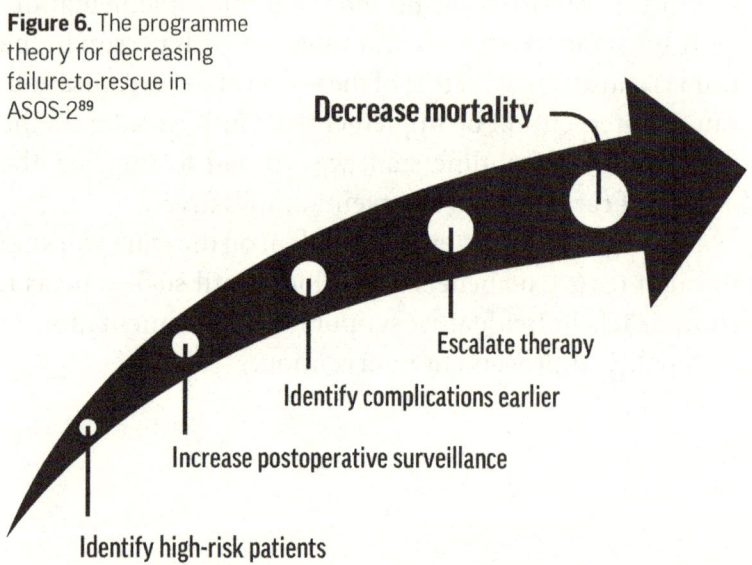

Decrease mortality

Escalate therapy

Identify complications earlier

Increase postoperative surveillance

Identify high-risk patients

The hypothesis is that, when staff numbers are insufficient, patients who develop postoperative complications are more likely to have complications that will progress and result in death. To decrease this excess mortality, we need to identify the patients at risk, then increase their postoperative surveillance on the ward, so that any complications can be identified earlier. We then escalate appropriate therapy for the complication, and hope the complication responds to the therapy, so that early mortality is averted. There are a number of 'ifs' in this process that can derail the whole intervention.

Education about the hypothesis and the programme theory are important. To implement the intervention successfully, it is important to co-design the intervention supporting the programme theory, to ensure that it addresses each step of the intervention. The intervention must be feasible to deliver. Collective competency is necessary for the delivery of the intervention. That is, each person can play their part in increasing the quality of care delivered. Therefore, an accepted degree of autonomy is necessary to ensure early implementation of the intervention, and this can be achieved by removing barriers to early care, such as the need for sign-offs by clinical superiors, characteristic of hierarchical structures.

Feasible interventions

Elliott Taylor studied interventions that were both efficacious *and* feasible to decrease death from maternal haemorrhage following caesarean section in Africa. The premise of the study was that to prevent death from haemorrhage in mothers in Africa, we need treatments that are available, deemed effective in the environment, and feasible to deliver. A consensus study was conducted with obstetric and anaesthesia leaders from across Africa to determine the essential interventions to prevent or manage maternal haemorrhage. Unsurprisingly, some of the efficacious interventions were unfeasible in the

African context: the availability of a specialist obstetrician and anaesthetist; early and comprehensive antenatal consultation with regular follow-ups; mentorship and support networks for non-physician surgical and anaesthesia providers; creation of a multidisciplinary peripartum haemorrhage response team with a rapid alert and call network, ensuring repeat caesarean sections are only performed by experienced providers; and accurate and quantitative measurement of peripartum blood loss.[101]

The inability to provide these efficacious interventions is instructive. Five of these six interventions were unfeasible due to the restrictions associated with a limited healthcare workforce. If we want to improve the quality of surgical care, and prevent mothers dying from bleeding, we need to co-design care strategies that are actually deliverable by the team available at the coalface. While guidelines exist on how to manage maternal haemorrhage, for example, these guidelines have little consideration of the austere environment in which healthcare workers are toiling in Africa. Elliott's work suggests that, to decrease maternal haemorrhage, we will have to upskill the healthcare providers, and create educational, training, and treatment guideline stepping stones relevant to the working environment. The alternative is for clinicians to try and follow guidelines drawn up in high-income countries, but these list interventions requiring resources that are usually unavailable in Africa. This essentially sets the carers up for failure. Guidelines that cannot be followed lead only to dead mothers.

Collective competency and autonomy

A sustainable workforce requires the entire medical team to share the emotional burden and compassion needed for managing patients in Africa.

– Nicky Kalafatis, *Earth Cast* S3E33

U ntil we have all the resources needed to deliver quality care, we will need strategies to navigate resource constraints. I would call these interim strategies 'stepping stones', where a response is tailored according to the resources of the local environment. To increase the capacity to deliver the intervention, and ensure it is implemented early, part of this response needs to consider the 'task shifting' or 'task sharing' aspects of the work, so early interventions are not delayed due to limited access to clinicians. Task shifting and task sharing are about the autonomy needed to deliver specific tasks to ensure the collective competency necessary for early and appropriate quality care.

Although the days of the surgeon barking orders are gone, the need to speak up remains. Good communication is not about barking from the top of the heap, but rather the ability to speak up from the bottom of the pile. ASOS-2 suggested that implementing interventions required teamwork and leadership within a flat hierarchy that is responsive to the needs of all team members. However, it appears that to make a difference in health, you should be able to speak up and be heard. In *Outliers*, Malcolm Gladwell demonstrates how cultures with steep hierarchies are associated with aviation disaster, using very visceral examples of pilots and co-pilots who could not bring themselves to speak up despite knowing their planes were in danger, which ultimately led to fatal crashes. 'The kinds of errors that cause plane crashes' he writes, 'are invariably errors of teamwork and communication.'[102] Similarly, nurses who cannot speak up to doctors, because they should 'stay in their lane' or they do not want to bother the doctor, potentially puts a sick patient at risk. If nurses do not have the freedom or ability to flag the patients that they are concerned about for fear of admonishment or scorn from senior staff, then the sick patient has no chance of salvation, and may ultimately die as a result.

Essentially, the healthcare system needs to support the nursing staff in being able to identify a deteriorating patient, intervene to assist them, and communicate the problem to a doctor. If a hierarchy, or an 'authority gradient' is causing a delay because the doctors have little respect for the nurse on the ward, then the patients are going to do badly. Calling for a doctor, and then having to wait for them without being allowed to start an intervention in the meantime, can be the difference between life and death, especially in a resourced-constrained environment. The team needs to trust *all* its members, and this should be reflected in the autonomy of those members. Every team member needs agency. A nurse who feels empowered to make a call on the deteriorating patient and has the autonomy to start therapeutic interventions while waiting for others has the power to save lives. This is agency.

How does one do this? By co-developing the quality-of-care interventions with the entire team of doctors and nurses, and then agreeing to 'outsource' some evidence-based interventions to staff at the coalface. The classic example is the golden hour in trauma resuscitation, where interventions are most likely to prevent death when instituted within the first hour. The same exists in surgery and critical care. Some complications kill patients quickly in the postoperative period. Bleeding kills mothers. A key principle must be to enable some autonomy for healthcare providers at the bedside, such as allowing nursing staff to intervene to save patients before more senior staff can get there.

Indeed, an analysis of nearly 130 000 patients from critical care in Brazil has shown that when controlling for other human-resource factors, increasing nurse autonomy was associated with increased critical care and hospital survival.[103] Nurses save lives. Let them do that by empowering them.

Deliverable interventions

The success of the Surgical Safety Checklist, and the failure of other interventions

The Surgical Safety Checklist (SSC) has become standard in surgical care. It ensures that common but avoidable errors are prevented through systematic checking of the patient and resource use from before to after the operation. It ensures that antibiotics are given timeously to prevent infections, and that sutures and swabs are documented to ensure that none are left behind in the wound. It's similar to a pre-flight checklist. The history of the SSC is documented in Atul Gawande's *The Checklist Manifesto* (2009).[104] In the first study of the checklist, conducted between 2007 and 2008, the outcomes of nearly 4000 patients from eight hospitals across five continents were compared to the subsequent 4000 patients operated on after the checklist was introduced. The SSC was an astounding success: postoperative mortality fell by nearly 50%, from 1.5% to 0.8%, and surgical complications from 11% to 7%.[105] Introducing simple checks of processes had a huge impact on outcomes. Certainly the true beliefs and values of the participating organisations were consistent with the expected benefit of the checklist intervention. The result was that the SSC was adopted by the World Health Organisation (WHO).

However, introducing process checks in surgical patients does not always improve outcomes. A laparotomy, an operation which enters the abdomen, has one of the highest complication and mortality rates in the UK, yet it is an essential operation in the treatment and management of many abdominal cancers in the elderly, making it a necessary and common surgery. To improve the outcomes, a quality improvement project was adopted to ensure that all the best care processes necessary for emergency laparotomy would be adopted across the UK's NHS. These included best care practices in the preparation and investigation of the patient prior to surgery, and during intraoperative and postoperative care. This was known as the Enhanced Peri-Operative Care for High-risk patients (or EPOCH) Study. Ninety-three hospitals across the NHS participated, with over 15 000 patients recruited into the study during 2014 and 2015. The primary outcome was death at 90 days postoperatively, and once the study was complete, there was no difference between the standard care group and best perioperative care group for emergency laparotomy. Both groups had a 90-day mortality of 16%.[88] This is despite the best care processes being set in place, the preparation of sites to provide the care, and local feedback on how the sites were doing.

This was similar to our own experience in Africa in ASOS-2, where our simple package to ensure increased postoperative surveillance failed to decrease in-hospital mortality or severe complications between the intervention and standard care groups.[87]

How processes contribute to implementation of interventions

While the EPOCH and ASOS-2 studies were running, subsequent studies of the SSC continued to document survival and complication benefits associated with the checklist.[106,107] In contrast why did EPOCH and ASOS-2 fail? How was it possible for the SSC to work, but for the surgical care pathways, which included best practice, to fail to change outcomes? Clearly, merely trying to implement processes of care known or expected to be associated with benefit, does not necessarily translate into benefit.

To understand why EPOCH and ASOS-2 failed, we need to understand what was happening on the ground. What were the barriers to providing optimal care? These barriers reflect the conflict between the processes needed to deliver a desired outcome, and the way in which the actual healthcare system is negatively impacting them. The processes may include numerous aspects of care such as identification of risk, communication of the clinical status of the patient, and implementation of quality-of-care interventions. It is incorrect to assume that an intervention will be implemented successfully during a study, so if the intervention does not work, we shouldn't throw the baby out with the bath water. Rather, we need to understand *why* the intervention did not work. And this comes down to intervention implementation or 'implementation fidelity'. It's exactly what PJ Devereaux had been alluding to in Prato a couple of years before: make sure the clinicians actually *do* the intervention. Rule number one.

When the leaders and teams were asked about what they would do differently in EPOCH, the following responses were volunteered: 'We would engage our colleagues better'; 'We will use the data-collection and analysis to support the change in how we provide care in the pathway'; and 'We will spend more time training our team in the proposed care pathway'.[108] In ASOS-2 the findings were similar, despite EPOCH coming from a high-resource environment and ASOS-2 from a low-resource environment.[89] These challenges to successfully deliver interventions to improve surgical care are universal.

To support care pathway improvement, many actions are needed to promote intervention implementation fidelity. A typical response in ASOS-2 was, 'We needed better engagement with the surgeons and the nurses and better education about the trial ... this was our main barrier ... I think people lacked understanding of what we were trying to do.' It is important to build and lead teams who are enthusiastic about the intervention. Leaders need to engage well across disciplines to form a multidisciplinary team. And the team needs to be educated on the hypothesis and the programme theory supporting the intervention. This should have been a key leadership component to implement the intervention in ASOS-2.[89]

Training is necessary to ensure that the team members understand the hypothesis, objectives, and reasons for the interventions. If any of their own beliefs run contrary to the hypothesis of the intervention or the components needed to deliver it, there will be resistance to constructive participation in the project. There was a comment that captured this: '[the] staff aren't always enthusiastic about the intervention when a "high-risk" patient by ASOS standards does not match high-risk in their mind. In that sense, buy-in from nursing staff is less than desired.'[89] Training, and then co-design, would have allowed the team to include other patients they considered high-risk independent of the standard criteria. This might have improved implementation of the intervention.

Even when the team agrees on the programme theory and interventions, it needs feedback on intervention fidelity. What processes are being delivered, how are they being delivered, and what are the resultant patient outcomes? The answers are important to ensuring compliance and making any modifications needed to achieve intervention fidelity within the local environment. For example, one team found that 'it was mostly the postoperative logistics that were a challenge … getting the patients to the right bed, the Bedside Guide, communicating with the nurses that the two-hour[ly] observations needed to be done.'[89] An understanding of the delivery of the intervention would have helped this site either galvanise their commitment to delivering the intervention, or modify their intervention strategy towards a more manageable solution. To ensure that the team understands the outcomes of the patients within their care pathway, and the care they received, it is important to provide regular, audited feedback.

ASOS-2 did not provide feedback. EPOCH did, but still failed to implement effectively. In EPOCH, only 11 of the 37 processes included in the optimal care pathway for emergency laparotomies had more than 50% of the sites trying to improve them.[108] In ASOS-2, only 38–57% of sites achieved intervention fidelity, depending on the definition of fidelity used.[89] A spectacular implementation failure by any stretch of the imagination. It could be argued that both projects have potential clinical efficacy, as the hypothesis and programme theories are good, but the real learning is about how we ensure implementation fidelity.

The intervention fidelity of a quality improvement process is key. In 2014, the Joint United Nations Programme on HIV/AIDS (UNAIDS) launched the 95-95-95 targets. The aim was to diagnose 95% of all HIV-positive individuals, provide antiretroviral therapy (ART) for 95% of those diagnosed, and achieve viral suppression for 95% of those treated by 2030.[109] This programme was originally supposed to be a 90-90-90 programme, but the mathematical success is substantially different between the two programme targets. Successful implementation in a 90-90-90 programme is 72% (90% x 90% x 90%), compared to the 95-95-95 programme at 86% (95% x 95% x 95%). The problem is also that, as the number of processes contributing to an intervention increase, the overall ability to effectively implement the intervention decreases. If you have 95% fidelity for every process, and you need, say, four processes to deliver quality care, then your implementation fidelity will only be 81.5% (95% x 95% x 95% x 95%), even if you have a team delivering 95% fidelity on every single task. Look at the overall fidelity below for a highly functioning team, based on the number of interventions needed to deliver a care package. If a care pathway requires 10 steps, then even a great team will only be able to achieve 60% implementation fidelity (see Table 7).

NUMBER OF PROCESSES	FIDELITY OF EACH PROCESS	FIDELITY OF ENTIRE PATHWAY
1	95%	95%
2	95%	90%
4	95%	82%
6	95%	74%
8	95%	66%
10	95%	60%

Table 7. The effect of the number of processes on intervention fidelity

The SSC had three processes (pre-, intra- and postoperative), ASOS-2 had five processes and EPOCH had a whopping 37 (and the clinician behaviour in EPOCH would suggest that only eleven were consistent with the true beliefs of the clinicians and feasible at the sites). A high number of processes are a major impediment to implementation fidelity. One is up against an increasing likelihood that some components of the intervention will conflict with the true belief and values of some team members, which may prevent implementation. Where an intervention package depends on the delivery of each intervention step, this could decrease the fidelity of the entire pathway, as shown in Table 7.

What strategies can we adopt to support the healthcare workers in delivering the intervention? Data from low- and middle-income countries suggest that there are many strategies, including supervision, training, and group problem-solving, amongst others. However, single, isolated support strategies do not appear to work. The poorest strategies are those in the form of printed job aids or information sheets, running at a median increase in performance of only 1%. This was part of the ASOS intervention: a bedside guide. Training and supervision appear to be better with a 10–20% increase in performance, and group problem-solving exceeds 20%. If group problem-solving is used together with training, performance may improve by over 40%.[110] This is important. Pierre Barker, a paediatrician by training who now passionately heads up the Institute for Healthcare Improvement (IHI) has pointed out to me that their quality improvement method is essentially built around structured group problem-solving (known as collaborative learning communities) and adaptive learning (a structured approach to systems analysis, data feedback and rapid learning). Their successful programmes are built around marrying problem-solving with training.

So where did we get the deliverable intervention wrong with ASOS-2? Firstly, the design of the intervention was wrong. We could not determine whether patients received increased postoperative surveillance, whether complications were identified earlier, and whether there was appropriate escalation of care for complications.[89] The intervention could have failed at any one of these points of the programme theory. Process monitoring of these steps should have been included in the intervention. Secondly, our educational preparation for the intervention was inadequate, through the general lack of on-the-ground team meetings and group problem-solving for the understanding of the hypothesis and implementation of the intervention. Instead, we had offered a simple online test on intervention, where incorrect responses triggered a short educational text. We did not assess whether team members agreed with the hypothesis, nor did we determine if the intervention was context-sensitive for the sites where it was being rolled out.

In our attempt to rapidly roll out a continent-wide project with the hope of identifying a generalisable intervention to decrease FTR, our intervention was fatally flawed in design, co-development of context-appropriate interventions, auditing of the processes to document intervention fidelity, and local team feedback on implementation and outcomes.

Processes and feedback

The role of processes in the success of quality surgical care

Interventions need to ensure that each step of the programme theory has at least one process metric measuring the fidelity of each step of implementation. This is important in ensuring that we work towards fidelity of the entire intervention. It is key that the performance of these process steps is fed back to the team to understand where and why performance may be sub-optimal, so that strategies can be developed to improve implementation fidelity.

To maximise the ability to realise success, it is important that the number of steps is limited, and that each intervention step is supported by evidence for efficacy. Do not include steps that are unlikely to improve outcome, because unnecessary steps will decrease intervention fidelity, and set the entire intervention up for failure.

A classic example of successful implementation can be found in the Enhanced Recovery After Surgery (ERAS) programme. Henrik Kehlet, a surgeon from Copenhagen, is a legend. He's a formidable personality (in his chocolate brown corduroy trousers) and an inspiration to a multitude of surgeons globally. More impressively, he has managed to cross the blood–brain barrier dividing surgeons and anaesthesiologists, so anaesthesiologists also consider him a true hero. He was convinced that patients spent too long in hospital, putting them at risk of complications. He knew we could get patients up and about and home earlier to prevent these unnecessary complications. He felt that we could make outcomes better if we removed all the barriers preventing patients from getting up and walking, and then allowed them to continue walking right out of the hospital after major surgery. He was correct. Get rid of all the bandages, tubes, and lines, and the patients would get up. We removed catheters, nasogastric tubes and the like, and the patients got up and went home. This led to the global movement of ERAS.

It has been a phenomenal success at improving the quality of surgical outcomes. The package has come a long way. Patients are now not unnecessarily starved before surgery. Instead they are optimised physically and nutritionally before operations, and they are not overly sedated, so that they wake up clear-headed. They receive anaesthesia and surgery with minimal impact to allow early mobilisation after surgery, and then they are vigorously encouraged to start moving and leave. Health economics has shown that the cost per surgical procedure has decreased for almost every procedure where ERAS has been implemented.[111]

However, the efficacy of ERAS has not been consistently demonstrated. Some studies have shown an incredible decrease in the postoperative length of stay, while others have not. Patients in Canadian and Dutch studies have got home quickly, but in studies from Spain, the patients hung around in the hospital for a long time. All the patients receive a standardised educational package to ensure that ERAS is implemented, but the difference between these studies may be found in auditing and feedback.[111] We know that education is important for implementation, but performance is way better when it includes group problem-solving.[110] Monitoring, auditing, and feedback allows a team to reflect on performance, and put mechanisms in place to improve that performance.

The ERAS group provided good data on the fidelity of processes in improving outcomes through spider diagram reports. Increasing adherence to more than 70% of the ERAS intervention recommendations results in a dose-response for decreasing surgical complications, earlier discharge, and 30-day morbidity, when compared to 50% compliance.[112] Tracking the processes to support the ERAS interventions ensures that we can provide better outcomes, in a dose-response manner.

There are also great examples in obstetrics and in surgery from low- and middle-income countries. Safe Surgery 2020 was a multicomponent intervention study to decrease maternal sepsis, postoperative sepsis, and surgical site infection. It was introduced at 10 intervention hospitals in the lake zone of Tanzania.[113] The multicomponent intervention planned to improve five areas of surgical quality: leadership and teamwork, evidence-based safe surgical and anaesthesia practices, sterilisation, compliance with sepsis outcome data reporting and provision of infrastructure support necessary for the project through a $10 000 grant.[114] The implementation study included a three-month pre-intervention period in 2018 and a three-month post-intervention period in 2019.

Processes were instituted to monitor adherence to implementation. The patient safety process adherence rate had six indicators, teamwork and communication had eight items, and the patient medical record completion rate was also monitored. The outcomes were recorded to ensure complete data for feedback to the teams.[114] The study resulted in an improvement in communication and teamwork by 25%, evidence-based practices by 33%, and a significant fall in surgical infections.[113] The caesarean section sub-study also showed a decrease in caesarean infection rates across institutions in Tanzania.[115]

Almost simultaneously, a similar implementation programme called Clean Cut ran in Ethiopia to decrease surgical site infections.[116] Clean Cut attempted to improve the quality of care through processes without investing in resources or infrastructure (which is a common scenario in low-resource environments, where you are expected to do better without all the tools). Clean Cut used three sequential steps to improve quality: team building; process monitoring; and feedback on process and outcomes. Note that the sequential structure of the processes are identical in sequence to the model proposed for improving quality of care. The first phase included team building and the modification of the SSC, led by local staff. The second step included assessment of compliance with quality processes, and the data collection of patient outcomes. The third step involved process improvement through process-mapping and feedback cycles, which included compliance and patient outcomes. Six processes were targeted, and process adherence was reported to the team, together with patient outcomes. This approach resulted in an approximately 50% improvement in process compliance, and a 35% reduction in surgical site infection.[116]

To shift systems the way Safe Surgery 2020 and Clean Cut managed to do, we need to focus on implementation fidelity for quality intervention processes. These quality metrics need to be informed by local patient outcomes. Therefore, in both Safe Surgery 2020 and Clean Cut, process adherence was closely married to patient outcomes in the feedback sessions.

Notably, these multimodal interventions appear to result in sustainable change. An implementation study to decrease surgical site infections in four hospitals in

Africa had a technical component (interventions targeting activities known to decrease surgical site infections) and an adaptive component (interventions to create a safety and audit culture). The adaptive component included safety webinars and, importantly, regular feedback on outcomes and process adherence with the technical components.[117] The effect was sustained for four to six months. For longer term sustainability, one really must build a culture of regular feedback, which includes tracking local outcomes and compliance with the technical component interventions necessary to improve the outcome.

So where did we fail with process support of the intervention in ASOS-2? We made two fundamental mistakes. Firstly, because we were determined to execute a rapid continental trial, we did not provide feedback on processes, so the intervention teams had no idea of their performance, nor could they initiate strategies to improve the fidelity of the proposed intervention.

The second deal-breaker was that we backed the wrong methods for healthcare worker practice support. We had provided printed aids and information sheets to place above the beds of high-risk patients, in order to flag the patient as high-risk and provide early care advice for staff should they complicate. However, printed aids have been shown to deliver a median increase in performance of only 1%. Really, we should have been on the ground training the team, which could have increased their performance by 10–20%, and then encouraged group problem-solving on how to maximise implementation fidelity during the feedback sessions. That way, we could have increased performance in the region of over 40%.[110] The logistics to do this are demanding, though, and this re-iterates the importance of strong local leaders who can build and support this training culture from within.

Resources

The ceiling effect of resources

E ven if we can get buy-in for an intervention, ensure people understand the hypothesis and the supporting programme theory, co-design a deliverable intervention, and ultimately ensure implementation through feedback analysis of intervention processes and patient outcomes, the peak performance of the intervention will ultimately be limited by the available resources. This is the ceiling effect of a limited-resource environment. We must be on the lookout for local performance indicators used by management, which may allude to resource constraints. Performance indicators will go some way to identifying potential resource constraints on a quality-care initiative.

When I moved to Cape Town seven years ago, I'd made the decision because the health system in KwaZulu-Natal was falling apart. The budget was too tight to maintain an oncology service in the province and a radiology service in my own tertiary hospital. South Africa was battling to provide healthcare across the provinces, and budget cuts were taking their toll. I was committed to the public service, but this was fast becoming an environment in which it would be too difficult to work. In contrast, the Western Cape was surviving. It had continued to provide good care despite limited resources and difficult economic times. It really stood out as something special in South African healthcare.

I moved to Groote Schuur in 2016, essentially returning to my roots. This is where I had trained in the late eighties and early nineties, when the new hospital had just opened. It's a hospital with a proud history, known globally for its innovation and groundbreaking work. Most famous in its reputation is the first human heart transplant, although it was much more than that. But when I returned to that same hospital it looked like it had not had a lick of paint since I left in 1993. The wards were still colour-coded in brown, blue, orange, and green. The chipped paint on the walls and stairs suggested that money had been better spent elsewhere. Nevertheless, two good things were evident, and these had probably contributed to the ongoing performance and stature of this great hospital. The first was that the management and staff were proud to deliver a fantastic service. The hospital management valued the opinion of the clinicians, and they were willing to take a chance on innovative ideas that might result in better care using limited resources. The second observation was that efficiency had become a cornerstone of healthcare delivery in the hospital. The performance indicators were centred around efficiency. As the budget got tighter and tighter, the value and role of efficiency became more and more important in ensuring that the best outcomes could still be achieved with less spend. And for a public sector hospital in Africa, it was very efficient. In the operating rooms, we targeted surgical starting times relentlessly to ensure that theatre time was not wasted, and that we understood the factors that could create barriers to delivering as much surgery as possible with the theatre time that we had available. The reason for late starts and patient cancellations were studied with a fine-tooth comb to ensure that as many patients got surgery as possible, and theatre downtime was avoided at all costs. I was proud to be part of this famous and efficient hospital delivering quality care against the odds.

But the last seven years have been instructive. The national health budget has not increased for the last few years, and as the health systems of the other provinces have deteriorated, more and more people have migrated to the Western Cape for care. This was all compounded by the Covid-19 pandemic. We were used to tracking surgical start times as a performance indicator, and originally targeted performance in the 90–95% range, but during 2022 the performance consistently dropped, reaching levels as low as 50%. As the performance has dropped the scrutiny of efficiency increased, almost to the point of obsession. Was it a lack of commitment from the doctors and nurses that led to this poorer performance, or was it something else?

The reality was that the deteriorating performance was a symptom of a bigger problem, which was tied up in two factors. As the clinical service demand has increased, the need to chase efficiency has increased along with it. In a system that is already highly efficient, however, small gains require tremendous effort. Chasing efficiency metrics will always lead you to a ceiling set by the availability of resources. No matter how hard you drive efficiency, and regardless of how committed your team is, optimal delivery will ultimately be determined by the available resources. And this is what we were experiencing at Groote Schuur Hospital. The resource constraints were becoming even more dire with the ongoing budget restrictions, together with the increasing patient burden. Resource constraints were impacting on the efficiency of the operating theatres: there were no syringes, no drugs, and the like.

Tinashe Chandauka (who you met at the beginning of the book) is in awe of Sue Fawcus (who we are all in awe of). When Tinashe discusses leadership and people who make a difference to care he speaks of the time that

Sue Fawcus was head of obstetrics at Mowbray Maternity Hospital (MMH). When the rate of wound sepsis went up, Sue looked for the cause. She'd be up in the ventilator shafts ensuring that they were cleaned, speaking to the porters about other factors that may be contributing to sepsis, and changing the mops used to clean the floors in theatre. Sue used sepsis as a performance indicator at MMH. Indeed, when management notes that performance indicators are starting to fall short, they should consider that the real reason may be related to resources. At Groote Schuur, decreased efficiency could mean decreased morale or work ethic, or inadequate resources to deliver surgery. At MMH, increased sepsis could mean increased antibiotic resistance, or poor infection control procedures.

Ant Reed, a lead anaesthesiologist in the Western Cape, is an expert in theatre management and surgical health systems. He confirms that there are performance indicators that tell you about the state of the system. People like Randy Heisner of Sullivan Healthcare Consulting and Jeff Peters of Surgical Directions have made a living identifying health system failures to improve the quality of care. Recently, Ant and I were together in an orthopaedic theatre when the surgeon stopped operating. He was waiting for an instrument to be sterilised. Sterilisation during an operation should be a non-starter for a surgical operating complex. It means there are not enough instruments to go around, which is a symptom of a system short on resources. It causes the surgical procedure to be delayed mid operation, and time is added to the operation. Fewer patients will get surgery if theatre time is lost due to the need to sterilise equipment.

When performance indicators are stubbornly resistant to improvement, we should consider the possibility that it's because of the ceiling effect of limited resources. These limitations may include a lack of equipment, limited patient bed capacity, limited operating theatre time, or limited theatre staff.[118] These all occur in low-resource environments, capping the performance of a quality care intervention.

Communication

Poor communication can break down the best attempts at improving the quality of care, even in a system that appears to have a functional organisational model. The process evaluations from both EPOCH and ASOS-2 suggested that leadership, with senior support and a collaborative, team-based approach, were important for implementation fidelity.[88,89] Conversely, we saw in the ASOS-2 process evaluations that a steep hierarchical team structure resulted in little teamwork, with poor implementation of the quality improvement intervention.[89] A recent systematic review of systems approach to healthcare delivery sums it up nicely: 'Most of the factors reported as contributing to success were related to people; engaging stakeholders, taking a team-based approach, enhancing communication, adopting a collaborative approach, and patient-centredness and physician-centredness.'[119] There is a need for education in the soft skills of communication in order to provide quality surgical care. The days of the barking leader are gone.

PART 3

The outside-in surgical resources model

> *There needs to be a multistate effort to ensure all sub-Saharan African regions have basic health infrastructure.*

– Tinashe Chandauka, *Earth Cast* S3E36

Capacitating a hospital and staff for surgery

It was a lack of surgical capacity that resulted in a young pregnant woman with a thoracic injury having to spend six hours on a motorbike to go to Kinshasa for surgery. Supporting a healthcare system to deliver neglected surgeries requires local hospital resources and educational stepping stones to provide these surgeries. This is the outside-in surgical model, and it has two components. Firstly, governments must work through the National Surgery Obstetrics Anaesthesia Plan (NSOAP) to address the resource shortages (physical infrastructure and the human workforce) to provide the scope and volume of surgical care required for population health. The second is to ensure that the skills and knowledge of a surgical team are adequate to deliver the necessary surgeries at the district hospital level.

Resources

The impact of limited resources on patient outcomes

New York, December 2019. Dr Isabella Epiu began her presentation at a closed Bill and Melinda Gates Foundation meeting on maternal outcomes with a slide showing a state-of-the-art anaesthesia machine. The machine had been covered with a tablecloth and teacups. This machine was beautiful (although I am professionally biased) but redundant in her home environment of Makerere University, Uganda. It had been gifted by an international donor, but was useless without the physical and financial support needed to ensure its operation. Isabella's work, conducted across five referral hospitals in Uganda, Kenya, Tanzania, Rwanda, and Burundi, demonstrated that, based on the WFSA international guidelines for safe anaesthesia, none (!) of the respondents had all the necessary requirements available to provide safe obstetric anaesthesia. Only 7% reported adequate anaesthesia staffing. There were a limited number of anaesthesia monitors, but even when available they were often non-functional,[120] much like the beautiful anaesthesia machine in her opening slide. These findings confirm why we identified the 'development of minimum provision of care standards for peri-operative healthcare providers (surgical, anaesthesia and nursing)' as the second highest perioperative research priority in Africa.[82] Basically, we do not have the resources for the care that we are expected to deliver. How might we adapt to address this challenge?

With the incredibly low volume of surgery in Africa, one strategy has been to use sedation alone to increase the volume of essential surgeries where no formal anaesthesia services are available. Ketamine is a low-cost sedative commonly available in low-resource environments, and it has a 'perceived safe' risk profile.[121-123] Formal protocols have been proposed to standardise the administration of ketamine in these environments. The 'Every Second Matters for Emergency and Essential Surgery-Ketamine' (ESM-Ketamine) package is a protocol to aid inexperienced physicians and non-physicians in the administration of ketamine to enable surgery without anaesthesia, and it has been reported as a safe alternative when there is no anaesthetist.[121] However, the ESM-Ketamine protocol remains controversial, and is not universally accepted.[124] Despite these concerns, it has been included in recommendations for doctors and midwives managing complications in pregnancy and childbirth.[125]

In Africa, sedation has also been used to increase access to surgery,[126] but the patients receiving procedural sedation by non-physicians have an eightfold increase in the odds of severe complications or death compared to those sedated by physicians.[126] This finding is even more significant when one considers that nearly a third of all procedural sedations for surgery in Africa were provided by non-physicians. This is naturally an extremely sensitive issue, and when submitting the data to a peer-reviewed journal we worked hard with the statistical editor to ensure that the signal of harm associated with the provision of sedation for surgery by non-physicians was real and robust. This is important, as it is easy to jump to the conclusion that the non-physicians alone were responsible for these poor outcomes. What we found however, was that the non-physicians were working in an environment that was significantly more resource-constrained than that of the physicians. It was as if their hands had been tied, and they were forced to do *something* to enable surgery, which in these cases was to provide sedation because general anaesthesia was not available. This was crucial for interpretation of our findings. The fact that non-physicians are required to provide sedation is more likely a marker of a poorly resourced facility. It was the resource limits of these environments that almost certainly drove the bad outcomes, and not the non-physicians themselves. Furthermore, the limited resources of this environment may mean that there's an inability to recognise and manage the complications of procedural sedation by non-physicians. The overall result is FTR when complications arise in the perioperative period, contributing to the high number of severe complications and death.[126] Ultimately, it is the environment's lack of resources and education that has forced non-physicians into this invidious position.

'A fundamental problem in providing surgical care in a low-resource environment is the inability to concentrate on the quality of care when one is struggling with the absolute basics,' says Isabeau Walker, a British anaesthesiologist who has spent her life developing the Safer Anaesthesia From Education (SAFE) programmes for low-resource environments.[127] These include paediatric and obstetric anaesthesia and theatre management programmes. These absolute basics she's referring to are the resources necessary to provide care, and the education to ensure that this care is delivered safely. It is therefore inappropriate to think that the ESM-Ketamine programme will safely increase the volume of surgery in Africa. This is because it will be required in the very environments where the resources are most limited: the monitors are insufficient, the skills and education are limited, and the ability to treat the complications are inadequate, which ultimately results in excess mortality. These working conditions are certainly not the same conditions in which the ESM-Ketamine programme was developed, in a more capacitated environment with a safety net of resources.

We have seen other examples of limited resources compromising quality of care. Although the SSC is a great example of improving outcomes through a simple intervention, it falls apart when the resources to support the processes of the checklist are insufficient, as evidenced by the decreased use of the SSC in countries with a lower HDI (Figure 7).[128]

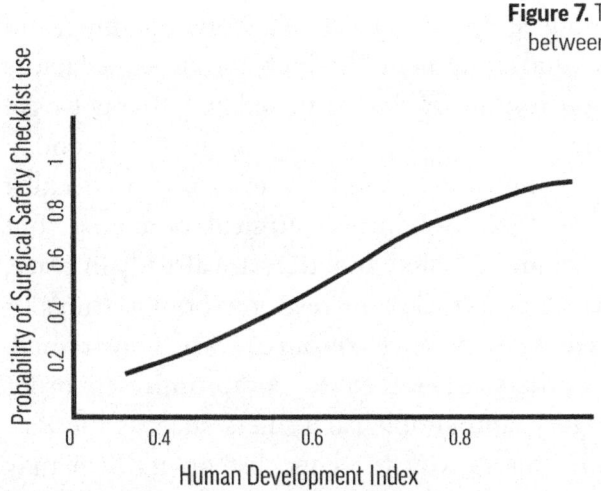

Figure 7. The relationship between the use of the SSC and HDI

Even more worryingly, the SSC is used less frequently in urgent versus elective operations in low HDI countries, while this is not the case in very high HDI countries.[128] Why is this? When the wheels come off, the structure that the checklist provides saves lives. That is why it is distressing to see less use of the SSC in less-resourced countries, and less use in urgent and emergent surgery.

Now imagine working in a low-resource environment without the resources needed to respond in the affirmative to some of the checklist items, such as the ability to provide preoperative antibiotics, or have blood available for a big surgery. I suspect that the tolerance for the SSC falls in resource-limited environments (and more so in their emergency situations) because the questions become redundant and irritating, especially when one is trying to do one's best in the circumstances. This opinion is supported by a programme in Uganda that attempted to implement the SSC. It showed that over 80% of the barriers to implementation of the checklist were associated with malfunctioning equipment, a lack of adequate staffing, and a lack of essential equipment,[129] which are the same factors that would push non-physicians to sedate patients to 'get surgery done'.[126] The key observation from the Ugandan surgical SSC study was the following: 'Using a checklist is an effective tool to improve surgical outcomes, but assumes that standard safety practices are already in place, which may not be the case in resource-poor settings.'[129] What we see is that once resources are constrained, healthcare workers are forced to compromise in order to allow surgery, and simple safety nets such as the SSC are removed. This is why the checklist on its own may not be an effective intervention in these environments. What is needed is a stepwise approach to strengthening a health system through ensuring sufficient resources and education to provide the necessary surgical care.[129]

We have seen how limited resources result in physicians and non-physicians being forced to provide care in a potentially unsafe manner. But how much does the availability of resources contribute to poor outcomes? If we can improve the resources supporting surgery, can we improve outcomes? The work by the NIHR Unit for Global Surgery gives us an idea of the proportional contribution of hospital resources and patient risk factors for mortality following cancer surgery. This allows us to estimate what proportion of quality of care is attributable to resources, and what proportion is attributable to patient risk factors (which is where the healthcare providers and their processes and interventions will affect the quality of care, as described in the inside-out surgical model. In this study, the country HDI and hospital resources contributed about 40% to mortality following cancer surgery globally, while the patient and disease factors contributed the remaining 60% of post-surgical mortality.[71] This makes a strong case for investing in adequate resources for surgical care. It demonstrates that despite the substantial role that clinicians and healthcare providers play in determining safe surgery for all, adequate resources are necessary to delivering quality care, and the absence of resources is responsible for nearly half of the deaths following surgery.

The National Surgical, Obstetric and Anaesthesia Plan

Emmanuel Makasa is the epitome of an advocate for surgical care and universal health. He was part of the famous World Health Assembly (WHA) resolution 68.15 where governments signed an agreement to ensure safe and affordable surgery for all.[130] He had followed a circuitous route to sit at that table. Emmanuel is a hustler with a strong moral compass. When I met him, his Twitter profile picture accurately captured his personality: a black and white shot of a suave, bearded man in a Stetson. Emmanuel is the middle child of 11, with five brothers and five sisters. He was involved in student leadership from a young age. Not on the frontline, but strategising and organising in the background. It is not surprising, then, that with the early death of his father when he was 21, he used his strategic organisational skills, and his affinity for numbers to ensure the financial security of his siblings. He describes how in Zambia, an intergenerational loss of wealth is almost ubiquitous, as the siblings split the wealth between numerous family members, leaving everyone with too little money to do anything meaningful. Instead, Emmanuel advocated for using his father's wealth for the education of his siblings to ensure they could be financially independent.

Because of his strong moral values, he flirted with the possibility of becoming a priest, but his first love was numbers and engineering. Being locked down in a mine somewhere in Zambia was not Emmanuel's idea of a life well lived, though, so he turned to his third career choice, medicine. Medicine was not for a numbers man and the rote learning was relentless, but because Emmanuel had a clear idea of his future, he moved through medicine comfortably. As a young doctor, he tried paediatrics but 'there were too many children'. He tried obstetrics next, but the unpredictable nature of delivery and the awkwardness of treating naked women led him at last to his true love: orthopaedics. A perfect combination of mechanics and compassion. It seemed like a match made in heaven, an effortless caring for Emmanuel.

He completed a master's in public health in Alabama, and then returned to Zambia to work as a specialist who would fly into remote locations to provide surgical care. With his public health background and his experience working on the ground in remote locations, he could not only see the problem of too little skilled surgery, but also what was required to change the situation. To effect changes through policy, he moved to the WHO in Geneva. When WHA 68.15 was signed, it galvanised a self-belief within Emmanuel. At that time he was not in the Zambian health ministry, but his take on the situation was, 'Well, I sat at the table [to sign the WHA 68.15 resolution], and I wasn't even in the ministry, yet I helped convince 194 countries to sign a resolution. Everything I need to do from now on to ensure safe surgery should be easy.' His strategy to promote surgical health advocacy is clear and simple: we need a hierarchy of priorities that include global health diplomacy and advocacy, regional health policy improvement, policy implementation for surgical health service delivery, and policy implementation research.

The global health diplomacy and advocacy for safe surgery is well on the road with WHA resolution 68.15, and the regional policy improvement and implementation is described in the National Surgical, Obstetric and Anaesthesia Plan (NSOAP) manual.[131] However, despite resolution WHA 68.15, little has changed, which essentially makes a mockery of the commitments of many governments to the process of ensuring safe and affordable surgery. This is a social injustice. The very people who represent their citizens, whom they profess to care about, have not led the change. It is clear that no county will reach the UN's SDGs without safe surgical care for all. Surgery is a core component of health, with a third of all hospital admissions requiring a surgical component to care,[132] and 30% of diseases requiring surgical care.[52] Fortunately, there is a solution and a template for governments to respond to the surgical needs of their populations. This is in the form of the NSOAP manual, which has been published to help governments create a local environment that can deliver surgical care,[131] in order to fulfil their mandate to WHA resolution 68.15. The NSOAP is a policy framework that helps to evaluate, strengthen, and establish a health system able to provide quality and sustainable surgical care for all.

At this point, only four African countries (Ethiopia, Zambia, Tanzania, and Rwanda) have responded to resolution WHA 68.15 and developed NSOAPs.[133] In typical Emmanuel style, he left the WHA meeting where resolution 68.15 was taken, and like a true leader and pioneer, returned to Zambia to start the NSOAP process there. Zambia was the first country in the world to have an NSOAP. Other African countries have also started NSOAPs, including Senegal, Nigeria, Madagascar,[134] and South Africa. In South Africa, we had a stuttered start to an NSOAP in 2015. It stalled, and we started our second attempt in 2020. NSOAPs are important to support adequate surgical provision in a country and to achieve health equity, but for an NSOAP to thrive it needs the support of a national health department.[133] Governments must take ownership of it, and clinicians and citizens must push governments to deliver. NSOAPs allow us to plan for a healthcare system that can deliver safe and affordable surgical care necessary for health equity, and it tracks the quality of the surgical service we are providing. Just as we expect to see the budget and expenditure of our countries, so too should we demand to see how our surgical system is planned and how it is delivering. It has been suggested that the key components of successful NSOAP implementation include: government ownership and support; agreed-upon target timelines; broad stakeholder involvement that includes frontline workers, with integration of the indicators into health management systems to track progress; and ensuring that the implementers and financing bodies are involved in the entire process.[133]

While we have seen improvements in the number of facilities and patient outcomes, these indicators also show us how far we still have to go. In Ethiopia, for example, maternal mortality has halved since 2000, and there has been an increase in surgical facilities from 108 in 2013 to 289 in 2019.[135] Despite these successes, however, the shortfall in achieving the minimum volume of surgery is enormous. Ethiopia provides about 112 surgical procedures per 100 000 population, nearly fiftyfold short of the recommended 5000 per 100 000 needed for an adequate surgical provision in a country.[41] The inability to provide an adequate volume of surgical procedures means that the resources to support surgery are insufficient, and therefore the ability to support other disciplines, such as critical care and acute care, are also compromised. In an Ethiopian survey, the surgical facilities could only perform a median of seven surgical procedures per day, and approximately 30% of the facilities had no specialist surgical or obstetric workforce members. Over 60% of the surgical facilities also did not have a physician anaesthesiologist. The advances being made in safe and adequate surgical healthcare provision in low-resource environments remain too slow and we therefore need to embrace and push for the NSOAP process in every country.

You can see the lack of NSOAP engagement at a governmental level when you speak to young doctors. Occasionally when working in the operating theatre, I meet a South African junior doctor (intern) who studied outside of South Africa, usually in China or Mauritius. They often chose to study abroad because they were passionate about medicine but could not secure a local undergraduate training post. I ask them how difficult it was to enter the South African medical system, with the regulatory approvals and intern placements. Typically, their response is that there is an inefficiency in obtaining registration, which takes a couple of years. They feel that it's so slow and inefficient because there are few to no job positions in which to place doctors coming into the system, and no money to support new doctors entering the profession, so there's no will to facilitate the process. This is despite the fact that we need more healthcare providers; South Africa is still short of the minimum workforce number defined for safe and affordable surgery.[33,136] One of the results of not engaging in the NSOAP process is this perpetuation of the workforce crisis in low-resource environments. An NSOAP demands that a country actively engage in a response to the surgical indicators and develop strategies on how to increase and capacitate the surgical workforce to provide universal healthcare.

In contrast, Tanzania is an illuminating example of the power of an NSOAP programme, and how return on investment for implementation is potentially massive. In implementing the NSOAP, Tanzania added 3% to the healthcare budget.[137] For this small additional cost, the scale-up in anaesthesia providers would be 25-fold for the country over a five-year period. This is a powerful outcome, and mind bogglingly massive, but it is only one component of the many benefits in providing an improved health system structure to upscale surgical care. The principle is that implementing NSOAPs can result in big wins. This builds capacity and will build the cross-cutting benefits on health by strengthening the surgical system. And the cost for these benefits? At the time, the 3% budget increase in Tanzania's healthcare expenditure amounted to $600 million over 7 years, or $2 per person per year.[137] Considering that surgical services contribute an estimated 30% to population health,[52] this is a tiny investment for the proportional increase in health capacity.

In Ethiopia's implementation of an NSOAP programme, the surgical facilities increased from approximately 80 in 2011 to over 290 in 2019, and access to surgery from 43 operations per 100 000 population to 465 operations per 100 000 population.[138] The increase in surgical facilities was based on an upgrading of facilities, and increasing staff with the necessary surgical skills.[56] These results are astounding. Increasing personnel 25-fold, and surgical facilities over tenfold, both within a period of under 10 years. Political will increases surgical capacity. These are compelling cases for the first part of the outside-in strategy for addressing the resource shortage with NSOAPs.

Remember the example of appendicitis in Africa. The current limited access to surgery is resulting in approximately 6500 to 8300 excess deaths per 100 000 patients due to inadequate surgical management of appendicitis alone, and at an additional $4.5 to $6.3 billion, these deaths could be averted.[42] Suddenly, the $2 per person per year seems totally inconsequential, if it was extended across Africa, and it would capacitate health systems to manage appendicitis and many other unmet surgical needs. This is the power of an NSOAP.

Unfortunately, the uptake and implementation of the NSOAP has been disappointing. The recent passing of WHA resolution 76.2 commits to the integration of emergency, critical, and operative care into universal health coverage, with a specific declaration that emergency, critical and operative care are part of comprehensive primary healthcare.[139] This is an extremely important resolution, providing more support for WHA 68.15. We need to ensure now that governments fulfil their NSOAP mandates.

Do more resources mean better quality of care?

If we improve the volume and scope of available resources, will we improve the quality of care? This is a fundamental question. A phenomenal study examined over 4000 healthcare facilities across eight low- and middle-income countries. It assessed WHO-recommended amenities, equipment, and medications necessary for various healthcare services. The investigators then conducted over 30 000 observations of clinical practice to identify whether it conformed with evidence-based recommendations. In this way, it was possible to determine the correlation between the recommended infrastructure for healthcare delivery and the quality of care delivered (i.e., providing evidence-based practice). While most sites had a moderate degree of infrastructure (at least 60% of recommended resources), the quality of care delivered was generally low, averaging 37% for sick-child care, and up to 60% for labour and delivery. The reality is that even when controlling for the resources necessary to deliver surgery for all, it does not guarantee quality surgical care. For example, when the outcomes of hospitals with similar levels of birth attendants were compared across middle-income countries, the maternal mortality still varied between sixfold and twelvefold across these countries, and neonatal mortality varied between threefold and fourfold.[81] Essentially, the correlation between resources and quality of care is low.[140]

So, should we even try to improve the resources available for surgery? Absolutely! There appears to be a low inflection point for resources below which the quality of care in the most resource-limited environments will be challenged, even in teams that are willing and able to provide good care normally. When you start from a low-resource base, there is a potentially large return in the quality of care. For example, implementing the SSC will require a minimum of resources that include staffing and functional essential equipment. In a Ugandan study, staffing and a lack of functional equipment accounted for over 80% of the barriers to implementing the SSC.[129] An NSOAP could potentially have a large impact on these barriers as a result. This same principle holds for making sedation safer in Africa.[126] Again, staffing would be key here, as would other equipment resources necessary to provide general anaesthesia and monitor patients.

In summary, increasing resources alone will not guarantee an improvement in the quality of care, but a certain minimum of resources is necessary to provide basic safety in surgical care. Above this minimum resource level, any subsequent improvement in the quality of care with additional resources becomes unpredictable. Once we have crossed the minimum resources threshold, then other factors affect the quality of care delivered, as discussed in the inside-out model.

Novel resource solutions

Africa presents a unique opportunity for novel strategies to provide surgical resources. This is what Emmanuel Makasa, Alex Torborg and I were discussing on a balmy evening in Pretoria in March 2020. We were there for the annual conference of the South African Society of Anaesthesiologists. (Little did we know that we would not have another face-to-face meeting for more than two years because of Covid-19.) It was a fascinating evening discussing global surgical health and, in particular, novel strategies to address resource limitations that compromise surgical delivery, especially with Emmanuel's extensive knowledge and Alex's understanding of paediatric care through her leadership of the African Paediatric Surgical Outcomes Study (ASOS-Paeds). The key discussions revolved around their understanding of the infrastructure limitations affecting surgery, and the novel strategies that people have used to circumvent these barriers in resource-limited environments. In particular, we discussed strategies for equipping and maintaining operating theatres, and effective theatre management.

Emmanuel's approach to novel strategies is simple: 'Stop showing countries how poorly they are performing. Rather, do something positive, and the money will follow.' Although the strategies are separate, they are potentially linkable for scaling access to operating theatres and the equipment necessary to support surgery. The first principle to equip and maintain a theatre effectively at a low cost, is to build and stock identical theatres, so that you can save money by buying things in bulk. A country's most powerful moment for financial negotiation for operating theatre resources is when it is preparing to implement an NSOAP.

Emmanuel sees an NSOAP as a *stimulus package for Africa.* 'Don't provide us with the crumbs of small incentives,' he says, 'but rather bring industry to the table when a whole country is negotiating to strengthen a surgical system through an NSOAP. Then you have real power to negotiate, and financial leverage.'

Building identical theatres allows us to realise the second principle of ensuring that all anaesthesia machines and surgical machinery are maintained. Technical support for operating theatre maintenance in low-resource environments is difficult and costly, especially when using a relatively low commercial volume in remote locations. If we don't get this right, we will see more of Isabella's anaesthetic tea tables instead of operations. The classic case study for circumventing this problem is the model developed by Garreth and Nicola Wood for Kids Operating Room (Kids OR). The model is simple but brilliant. They build identical operating theatres across the globe, and then when technical support is needed, it is delivered remotely by a technician in an identical model operating theatre in Scotland. It is possible to communicate where the problem lies, and then provide the support for a remote repair of the theatre. This model has been highly effective. There are now over 50 Kids OR operating rooms in Africa and Latin America, and it is estimated that they provided the infrastructure for more than 80 000 operations since the inception of the charity in 2018 (https://www.kidsor.org/our-work/). This is a great model for sustainable operating theatres in Africa.

The third principle is to then ensure that operating theatres are managed effectively. Many operating theatres currently do not run 24 hours a day, but they should. Any theatre downtime could be used for private surgical patients and billed for. This exploits the financial potential of having a functional operating theatre. Non-profit network CURE International has leveraged this principle successfully.

It could be argued that the current resource requirements for surgery in low- and middle-income countries should not be seen as a barrier, but as an opportunity for thinking differently about resourcing surgery. It is important to remember that setting up operating theatres is not prohibitively expensive. Construction costs and equipment account for about 20% of the cost. Rather, it is the ongoing staffing of the operating theatres that is the main expense (about 30%).[141,142] It is possible that these novel strategies could further drive down the costs of establishing and maintaining operating theatres in Africa.

Making sense of the relationship between resources and processes

The outside-in surgical model is about *resource* capacitation and the inside-out surgical care model is about *process* capacitation. These two models work in tandem. Neither model can work effectively in isolation. The relationship between resources and processes on the quality of care is shown in the Figure 8.

The figure represents a simple yet appropriate hierarchical strategy for 'quick wins' in improving the quality of surgical care in low-resource environments. In the bottom left corner, when both resources and processes are inadequate, a strategy that targets resources should be adopted first. When resources are so limited, it sets up even the most committed healthcare providers for failure. We saw this in ASOS when non-physicians were forced to

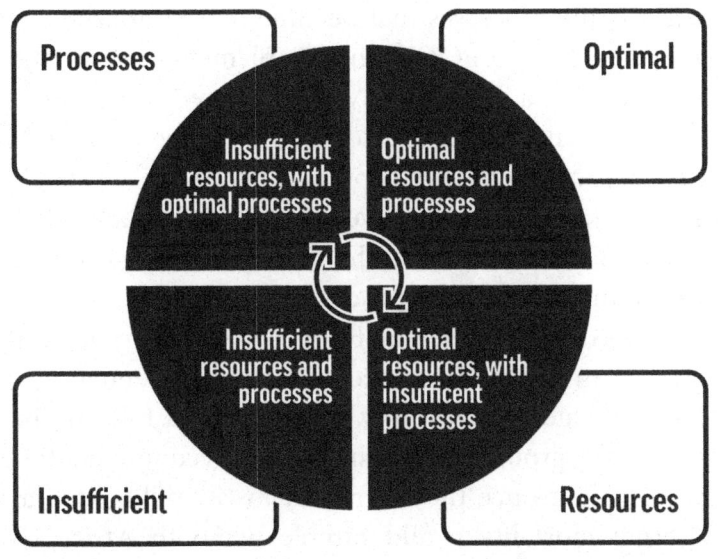

Figure 8. The relationship between resources and processes in delivering quality care

provide sedation to allow for surgical care, and how it had a negative impact on morbidity and mortality.[126] These data suggest that there is a minimum resource level that should never be accepted in healthcare delivery. This is similar to the observation that most of the barriers to implementing the SSC are related to insufficient resources (both human and equipment).[129]

Only once this minimum resource threshold is reached can processes then contribute to increasing quality of care. The ultimate quality of care will be limited by the ceiling effect of the available resources (the top left corner). This is what I believe we are starting to experience at Groote Schuur Hospital.

When resources are optimal, which is closer to the situation in the NHS EPOCH study[88] (bottom right corner), then it is the processes that become more important. We have seen from EPOCH that implementation of these processes in a relatively well-resourced environment is certainly not easy. The top right corner of sufficient resources coupled with optimal processes appears to almost be a unicorn. However, it could be achieved if the delivery of care is based on the principles of the inside-out surgical model to ensure process capacitation.

In 1998, the Confidential Enquiry into Maternal Deaths (CEMD) in South Africa led to 10 recommendations to decrease maternal mortality.[143] Sue Fawcus told me how excited the group was about the 10 recommendations. They felt that once they were out in the public domain, maternal mortality would tumble in South Africa. The recommendations were robust and based on both good data and expert interpretation of what was contributing to maternal mortality in South Africa. However, the decrease in mortality was not nearly as spectacular as expected. Sue relates how deflating this was for the group.[144] The majority of CEMDs globally do not have implementation strategies linked to the recommendations made by their committees, but South Africa *does* have an implementation strategy,[145] so the disappointment was even greater. The failure suggests that the process capacitation of the inside-out quality surgical model is needed to ensure optimal implementation of these recommendations.

To achieve a functional surgical health system, we must work inside organisations with the inside-out model to optimise processes and implementation, and outside the organisation to provide the resources necessary for surgical care.

Education

The scope and challenge of the education needed for quality surgical care

To determine the role of education in increasing the quality of care, we could conduct an experiment where we control for the resources available and determine the impact of education or supervision on patient outcomes. This is what the investigators in the Service Provision Assessment in Sub-Saharan Africa did, to assess the impact of in-service training or supervision on the quality of sick-child and antenatal care. What they found was that the quality of care was generally poor, with only about 40% of evidence-based interventions applied in sick-child and antenatal care. The improvement in the quality of care following the educational or supervision interventions was small, amounting to one additional evidence-based intervention administered out of 18 sick-child interventions (a 6% improvement) and one additional intervention of 40 antenatal evidence-based interventions (or a 2.5% improvement).[146] The effect of training was small. Granted, it is difficult to assess the quality of the educational training and supervision from this study, but other studies have suggested that supervision or training alone has provided about a 10–20% increase in healthcare worker performance.[110]

In an attempt to improve maternal outcomes in South Africa, a two-day 'skills and drills' course was held for obstetric teams from the 12 worst-performing healthcare districts. The course was built on the Kirkpatrick training model, and the objective was to deliver the Essential Steps in Managing Obstetric Emergencies (ESMOE) course to the maternity care providers in the district teams with the worst maternal mortality. The result was a significant decrease in direct maternal deaths (driven predominantly by a decrease in haemorrhagic deaths) and indirect maternal deaths (driven predominantly by a reduction in non-pregnancy related infections).[147] These sites had started from a really low base with an institutional maternal mortality ratio of 206 per 100 000 live births. When one considers the surgical component, the case fatality rate for caesarean section dropped by just under 15%. This was not significant in the study, but there was a clinically significant decrease in haemorrhagic deaths at an RRR of 36%. Education had decreased maternal mortality. While the data presented in these examples suggest that education is not a panacea, it is possible that the more decisive action needed in rapidly fatal complications, such as acute haemorrhage, may be positively impacted by education.

Although an adequate volume of education with extensive coverage to include most of the healthcare providers is important in delivering safer maternal and caesarean section care, it is apparent that not all outcomes are going to be improved by education alone.[147] Here is a summary of our understanding of factors affecting quality surgical care. Resources are needed to provide the minimum for an acceptable environment to deliver safe surgery and anaesthesia, and will ultimately determine where the ceiling effect comes into play in local site performance. The quality of care still varies tremendously between surgical sites with similar resources, but could be improved by process capacitation and implementation. Education alone won't improve the quality of a surgical system in sub-Saharan Africa, but education is essential to get the full benefit of adequate resources, processes, and implementation. The volume of training that is needed to improve outcomes is unclear, and the impact of the educational intervention will only be evident on some patient outcomes. At this point, we do not know which outcomes, although it is likely that education is important in successfully managing maternal haemorrhage, which is the leading cause of maternal mortality in Africa.[2] Educational interventions may be more impactful for acute complications that deteriorate rapidly, such as haemorrhage and anaesthesia-related complications, because knowledge allows for more decisive action. In Africa, it is these rapidly progressing complications that are most important in maternal mortality[2] and in unnecessary deaths associated with anaesthesia complications in children.[65]

The scope of education required to provide a safe surgical service is mind-boggling. My own path has been instructive. When I started my medical training, I aspired to be a 'super general practitioner (GP)'. At the time they were prevalent in South Africa: a vast country with small one-horse towns where the population was cared for by the lone town GP. This was the omnipresent doctor, all-seeing and all-knowing. He or she knew everyone in the town, their personalities, their secrets and frailties, both physical and psychological. Yet, at the drop of a hat, they could leap in and wield a surgical scalpel competently and swiftly to save a life. They were skilled and confident. I prepared myself for this throughout my varsity career. I collected obscure textbooks with names like 'Primary Surgery', featuring step-by-step guides on how to do an appendicectomy and the like. I filled my textbooks with practical annotations on how to manage everyday surgical problems, resourcefully transcribed during training by listening intensely to my consultants, who spoke from practical skill. Groote Schuur Hospital and UCT have a proud tradition of pioneering surgery, and it was evident in the training I received.

Towards the end of my undergraduate training, I took a road trip around Zimbabwe. It was there that I found where I wanted to be. I drove east from Masvingo to the Eastern Highlands, which run off the plateau towards Mozambique and the Indian Ocean. In this verdant forest, moist and misty, I drove through Chimanimani village. Just off the dusty jeep track was a small medical clinic, unpainted, with a red cross on the wall. It looked like the place where the village's one doctor could hold the fort and make a difference. It felt like a calling. The perfect place for me to be a Super GP. It was Africa at its most beautiful, and most wild. I was on track to complete my training; just two more years, my final year and internship, and then I would be ready to return to Chimanimani.

While I was enjoying Zimbabwe and imagining my future, Sue Fawcus was working down the road in Masvingo and contributing to the first documentation of maternal mortality for the region. Our paths would cross more than 25 years later in Cape Town. At the time, I was unaware that Masvingo had a maternal mortality rate of about 168 per 100 000.[4]

Aspiring to be the hero of Chimanimani, I worked hard to get my fifth-year elective placement at the hospital of my choice – Victoria Hospital in Wynberg, Cape Town. This hospital was the 'school of the all-rounder' and the super GP. It was a small family of competent career doctors who had dedicated their lives to teaching safe principles of medical practice for the non-specialist. It was a gem of a hospital. Here one learnt how to treat heart attacks, do essential surgical operations such as appendicectomies, cholecystectomies, and fixing fractures, give a safe anaesthetic and resuscitate a tiny baby that was severely dehydrated from diarrhoea. A year in this environment with its great mentors would set me up nicely to become a great GP. And if I impressed the local doctors during my elective, there was a chance of getting my internship placement there too. It would be great. Things were on track. I got my elective in fifth year and spent four weeks doing paediatrics. I managed to pull the wool over their eyes, and was offered an internship at Victoria. I would be joining the family of docs who did their work diligently in the morning, then downed tools to connect with each other and discuss problem patients in the small tearoom with the veranda overlooking the beautiful palm trees of the parking lot. Afterwards, they returned to the wards, operating theatres, and outpatient clinics to continue the work. It was a happy place.

But as I neared the end of my undergrad training, I started to see the enormity of the task of being a competent super GP. There was a slow realisation that a super GP was not part of a specific training programme but a generalist who maintained and augmented the many and varying skills and knowledge of medicine and surgery. Indeed, a super GP may well be one of the hardest jobs in all of medicine. One had to be skilled enough across the range of medicine and surgery that you could practically bail yourself out of trouble, and competent enough that you could ensure the safe passage of a sick patient over a far distance to a larger centre if necessary. This reality started to hit home while doing my internship, and I pivoted towards anaesthesia: a more controlled environment, with clear speciality boundaries. My mentors at Victoria were super understanding. Often when I was meant to be on the blood side of the blood–brain barrier during surgery, they let me to sneak back onto the brain side and sit and learn with the anaesthetist. I felt more secure in the corralled space of an aspiring specialist anaesthetist, behind the green sheet that was the blood–brain barrier separating me from the surgeon and the bloody surgical field. Following the advice of Margie Lavelle, my anaesthesia mentor at Victoria, I moved to Edendale in KwaZulu-Natal after my internship to continue my training. I pursued a diploma in anaesthesia under the peerless, motherly teaching of Jenny King, instead of the planned Chimanimani adventure.

Edendale was wild. This was shortly after the first democratic elections in 1994, and the country's triumph was marred by continued Inkatha–ANC violence, where the stronghold of the Inkatha Freedom Party in KwaZulu-Natal tried to maintain political and tribal relevance in a fast-paced political environment. The anaesthesia training was solid, though, and the exposure was unbelievable. As a mere medical officer, I spent one New Year's Eve managing three stabbed hearts in a row. It was mind boggling. This was straight from the pedagogy of 'see one, do one, teach one'. Edendale was a five-storey hospital, with old red brick floors. I wasn't sure if that was an intentional plan to hide the blood on the floor. The hospital had that sweet smell of dry blood and alcohol, especially in the surgical wards and theatre. It felt like the floors were always awash with blood. If it wasn't a knife in the heart, it was a knife in the abdomen, or a mother frothing and fitting with eclampsia on a hard metal stretcher that always looked like it should have been washed before the patient was placed on it.

Outside of the crazy anaesthesia training, and the brutality of the trauma and filth and blood of the hospital, my colleagues and I tried to earn some extra cash by moonlighting when we could. We'd step from the harsh world of the massive tertiary Edendale hospital, filled with dirt and horror, into the neat, clean, and sterile world of private medicine in South Africa. There were a few locum opportunities doing the rounds in our little community: a small GP practice locum in a town outside of Pietermaritzburg, and a city-slicker alternative locum 50 kilometres down the road in Durban. I had been lined up for the small-town GP locum, but for some reason (which evades me now), I did not go. Thank goodness, as it turned out! A colleague went instead. He had the courage to leave Pietermaritzburg for the weekend and drive the 50 or 60 kilometres to locum for the town GP, who had taken the weekend off to go fishing. My colleague was doing the Saturday morning ward round in the small 'hospital', when he got to the bedside of a woman who had been recently admitted with a complicated term pregnancy. He read through the patient's notes and talked confidently about her obstetric problems with the nurse who was rounding with him. Eventually (and appropriately proud of his diagnostic skills) he announced that she would need to go to theatre for a caesarean section. The nurse did not turn to call a surgeon, just stood and stared at him. He broke out in a sweat as it suddenly dawned on him that *he* was the surgeon. He had only assisted at a caesarean section as a student, and now he would need to do one on his own, without an assistant. That took plenty of courage and stupidity. When he recounted the story, my dreams of being a super GP died. Instead, I kept doing my city-slicker locums down the drag in Durban. I provided night cover for patients with anxiety and kids with sore throats. I would sneak into the procedure room during consults to flick through my textbooks to find diagnoses, treatments, and drug doses. I was anything but a super GP. I was an incompetent generalist.

I had had grandiose visions of being this knight in shining armour who could face any medical condition and immediately know what to do and, more importantly, how to do it. It was clear now that I was not a knight but a wimp. I realised that being a true all-rounder required a level of medical and surgical skill that only a very select group of individuals would ever achieve. Despite this revelation, my perspective was also limited. I only saw the challenge from my own personal context and individual competence. I had started to understand the immense and broad competence needed, but I had not even considered the environments in which super GPs work, and how these environments further contribute to the difficulty of delivering quality medical and surgical care, and the risk of failure.

What education is needed to provide quality surgical care in these environments? And how do we disseminate knowledge and education there? Atul Gawande discusses the complexity of modern medicine in *The Checklist Manifesto*,[104] and how medicine has responded with the emergence of numerous specialities and super specialists across the field. While this transformation of modern medicine has resulted in improved outcomes through amazing insights from the many subspecialities of medicine, and the honing of unique skillsets to respond to all its challenges, it has also created a massive gulf between the medical aspirations of high-income countries and the lived reality of rest of the world. With an insufficient number of healthcare workers in low-resource environments, there is a need for generalists to provide competent care across a broad range of conditions. The need for a super GP has never been greater than now: due to the population growth in low-resource environments, the global demand for the competent all-rounder is increasing exponentially.

But being a generalist is arguably the hardest 'discipline' in medicine. It is predicted that by 2100 the global population will be 10.9 billion people, with only 1.3 billion residing in high-income countries.[148] The remaining 9.6 billion will be in Asia and Africa, with 4.7 million in Asia and 4.3 million in Africa. The skill and scope of the super GP, who is both a rural doctor and a rural surgeon, has been largely ignored and lost as medical students hurtle towards super-specialist aspirations in high-income countries. Yet close on 90% of the world's population is going to need care from super GPs by 2100.

In providing healthcare in resource-limited environments, we find ourselves at a fork in the road. Many now see medicine and medical education in terms of a high-complexity, high-cost model in high-income countries, and an alternative low-complexity, low-cost model in low- and middle-income countries. This model is flawed, and does not consider the alternative, which has been summed up beautifully by two of my colleagues. Allan Taylor, a neurosurgeon in Cape Town states that, 'It is not about how can we dumb down modern healthcare for low-income countries. Rather, how do we provide excellent care associated with good outcomes despite limited resources?' Silke Dyer, an obstetrician and gynaecologist in Cape Town asks, 'How can we provide rational excellent care, at a reasonable cost which is appropriate for all?'

Reforming education is a key component of responding to this challenge. Understanding the needs of healthcare workers in Africa may provide some direction for educational initiatives needed to improve surgical care.

According to African researchers, the top two research priorities for perioperative care in Africa are to 'develop training standards for perioperative healthcare providers' and to 'develop minimum provision of care standards for perioperative healthcare providers'.[82] This is crazy, right? Surely, we have training standards for healthcare providers, and surely medicine has baseline monitoring standards for perioperative care? And yes, we obviously do. But they were all developed in the high-complexity, well-resourced environments of high-income countries. They are not fit for purpose outside of those environments. Those top two research priorities tell us so much about the current situation in Africa, and about providing care in low-resource environments. Dolly Munlemvo, an anaesthetic colleague in the DRC, bemoans the fact that the patient outcomes vary so much across institutions when comparing procedures of similar complexity, reflecting the variance in quality of care.[81] Dolly speaks passionately of a desire to 'harmonise' practice through the standardisation of care and practice protocols. 'In the same country, the gap is huge among hospitals. In the DRC, in the very same country, you can find people who are doing a great job, but others are just doing badly.' He believes that training is a big contributor to the variance in quality of care, as did most of the clinicians across Africa who participated in our priorities consensus process.

To understand the educational challenge Dolly faces in the DRC, we need to look at the three categories of surgical care providers: anaesthesia, surgery, and critical care. In anaesthesia, the ability to respond to the current training standards is difficult when the number of physician anaesthesia providers in the DRC is 0.13 per 100 000,[149,150] which is a mere 3% of the required number of anaesthesia providers for a minimum safe service.[151] Conversely, for every current provider in the DRC, another 32 are needed to reach the recommended minimum for safe surgical care.[33] Achieving this objective is both daunting and debilitating in expectation. Furthermore, because a 33-fold jump to physician providers is not possible, the need for task shifting becomes real. The educational challenges in the DRC are not unique. This situation is nearly universal across Africa.[149] However, the recommendations for training, and scope of practice to respond to this challenge do not exist.[152] Isabeau Walker comments that, 'In these low-resource environments, anaesthesia providers may be very skilled, but with a knowledge which is extremely limited, as they are essentially "trained on the job", and their knowledge is based on what their mentors taught them years ago.' Now add a work environment where the crucial resources for safe care (many of which our high-income country colleagues would take for granted) are absent, hampering the delivery of safe surgical care. In a study of low- and middle-income district hospitals, a quarter of hospitals did not have a reliable oxygen source, a third did not have reliable electricity, 70% did not have a pulse oximeter, and 47% did not have dedicated postoperative care.[153] In the ASOS-Paeds study of surgical outcomes in Africa, a third of anaesthetists and surgeons across Africa considered their operating theatres unsafe for surgery for children less than a year old.[3] So, published standards of practice that consider carbon dioxide detectors and pulse oximeters as 'highly recommended' set up providers to fail in these low-resource environments as they cannot fulfil these recommendations,[154] just like the Ugandan study that showed that it was impossible to complete the SSC because the resources for doing so were unavailable in many cases.[129]

Indeed, when we were looking at risk factors associated with Covid-19 critical care survival and mortality in Africa, we found that it was impossible to measure the oxygen saturation in every patient in the intensive care unit, even though this is considered a most basic requirement for a sick patient.[155] In this light, the priorities set by African clinicians for training and monitoring now make sense.[82] We have to provide training and monitoring standards that are context-sensitive to low-resource environments. These observations are consistent with Nicky's evaluation of the CanMEDS training model, which found that the whole educational model was encapsulated in an awareness of the South African context.[98]

In summary, healthcare providers in Africa are aware of their working environment and its limitations. They are also acutely aware of where education and recommendations need to be addressed to ensure the delivery of safer surgical and anaesthesia care. The challenge now is to plan, design, and deliver these adapted educational programmes in Africa and other resource-poor environments.

Educational stepping stones to improve care

To respond to this educational challenge, we must first provide stepping stones to help bridge the divide from the current under-resourced reality to the internationally prescribed minimum training and monitoring standards. In setting their own training and monitoring priorities, healthcare providers in Africa are asking not to be berated because they don't have an oximeter or a carbon dioxide detector, but rather for us to accept their current circumstances and help them provide a safe framework within which to work to minimise the risk of harm. The response needs to be done in a realistic timeframe to reach the prescribed training and monitoring goals. The Tanzanian NSOAP is a classic example of how a country has responded to the challenge. At the time of the development of the NSOAP, Tanzania had 0.46 surgery, obstetric, and anaesthesia (SOA) physician providers per 100 000 population.[137] This is well short of the recommended minimum of 20 SOA physicians per 100 000, and so a decision was made to target 2.27 per 100 000 by 2025, which remains a massive fivefold increase in workforce. This target was based on the calculation that they would then have enough physicians to supervise non-physician staff to further increase capacity and build a bridge to safer care through task shifting. Anaesthesia providers were particularly sparse at 0.09 (physicians and non-physicians) per 100 000 at the beginning of the NSOAP development, but would increase substantially to 2.23 per 100 000, requiring the training of 567 anaesthesiologists and 1100 nurse anaesthetists by 2025.[137] This is a scale-up of nearly 25-fold from the current state. Clearly, early funding must be earmarked for human resources. The strategy was to provide an opportunity to phase out non-certified practitioners, and replace them with three-year trained practitioners, ensuring an appropriate educational platform sensitive to the context in which surgical and anaesthesia care is to be delivered. What is truly incredible, however, is that through appropriate planning and management, this massive scale-up comes at a projected increase in healthcare expenditure of $2 per capita per year over a seven-year period, which was calculated at 3% of the current per capita health expenditure.[137] What a wonderful return on investment.

As the Tanzanian NSOAP model shows, a stepping-stone response requires a mix of physician and non-physician providers, which necessitates task shifting. It is this realisation that resulted in the approach of the SAFE courses, as described by Isabeau, where the objective was to support the anaesthesia providers with the knowledge and skills to provide safe anaesthesia even in low-resource environments. SAFE – Safer Anaesthesia From Education – is a joint project developed by the Association of Anaesthetists and the World Federation of Societies of Anaesthesiologists (WFSA). The realisation was that local physicians were the experts and outstanding trainers (partly because they also understood the context), but needed support to provide education for the non-physicians and non-specialists. The SAFE courses provide a 'training of trainers' strategy to create a sustainable training model. This is also a stepping-stone approach to a context-sensitive educational programme.

The SAFE model works.[156] A three-day SAFE paediatrics anaesthesia programme conducted in Ethiopia, Kenya, Malawi, Uganda, and Zambia, with six lectures, 10 modules of low-fidelity simulation, and over 95% non-physician participants, demonstrated that pre- to post-course knowledge and skills increased significantly. More importantly, it was retained at six months. Preparation, perioperative care, resuscitation, communication, and teaching were all assessed, through face-to-face interviews, as having positive behaviour change over six months.[156] This has important implications for rapid improvements in the quality of care through simple educational interventions.

As there are no standardised educational programmes for non-specialist anaesthesia providers across Africa, the SAFE programmes provide an important step forward in providing educational standards for safe anaesthesia for obstetrics, paediatrics, and theatre management.

A local critical care nurse was telling me about his experience in the Eastern Cape, a poor province with a collapsing health system. Diabetic comas are a medical emergency driven by uncontrollable high-blood-sugar levels. It is life-threatening. This is core emergency care in any environment. As such, the critical care nurse frequently responded to these emergencies, but the matter was not as simple as it should have been.

'Bruce, it was really difficult to treat these patients,' he complained.

'Why?' I asked, 'This is a common medical emergency, and you are working in intensive care.'

'Well, we didn't have glucometers to measure the blood sugar level,' he declared, somewhat ashamedly.

He had no reason to be ashamed. He cared, but he was providing care in a difficult environment and struggling to make the step from education and knowledge to delivery of care. It is quite incomprehensible that he could not measure the glucose level to treat a diabetic emergency; any member of the public can buy these monitors over the counter and they are relatively cheap. This is obviously an extreme example, but it highlights the need for education and knowledge to be transferable to the clinical environment in which healthcare workers operate. Otherwise, the education is meaningless.

Group problem-solving can be used to cross the gap from education to local delivery of care. Education or training is important, but on its own does not improve the performance of healthcare workers much more than 10%,[110] especially when the working environment is unable to support all the interventions needed to deliver care.[101] Group problem-solving substantially increases healthcare provider performance to over 40%.[110] This is because the team members, with their collective education and knowledge, engage with the unique challenges of the local environment to determine workarounds that enable them to provide as many interventions as possible within their resource constraints. Group problem-solving helps translate educational theory into clinical practice.

The quality of surgical care varies tremendously, and even across Europe postoperative mortality differs nearly 16-fold between countries, even after adjustment for confounding variables.[31] We know that merely providing resources or education alone will not adequately or reliably address the quality of surgical care. Furthermore, we also know that the provision of care is intricately linked with processes necessary to deliver the surgical care. So how do we maximise the success of many wonderful educational activities, such as SAFE courses and ESMOE, which are happening across Africa to improve surgical outcomes? SAFE courses, ESMOE, and others have all shown improved knowledge about how to manage critically ill mothers and surgical patients, yet the data doesn't demonstrate the massive improvements in the surgical outcomes that we would like to see. I think the fundamental issue is that the healthcare providers rarely return to their work environment and ask, 'How do I implement what I have just learnt on that course in *my* environment?' Without that question, they will never develop the workarounds needed to deliver the care they have learnt about.

For example, it is too late when you find yourself in an emergency and ask for the defibrillator, only to find that it is a ward away. That valuable minute or two spent fetching the defibrillator could be the difference between life and death. Sometimes the resources necessary for the treatment taught on a course do not even exist in the local environment, leaving the healthcare worker stumped. On returning to one's place of work, it is necessary to check in, and work out how to apply the knowledge. This is the group problem-solving that transforms theory into site-specific practice after a training course, and it's the reality of working in Africa and other low-resource environments. It's exactly what Elliott Taylor showed when he attempted to identify which interventions are both efficacious and feasible for treating maternal haemorrhage in Africa.[101] Nine interventions that were considered efficacious in preventing or treating maternal haemorrhage were not feasible in Africa. So if you are on a course on how to manage obstetric haemorrhage, and one of these interventions is part of the management algorithm, such as ensuring that a repeat caesarean delivery is only performed by an experienced provider, or the availability of a specialist obstetrician or anaesthesiologist, then it will simply be impossible to follow the algorithm.[101] We have to take the educational package and group problem-solve it to ensure that it is context-specific, meaning that it's cognisant of the interventions missing from the local environment.

Proposed medical and surgical guidelines are often inappropriate for more resource-limited environments. This is a potentially massive barrier to the delivery of quality care. Stepping stones not only bridge education across different levels of healthcare providers, but also provide context-specific treatment algorithms and guidelines. These are not the gold standard treatments or guidelines of high-income countries because those currently cannot be achieved in a resource-limited environment. A great example of context-relevant educational materials and treatment guidelines can be found in the work of Professor

Johan Fagan, the head of ear, nose and throat (ENT) surgery at the University of Cape Town. He is an avid biker, and it is not uncommon to see him in his leathers after work as he heads home. Johan has a three-pronged approach to creating context-specific ENT surgical care. Firstly, he hosts international fellowships within his department for surgeons from other parts of Africa.[157] This is hugely important, as many countries do not have ENT training programmes. To ensure home-country retention and sustainable change for the trained fellows, he provides continual support through virtual case discussions with past and present fellows. Johan's drive and commitment cannot be underestimated. He chairs a monthly educational meeting with the fellowship network, in addition to two one-hour meetings per week, where fellows from across the continent can discuss difficult cases and challenges with all attendees. They are essentially group problem-solving surgical treatment and management options for the patients in their own environments. This ongoing mentorship and collaborative learning are key to the success of the programme, and fellows have since established their own fellowship programmes.[158]

The second approach is the delivery of open access educational resources to overcome the limited access to such resources, which are often both unaffordable and inappropriate for the environment. Johan started an open access ENT textbook, which documents all the known ENT surgical approaches. In a way it has led to a revival of the 'old', where surgeries now considered obsolete are documented and practiced in environments where they are still fundamentally relevant due to either limited equipment, skills, or therapeutic options. The textbook has had over a million downloads, and it won UCT's

Open Textbook Award for 2023. Ironically, it is heavily downloaded in high-income countries too. Johan's work has relevance, as his commitment is to the training for ENT specialists for Africa, and those surgical operations that were disappearing are now being used in an environment where full access to other therapies are not available.

The third and final approach is the provision of resource-appropriate ENT surgical practice guidelines developed by local experts, which provide treatment guidelines according to the availability or unavailability of diagnostic and therapeutic resources.[159] These guidelines have taken the concept of group problem-solving to the highest level by including African and global leaders in the development process. The guidelines are available at https://developingworldheadandneckcancerguidelines.com/. One can simply click on a diagnosis category, and an agreed-upon consensus practice guideline will be displayed, documenting the path to the best care that can be provided based on the resources available at that site. This is the ultimate stepping stone. It is fit for purpose and does not leave healthcare providers stranded at the coalface, helplessly trying to figure out what they can provide with the resources they have. Developing similar guidelines should be an aspiration in all disciplines for surgical, obstetric, anaesthesia and critical care in Africa.

Johan's educational approach is simple: mentor local leaders and experts, ensure access to appropriate educational material, and ensure that treatment guidelines are context-sensitive and deliverable. This strategy exploits smartphones and internet access for educational support across Africa.

Improving competency

The most common approach to learning is intuitive or tacit knowledge, characterised by pattern recognition. In Africa and other low-resource environments, however, where the surgical volume is low and the care is provided predominantly by non-specialists, generalists, and non-physicians, it is likely that healthcare workers may not have enough experience in the complications associated with care to develop the necessary pattern recognition for safe management. For example, a spinal anaesthetic is frequently used for caesarean section because it is simple, generally safe, and removes the need to secure the airway with an endotracheal tube, which in itself is potentially difficult and dangerous because the airway swells during pregnancy. However, sometimes the height of the local anaesthetic block on the spinal cord reaches the nerves that supply the diaphragm necessary for breathing, resulting in difficulty in coughing and a soft voice. If allowed to progress, this will result in the inability to breathe and a respiratory arrest if the airway is not secured with an endotracheal tube and the breathing supported. In these more complex or unusual situations, the anaesthesia provider needs factual knowledge and theories to analyse the situation and manage it appropriately. In high-income countries, this learning tends to happen through reading and teaching which is then exposed to practical experience to create practical knowledge. In low-resource environments, the process is often inverted. The clinician often gets experiential learning first (the 'see one, do one, teach one' model), and then later supplements it with reading.[160] This is exactly how my early anaesthesia training in Edendale Hospital was conducted.

The challenge in low-resource environments is linking the experiential learning to theory, such as linking the mother with the spinal anaesthetic and a soft voice to the theory of a high spinal and how to manage it. Reflection is considered ideal in education theory, to deepen the knowledge, but there is little time for reflection or people to mentor reflection in an understaffed, resource-limited environment.

Nicky Kalafatis considers competence to be the biggest challenge to safe surgical care in low-resource environments.[97] While there is a need for training in resource-limited environments, collective competency becomes extremely important. If training or knowledge is limited, then the surgical team needs to provide collective oversight to ensure patient safety. Nicky makes the point that the SSC is partly based on collective competency, where we share our understanding of the surgical case and our insights into potential problems that may arise. By sharing potential problems, the surgical team are ensuring that they can share the different competencies across the team in the operating theatre should they need to manage a complication. Furthermore, low-resource environments require task sharing to compensate for the limited human resources, and task sharing requires collective responsibility for the care of the patient across all the levels of participating healthcare providers. The results from the ASOS-2 trial suggest that we must ensure that collective competency extends across the entire healthcare team. A nurse needs to understand what a deteriorating patient looks like, and then needs to know how to communicate the deterioration to the doctor on the ward, so that the doctor understands the gravity of the situation and responds swiftly and appropriately. The SAFE courses have gone a long way towards developing collective competency, which can certainly be augmented with stepwise plans and cognitive aids.[160] Nicky is adamant when she states that, 'The bottom line for me is that we have to move away from individual competence into the realm of fitness for purpose and collective competence.'

In the UK, it is normal for anaesthetists to work with an operating department assistant or ODA. An ODA is the 'right-hand man' of any anaesthetist. Early in my training, I was anaesthetising a patient and, as soon as they lost consciousness, I lost the airway and was unable to intubate the patient. The time between life and death is extremely short here, as the patient cannot breathe and will desaturate quickly. I could feel my vision narrowing as my anxiety grew. Suddenly, I felt the ODA place a bougie in my hand. He had clearly been watching, understood the situation, and so provided support through his knowledge and experience. The bougie was the correct answer. I managed to introduce it into the airway, railroad the endotracheal tube to secure the airway, and oxygenate the patient with no harm caused. This was collective competence at the bedside, and it is powerful for quality of care. For example, when an anaesthesia nurse assists an anaesthetist, then 30-day mortality is halved compared to an anaesthetist working without assistance.[161] Without the assistance of that ODA, I could have been part of this grim statistic.

The Lancet Commission for Global Surgery suggests that the ability to deliver the three bellwether surgical procedures (a caesarean section, a laparotomy and an open reduction of a fracture)[33] will ensure that a hospital has sufficient resources to provide safe surgical care. Zane Farina believes that the ability to perform the bellwether procedures carries the additional value of cross training, because the skills learnt for each procedure are transferable to the management of complications across procedures. He is correct to suggest that a hospital that is only able to provide caesarean sections (and maybe some other minor surgical procedures), is dysfunctional, and to improve it must address the absence of the other two surgical procedures. If you can perform a caesarean section, you may be able to manage massive haemorrhage, but the anaesthesia provider may not be comfortable managing an airway. If you are also conducting laparotomies, then the anaesthesia provider will be comfortable managing an airway, as these procedures routinely require endotracheal intubation, and this will ensure increased safety when a pregnant woman requires an endotracheal tube or a general anaesthetic, as opposed to a spinal anaesthetic. If there is no cross training, it is likely because the environment lacks the resources to support the different types of surgery necessary to develop cross training. A study in Uganda showed that due to shortages of personnel, drugs, equipment, and training, only 23% of anaesthetists have the facilities to deliver safe anaesthesia to an adult, 13% to deliver safe anaesthesia to a child and 6% to deliver safe anaesthesia for a caesarean section.[162] Therefore, if you are only able to provide anaesthesia for caesarean delivery, it is certain that your ability to provide safe anaesthesia for other adults and children will be compromised due to limited resources *and* limited cross training, compromising the ability to develops the skills and proficiencies needed to provide safe surgery for all. Zane clearly states that to address the fundamental problem of maternal mortality, district hospital doctors need to upskill through cross training by performing the non-caesarean section operations such as ordinary laparotomies or fracture fixation. His reasoning is that it prevents obstetric care being delivered by a provider with a limited arsenal of anaesthesia skills. So instead of only been able to provide a spinal anaesthetic for a caesarean section, or an evacuation of a retained placenta under sedation (uncomfortably), a broader skillset is available thanks to the practice of the other two bellwether operations. It is these skills that are life-saving for mothers in times of trouble, and they were missing at the sites we studied where non-physicians had to provide sedation for surgery, because these hospitals only had the resources to deliver sedation and did not have the resources or the cross-training to manage complications.

Zane is adamant that

> We will not make a difference until we are doing SAFE courses and the district hospitals are also doing their bellwether procedures. These true generalists are actually "multi-specialists" and allow care provision for many rural communities that would otherwise go without care. However, to work as a multi-specialist in a rural setting is taxing, both personally and professionally.[33]

This was my problem when I realised that I was not up to the task of being a super GP; as Zane correctly says, they are actually multi-specialists. Half the problem is that these multi-specialists are not recognised as specialists by professional medical colleges, and the ability to cross-train and provide adequate care in resource-limited environments will not change, until these multi-specialists are recognised as such.

While we have focused on the three bellwether surgical procedures, the World Bank has identified 44 procedures that these multi-specialists must provide at the district (or first-level) hospital.[57,58] Essential trauma services, including the expeditious management of pneumothoraces and haemothoraces (air and blood in the chest cavity), with a tube thoracoscopy is considered an essential procedure.[58] The inability to provide this procedure is what nearly killed the young pregnant woman in Bandundu, DRC. Neglected surgeries are the missing surgeries or surgical skills at district hospitals, despite being among the 44 essential surgical procedures for the super GP.

The Western Cape in South Africa could be considered a desirable and well-resourced environment in an African context. South Africa is an upper middle-income country, and the Western Cape has traditionally been viewed as functionally good and medically desirable, with a strong history of landmark medical achievements, from the first heart transplant to HIV and AIDS advocacy and world-class science. Yet, examination of the district hospitals in the Western Cape show that a third have no budget for surgery, and a fifth have no functional operating theatre.[163] This puts the challenge facing lower-resource environments in context: we cannot even reliably provide appropriate district-level surgery throughout a comparatively well-resourced African environment.

This brings us to the competencies for surgeons in district hospitals. There is no standard training programme for these competencies. This impacts on what surgery can be delivered in these environments. The challenge is to roll the competencies of surgeons from 20 different specialities into a single multi-specialist surgeon, which is what district hospitals need. Kat Chu, a general surgeon and head of global surgery at the University of Stellenbosch, has worked extensively in humanitarian surgical programmes. At a meeting, she puts up a slide from the very textbook

I once owned when I still aspired to the great heights of the super GP: *Primary Surgery, Volume 1*. On her slide is a list of some of the common procedures in a rural hospital: a caesarean section (obstetrics), a laparotomy (general surgery), a fracture reduction (orthopaedics), packing a bleeding nose (ENT), draining a pericardial effusion (cardiothoracics), draining a subdural haematoma (neurosurgery), inserting a suprapubic catheter (urology), managing an infected hand (orthopaedics), doing a skin graft (plastics), repairing a severed artery (vascular), and the list goes on. Our challenge is to create a multi-specialist surgical and anaesthesia course that is accessible and achievable in low-resource environments, both in training and in the maintenance of the clinical service during training. Kat speaks passionately about the need for a central 'hub' hospital to support isolated rural surgeons at the district 'spoke' hospitals. The central hub surgeons and hospital need to consider themselves responsible for all patients within their catchment. This is like the role that Zane plays in anaesthesia care in KwaZulu-Natal, and that Johan Fagan plays in his weekly virtual African ENT surgical management meetings. The benefit of the hub-and-spoke model is that it creates an understanding of the surgical needs in the district hospital, the challenges faced, the support needed for delivery of appropriate surgical care, and when referral is required. Until we reform surgical and anaesthesia education to address the many procedures required at the district level, and enable cross-training by enabling the delivery of all basic surgeries, we will not be able to provide safe care in low-resource environments.

We need to capacitate the surgical team at the district-hospital level so that they can provide the necessary surgeries in this environment. This includes working towards a personnel structure that is sustainable for surgical provision, so that these providers have functional communication networks for external mentorship, the knowledge and educational materials at hand for self-development, and context-specific guidelines. Human resource capacitation can be done locally and externally.

The personnel at a district hospital must be able to make and deliver on the brave decisions expected of a super GP across many medical and surgical disciplines. To make these brave decisions, the medical officer needs to be trained to make decisions that are acceptable in terms of potentially successful management of outcomes and complications across many disciplines. These include, for example, the baby with diarrhoea in the clinic, to the mother bleeding with a preterm fetus, to the surgical patient with an open fracture from a road traffic accident. This is the reality that faces doctors providing care in district hospitals. Education and training for a package of care will not guarantee a functional and sustainable district hospital until it has the necessary human resources to support it. Modelling suggests that a functional district hospital requires at least eight medical officers, of which one needs to be a family physician.[164] If you have adequate human resources, you then need to retain them within the district hospital environment, which is difficult. Steve Reid, professor of primary health care at the University of Cape Town, describes his group's work in district hospitals in KwaZulu-Natal. It suggests that the work environment needs to develop the characteristics of a learning system within the hospital, and this insight is supported by the literature. This learning system has six components, which are important if the hospital is to continue to function and improve. These include leadership, teamwork, a culture of change, resources for learning, formal education (the factual knowledge component), and reflective practice (which is considered informal learning). The interesting observation is that these six components are almost the same concepts needed to support quality improvement and implementation. Reflective practice could be considered equivalent to regular meetings to ensure compliance with quality improvement interventions, or group problem-solving.

Communication has been shown to be critical to hold the inside-out quality surgical model together, and this extends to the learning system of the district hospital. The functional communication networks need to extend outside of the hospital too, to an environment of external mentorship. The external mentor may be a local expert in a specific discipline working at a central/hub hospital and may support or mentor several district hospitals or 'spokes' across many countries, as demonstrated by Johan Fagan. Support can be provided via a number of social media platforms, including WhatsApp.

The external component of human resource capacitation through education is probably best personified by Johan Fagan's work described earlier. This model could be adopted by all disciplines across Africa who do not have dedicated training programmes in various countries. What is beautiful about his educational strategy is that it acknowledges the contextual challenges surgeons face in low-resource environments. It provides comprehensive open access educational material through the online textbook, which covers procedures that are disappearing in high-income countries but may still be relevant in an environment where access to chemotherapies and other treatment regimens are not available. The second component supports the surgical decision-making, which is cognisant of the environment and the resources available to the surgeon, through the context-specific guidelines. Finally, the third component is the ongoing mentorship through fellowship and virtual management meetings.[157] These fellowships have resulted in sustainable change, with nearly 100% retention of trainees in their base countries. These educational interventions can increase head and neck surgeries more than threefold per annum with each surgeon who is upskilled, without increasing the number of healthcare workers.[157] Furthermore, this strategy provides evidence that these fellowships can be provided by middle-income countries within Africa (such as South Africa), as opposed to high-income countries.[165] This is a good example of South–South mentorship, as opposed to the North–South learning.

It would be fair to say that the experts and skills needed for training in low-resource environments are already on the ground in Africa. Johan's educational strategy has overcome the limited access to education and training, which in mostly unaffordable and often inappropriate and inaccessible in low-resource environments. He has exploited the power of smartphones and internet access for sharing educational materials, and setting up virtual platforms for educational support and mentorship. This model could and should be replicated for other surgical disciplines in low-resource environments. My only critique of these fellowships it is that they are fundamentally focused on individual (procedural) competence. Really, we need to consider adding quality improvement implementation science to any fellowship, to address the importance of leadership, the development and maintenance of multidisciplinary teams, and an appreciation of collective competency strategies.

In summary, we need to do the following to strengthen district hospital surgical services. We need to ensure that the healthcare providers receive education in the package of emergency and essential surgical procedures prescribed for district hospitals. We need to ensure that the appropriate equipment and resources are available to deliver these procedures, over and above the three bellwether procedures. We need to ensure that there is collective competency, clinical leadership, and teams characterised by a flat hierarchy. Finally, the collective competency needs to extend externally to support surgeons and anaesthetists at regional and tertiary hub hospitals.[166] The role of a multidisciplinary team is probably best summarised by Kat Chu and colleagues who state that 'successful surgery should be defined by the patient and is best achieved by a co-ordinated, multidisciplinary team, embedded in a culture of collaboration and safety.'[167]

Scaling education and care

The Utstein Abbey is a beautiful Norwegian medieval monastery that lies about 30 kilometres north of the port town of Stavanger. It is a small monastery, with imposing high white walls and steep roofs, standing on the southern bank of Klosterøy Island, overlooking the marshes and fjord across to Fjøløy Island. Founded in the 1100s, it was placed in its current location by King Magnus VI of Norway in the 1200s, and it was the home of the Augustinian Canons.[168] It has a small central courtyard, with rooms running on the perimeter. It housed about 12 monks, along with the many people who worked to maintain the building, cook meals, and work the lands.

This little monastery has supported many people thanks to its extensive lands. The highly prized sheep feed on the very salty grass that runs down to the marshes on the coast, and the slow-roasted leg of lamb is a local delicacy. It is a particularly satisfying meal, and has you coming back for more. One can imagine the monks sitting in the beautiful dining hall, with its low entrance and ceilings being sooted up by large candles billowing smoke, while looking through the hazy windows over the waters below. This existence came to an end in 1537 with the Reformation, and Utstein Abbey passed through the hands of various noblemen until it was returned to the state in 1899. It now is a museum and a site for music recitals in the high-arched church, where the acoustics are something to behold.

Over the last 50 years, Utstein Abbey has been the venue for resuscitation guideline development, and become synonymous with resuscitation innovation and practice globally. This is because of Åsmund Laerdal, who started a toy and doll company in Stavanger in 1940, and experienced an unfortunate event with his child, Tore. Tore was two years old when he fell in the cold waters of a Norwegian fjord, and it was his father who fished him out.[169] Hypothermia is actually protective for near-drownings, and fortunately Tore was fine. In this traumatic experience, Åsmund observed two significant things: that he had to clear the mouth of his baby boy to ensure that he could breathe, and that very few people knew how to resuscitate a child. Åsmund was acutely aware of the need for training in resuscitation. The extraordinary number of near-drownings in the cold Nordic waters probably contributed to this awareness, along with the opportunities for survival due to the protective effects of profound hypothermia.

By a strange twist of fate, Dr Peter Safar, the world

leader in early research on resuscitation, would meet Dr Bjørn Lind from the Stavanger Hospital (not far from Åsmund Laerdal's offices) at a Scandinavian anaesthesiology congress in Norway. Peter Safar was an Austrian anaesthesiologist working in Baltimore in the USA at the time, and had demonstrated that expired air and mouth-to-mouth or mouth-to-mask resuscitation was possible and potentially lifesaving. But he needed mannikins for training in this technique. Dr Bjørn Lind's local knowledge of both Åsmund Laerdal's experience and his successful toy doll business would prove pivotal in the quest for global resuscitation training. Having almost lost his son, Åsmund was naturally receptive to the need for mannikins for resuscitation training, and his experience working with plastics had given him the skills and knowledge to develop mannikins that would respond to the mechanics of resuscitation manoeuvres with head tilts and responsive airways and chests. The rest is history. Laerdal is now an industry leader in resuscitation equipment, and his 'Resusci Anne' is the most well-known resuscitation mannikin around. Resusci Anne's face was fittingly taken from the death mask of a young woman who drowned in the River Seine in the 1880s. Her face is calm, youthful and innocent, yet poignant enough to remind us of unnecessary avoidable deaths.[169]

The work and friendships of Peter Safar, Bjørn Lind and Åsmund Laerdal resulted in the pivotal moment of the first International Symposium on Emergency Resuscitation, held in Stavanger in August 1961. It had global attendance, and the recommendations were published in a special edition of the *Acta Anaesthesiologica Scandinavia*, with a recommendation that mouth-to-mouth resuscitation be taught in all schools.[169]

Laerdal went on to produce many simple, low-fidelity mannikins that are now key to resuscitation training across Africa. Why are simple mannikins so important? Firstly, they are accessible and functional in low-resource environments. Secondly, we know that they have similar educational impact to high-fidelity mannikins, as demonstrated by data on simulations for education from the SAFE courses. It is the realism of the simulation used in training that is important for the educational response, and not the realism of the mannikins. The data suggests that simulations using simple mannikins are not inferior to those using high-fidelity mannikins for retention of skills performance at a year after training.[170] Data also demonstrates that a similar stress response can be achieved during simulation training with a low-fidelity mannikin when compared to a high-fidelity mannikin, supporting the delivery of a realistic simulation.[171] Finally, education using low versus high-fidelity mannikins has shown no difference in knowledge acquisition.[172] The importance of ubiquitous mannikins across Africa therefore cannot be overstated. And where mannikins are not available, improvised low-fidelity mannikins could be used. Rowan Duys uses mannikins made from pillows, linen, and gloves when providing simulation training in low-resource environments (Figure 9).

Christian Kampik, a German anaesthesiologist who has spent his professional career in South Africa, conducts simulation training across Africa. When we chat, he stares at me over his reading glasses and intensely educates me, emphasising every point with a head nod as his ponytail swings behind him. He speaks about the simple things that one can do to increase the realism of simulations. These include: doing the simulation in an operation room;

dressing up in theatre clothes; using apps that provide patient monitor readings of heart rate, blood pressure, and oxygen saturation; and doing simple workaround jobs on low-fidelity mannikins to make the mannikin more 'responsive', so that the simulation instructor can then manipulate the mannikin to make it look like it is breathing. Christian inserts a tube through the neck of a Laerdal mannikin, running it under the doll's clothes and over to the instructor in the corner of the room, who can then breathe for the mannikin, through the tube into the trachea, or obstruct breathing. With a bit of ingenuity and imagination, Christian can pack the low-fidelity mannikins, and the bits and pieces needed for a few workarounds, into

Figure 9. Rowan Duys' low-fidelity mannikins in the Eastern Cape. Photo © Simon le Roux.

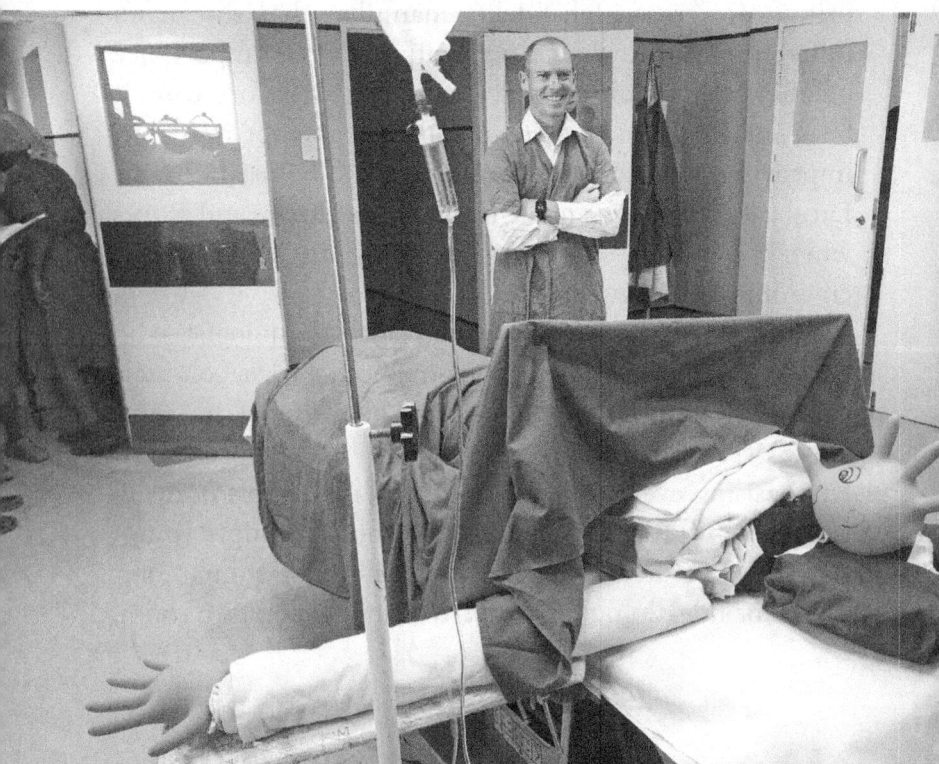

a single suitcase, and an app for a bit more feedback in the simulation, and then he can essentially travel anywhere to provide a fairly realistic simulation.

Good educational courses and simple, low-fidelity mannikins used in realistic simulations can result in knowledge and skills retention for six to 12 months. This is all accessible in a low-resource environment. First-prize would be to ensure that the teaching is context-sensitive and that the simulation is adapted to the available resources. This would eschew the need for group problem-solving when healthcare workers have to implement the training at their hospitals.

Conclusion

The Donabedian perspective[78] on quality of care considers the relationship between structures (e.g. resources, adequate staffing), processes (e.g. adequate ward routines for monitoring patients), and outcomes.

When considering the resources for safe surgery we know the following. Surgical healthcare providers need education and training that is context-sensitive, with management plans that are also context-appropriate, and mentorship to support their decision-making and delivery of care. All training should focus on collective competency, which allows everyone in the team to contribute to better outcomes, while simultaneously supporting the delivery of care to the patient. An emphasis on ensuring the capacity to cross-train is necessary if we don't want to end up with unwanted complications and deaths.

We must acknowledge the importance of tracking processes that are key to ensuring the implementation of evidence-based care. We have shown that studies of complex interventions from high-income settings, e.g. EPOCH[108] and low- and middle-income settings e.g. ASOS-2[87] cannot improve the quality of care through process improvement alone. Improving outcomes (the quality of care) requires triangulating resources (which include the infrastructure, the equipment, and the people needed) with evidence-based interventions and the processes needed to implement and track the success of the interventions.[129] To improve surgical outcomes, we need to marry clinician researchers (who have the expertise to provide the evidence) with implementation scientists (who have the expertise to ascertain whether the interventions are implemented). While clinician researchers focus on the science and the evidence, implementation scientists consider the people and the processes. We need these two groups to meet, so that the evidence, people, and processes work in unison to improve outcomes.

Finally, we need to track outcomes, and meet and reflect on the performance of the quality of care that we are delivering. Feedback on processes and outcome data completeness is then necessary to drive quality improvement through implementation. One needs to develop a culture of quality care. We need to be able to review our performance on the implementation of these evidence-based interventions if we want to improve care. We need to embrace the process of group problem-solving if we are to ultimately make surgical care better.

In the resource-limited environment of Africa, we need to accept that there are ceilings to any quality care initiative. Low ceilings are imposed by the limitations of ineffective stakeholder and leadership engagement. These are soft ceilings. The hard ceiling is that of severe infrastructural and resource limitations, which cannot be bypassed without more resources.

In conclusion, the challenge to improving quality of care is that it is more often than not a complex intervention in a complex environment.[173] Unlike simple interventions, such as a medication being evaluated in a drug trial, complex interventions are commonly designed to change institutional processes and systems and/or human behaviour or interactions. The number and adaptability of interacting components and people involved affect the level of complexity of the intervention, making it hard to define exactly what is delivered, and which of these are the 'active ingredients' that are most influential on the target outcomes.[174] Finally, this is also complicated by the negative impact of sequential or multiple processes on fidelity. We must therefore do everything possible to simplify complex interventions if we are to successfully improve the quality of surgical care.

PART 4

Advocating for
safe surgery

S urgery results in better population health, and is key to ensuring the delivery of many of the UN SDGs. SDG 3.1 is to reduce maternal deaths to less than 70 per 100 000 live births and SDG 3.2 is to decrease neonatal deaths to 12 deaths per 1000 live births.[84] Maternal and neonatal mortality will both decrease if we increase access to caesarean sections until we reach the safe inflection point of 19 caesarean sections per 100 live births.[27] Africa is currently running at about five caesarean sections per 100 live births. A caesarean section rate of less than 7.2 per 100 live births is associated with a maternal mortality of 463 deaths per 100 000 live births and a neonatal mortality of 30 deaths per 1000 live births. Providing 19 caesarean sections per 100 000 live births results in a fall in maternal mortality to 36 deaths per 100 000 live births and neonatal mortality to seven deaths per 1000 live births.[27] This equates to a potential twelvefold reduction in maternal mortality, and fivefold reduction in neonatal mortality. Although simply increasing access to caesarean sections would not ensure mortality figures within the SDG targets, the associated systems requirements to increase the ability to deliver more caesarean sections will certainly contribute to improving maternal and neonatal outcomes.

SDG 3.2 is to reduce neonatal mortality and preventable deaths in children under five. We know that neonates born in Africa have a mortality at least double that of high-income countries following caesarean section,[2] and increasing access to caesarean sections will decrease maternal mortality.[27] Children having surgery in Africa have an elevenfold higher mortality than high-income countries.[3] Currently, anaesthesiologists and surgeons working in Africa consider nearly half of the operating rooms unsafe for neonatal surgery and one third unsafe for surgery in children under one year old.[3] There is an enormous opportunity to improve child health in Africa with adequate surgical provision.

SDG 3.3 aims to reduce the incidence of HIV infection, tuberculosis, malaria, hepatitis B, and neglected tropical diseases.[84] Circumcision, a simple procedure, is associated with HIV prevention. In Africa, however, it is associated with mortality through surgical sepsis, where sterile surgical conditions are unavailable. Safe surgery will decrease HIV infection through safe circumcision. SDG 3.4.1 aims to reduce premature mortality from cardiovascular disease, cancer, diabetes, or chronic respiratory disease by one third by 2030.[84] Safe surgery will contribute at least a third to the management of these diseases to ensure comprehensive medical care.[52] Target 3.6 aims to halve the number of deaths from road traffic injuries by 2030. Target 3.8.1 is to achieve universal health coverage of essential health services, including reproductive, maternal, newborn and child health, infectious diseases, non-communicable diseases, and service capacity and access among the general and the most disadvantaged populations.[84] Surgery is needed to support and achieve these goals.

Target 3.c aims to increase health financing and the

recruitment, development, training, and retention of the health workforce in low- and middle-income countries.[84] We have also shown how a small increment in a health budget, in the context of a comprehensive NSOAP, can provide a substantial change to the delivery of a surgical service.[137] We also need to rethink education to enable an increase in the quality of surgical care we can deliver, while also retaining surgical providers.

SDG 5 is gender equality by 2030.[84] Women in vulnerable populations face gender-specific barriers in accessing healthcare as well as the burden of many sex-specific conditions, including gynaecological disease and the vast majority of breast pathology.[73] These diseases commonly affect women in the prime of life and, as such, have substantial societal consequences due to the complex effects on their children and families, not to mention the economic impact.[73] Through the work of ASOS and ISOS, we have shown that women living in Africa have double the odds of severe postoperative complications following elective non-obstetric, non-gynaecological surgery compared to international incidences.[72] The gender inequality in surgical care is larger in Africa than the rest of the world, and this needs to be urgently addressed. This may extend to the critical care environment, where the data from Covid-19 admissions in Africa suggested that men possibly had more access to critical care and, once in critical care, received more care than women.[155]

SDG 8 aims to promote inclusive and sustainable economic growth, employment, and decent work for all.[84] The aim of SDG 9 is to build a resilient infrastructure, promote inclusive and sustainable industrialisation, and foster innovation.[84] Neither of these two goals are achievable without a healthy population. Delivery of essential surgery will increase the quality of life for about a third of the population.[52] SDG 17.18 calls for capacity-building support to increase the availability of high-quality, timely, and reliable data. The surgical indicators act as a benchmark for countries, but we still need mechanisms to ensure accurate reporting from the facility level to the ministries of health to the WHO and the World Bank Group.[84] This would allow benchmarking and monitoring of progress with surgical delivery. This brings us full circle to why we need NSOAPs.

These are solid arguments for why we need to advocate for NSOAPs and adequate surgical provision. However, a functional surgical health system in one country or region can still be severely compromised if adjoining countries cannot provide adequate healthcare. Diseases do not follow political boundaries; mosquitos happily cross country borders and so does malaria. A regional strategy was adopted to address this, with the Malaria Elimination Eight Initiative (E8 programme) in sub-Saharan Africa. If Botswana can eradicate malaria but Zambia can't, then that eradication is futile, as the mosquitos will continue to cross national borders. People in need will also overcome any country borders to survive. Therefore, we need regional strategies to solve health problems. For an example of how patients in need migrate, look at how the Western Cape province in South Africa is being required to provide care for increasing numbers of patients from the Eastern Cape, where the public healthcare service is on the verge of collapse. It is for these reasons that we need a regional strategy for surgical health in Africa.

Advocacy

Change requires more than righteous anger. It requires a program, and it requires organising.

– Barak Obama

The changes we need to make to deliver safe surgery require advocacy.

We have seen how indicators were an important catalyst to improving maternal outcomes. The success of tracking indicators in maternal health and obstetrics is evident, with the associated falling maternal mortality. Now we need to monitor and document surgical outcomes so that we can understand what is needed to ensure universal healthcare.

Surgery has had four landmark global health advocacy victories. At the 68th World Health Assembly in May 2015, the World Health Assembly passed WHA resolution 68.15 titled 'Strengthening emergency and essential surgical care and anaesthesia as a component of universal health coverage'. This established surgery as a cornerstone of universal healthcare.[130] It had been a long time coming. There was a growing appreciation that to provide universal healthcare, the surgical component of diseases needed to be adequately addressed. Importantly, there was an awareness that provision of the resources and infrastructure needed to provide surgery also contribute to establishing an enabling healthcare environment to provide other healthcare.[33] What is truly mindboggling is that it took us until 2015 to recognise that surgery is essential for universal healthcare. Where had we been for so long?

The upshot of this was the second victory: WHA resolution 70.22 was passed in 2017, where WHO member states agreed to report their SDG progress every two years.[131] This included the perioperative mortality rate (at and around the time of surgery) in the 100 core health indicators, and the other five indicators of surgical care as categories in the 100 core health indicators.[175] At last there was a global agreement to track surgical outcomes. The World Bank health indicators include workforce, volume of surgery, and financial protection indicators.[176] Unfortunately, the access to surgery and perioperative mortality rate indicators are currently not included as the data is not readily accessible. This is concerning: the perioperative mortality rate is the only quality indicator of surgery, but because it is not readily available, it is not reported in the World Bank 100 indicators. It has been agreed that the perioperative mortality rate is globally important, but if it is not being reported, it may send the message to the public that it this metric lacks significance. Even if we don't have the numbers, I would prefer that the indicator appeared on the list followed by a field showing that the data is 'not available'. This will at least flag the importance of the indicator, and the need to find ways of making the data available.

The third global advocacy success was achieved in Richard Horton's opening address at the 72nd World Health Assembly in 2019. As editor-in-chief of *The Lancet*, the pre-eminent global public health journal, he had canvassed the global community on Twitter, asking which top global health concerns he should communicate to country leaders at the opening of the assembly. He presented five global health priorities, of which one was safe surgery for all. The international community had spoken and were calling for global attention to surgical health.

Finally, in 2023, the WHA committed to a new resolution, 76.2: 'Integrated emergency, critical and operative care for universal health coverage and protection from health emergencies', also known as the ECO resolution. This resolution states that emergency, critical, and operative care is integral to comprehensive primary healthcare. This is a huge step forward at an international level, as it recognises that universal healthcare is impossible without emergency, critical, and operative care.

The international advocacy work led by John Meara, Emmanuel Makasa and others has paid off with these four victories for surgical health and advocacy. John is the plastic surgeon-in-chief at Boston Children's Hospital, a professor of surgery at the Department of Surgery at Harvard Medical School, and the founder and director emeritus of Harvard's Program in Global Surgery and Social Change. He is soft-spoken (unusual for surgeons) with a baby face, and has led advocacy for safe surgery, particularly through his role as co-chair for the Lancet Commission on Global Surgery. Identifying the need for global monitoring of perioperative mortality was a major success, providing a platform to document the progress to universal healthcare coverage. If only this had been delivered as promised, though. Shortly before the Covid-19 pandemic, Emmanuel Makasa lamented to me that 'The WHA resolution [68.15] was agreed by many, but it has been supported by few.' In a 2016 study of the 215 countries on the World Bank's list, the most commonly reported indicator was 'specialist surgical workforce density' (71 countries, 33%), yet 'access to timely essential surgery' was reported by only 33 countries

(15%), and 'perioperative mortality rate' by 29 countries (13%).[177] Essentially, we have little idea of the quality of surgical care in seven of every eight countries in the world. Therefore, we cannot track surgical outcomes in nearly 90% of countries globally, making it difficult to develop the impetus needed to improve the quality of surgical care. To mimic the influential work of Florence Nightingale, Andrew Topping, the Cape Town flying squads, the CEMD, and others, it is imperative that we push to track surgical outcomes in every country. We currently have important surgical indicators as part of the core health indicators dataset, but the reporting compliance is unacceptably low, and there appears to be no teeth to make this happen. We must change the current non-compliance for tracking surgical outcomes through advocacy. Without it, surgical health (and by extension population health) will remain poor.

Financing health

Surgical health financing is often perceived as competition to other medical fields. However, we advocate and campaign for projects that strengthen the entire system and workforce.

Lydia Cairncross, *Earth Cast* S3E35

How we spend money on health

My father was a difficult man. Intellectually sharp but with a personality that meant he spent his life swimming upstream. He would argue and keep pushing back. He couldn't see the point of doctors – 'Bloody money grabbers!' He was resilient, and strong as an ox. An arteriopath from a life of heavy smoking, he had coronary artery disease, aortic disease, and carotid disease. He had successful coronary artery bypass surgery when I was at university studying medicine. A ruptured aortic aneurysm, with an expected mortality of 20–50% when I was a qualified anaesthesiologist. I was in San Francisco at the time. I spoke to my mother as he was being wheeled into the operating theatre and explained the poor prognosis. However, as always, he was home within a few days, ready to complain about doctors when I returned from the US. 'They charge a fortune and I feel awful!' he moaned. He *did* look awful, which is not surprising considering that he had just survived a life-threatening surgical emergency, and clearly bled a torrential amount. He was as white as a sheet. A few years later, he went on to have a transient ischaemic attack (a little stroke that resolves, fortunately) and underwent a carotid stent to prevent it happening again. I thought he would complicate with a stroke, but again he flew through. He was living proof of the benefits of surgery. Three big operations with no complications. Amazing, really. His life was a good 20 to 25 years longer than it should have been, due to successful surgery. He was mentally sharp to the end. But he never liked doctors, and would have a go at me at every opportunity. Until his death, I battled to persuade him of the value of medicine and surgery. He could not accept what healthcare cost, but he was never out of pocket. I think that if he read this chapter now, he may have changed his tune, but he wouldn't have capitulated easily. He would have worked me over with some challenging arguments. I hope that, had he read this, he would have focused his anger on the system and governments, and how poorly organised the funding of healthcare is, rather than taking his usual position and targeting healthcare providers such as myself. I hope, too, that this chapter makes you unhappy and indignant with the surgical care funding currently provided by governments, non-governmental organisations (NGOs), and others.

Here is a refresher of what you have read. Maternal mortality numbers suggest that a mother dies every 1.75 minutes, 24 hours a day, 365 days a year.[7] The number of people in Africa who cannot access safe and affordable surgical care is approximately one billion, out of a population of a little over a billion.[33] At least a third of all diseases need surgical care. And universal healthcare cannot be achieved without surgical care.

So, what do we need to do to rectify this? It is estimated that global universal healthcare would cost about a $1 trillion per annum. The WHO defines universal health coverage as 'access to needed essential health services, without financial hardship'. Universal coverage is comprehensive. It includes the full range of care from health promotion and prevention to treatment, rehabilitation, and palliative care.[178] To achieve universal health coverage, health financing requires about $100 per capita to achieve an essential package of 218 interventions, and $50 per head for a basic package of 108 'highest priority interventions'.[179,180]

The cost of providing 80% coverage for essential universal health coverage across the 21 essential universal health packages for safe maternal and newborn health would require $2.70 per capita in low-income countries and $3.70 in low- and middle-income countries.[181] This is an increase in the current expenditure of $1.60 and $2.10 per capita respectively.[181] So for an additional $2 per capita per annum, we can achieve 80% coverage of the SDG goals for maternal and newborn health, at an incremental cost of $1.2 billion in low-income countries and $5.6 billion in low- and middle-income countries.[181]

What about doing the same for all surgeries? The per capita cost for providing 80% essential health coverage for surgery is $5.10 in low-income countries and $7.40 in low- and middle-income countries.[181] However, here the incremental cost is approximately three times more than what is required for maternal and newborn health, due to the current low expenditure on surgery: $4.4 billion is currently spent on surgery, but $17 billion for maternal and newborn health.[181] The discrepancy between the funding required for maternal and neonatal health, compared to surgical health, shows the current disparity in health expenditure between these two health categories, where maternal and newborn care receives three times as much financial attention as surgery.

Globally, $1 trillion would provide sufficient financing to achieve essential universal health coverage for all.[179] $1 trillion may sound like a lot of money, but in context it is not. In fact, it is an eighth of what is currently spent on health globally. In 2018, the global health expenditure was $8.3 trillion dollars,[182] with 60.7% of that total coming from government health spending, 20.6% from prepaid private spending, 18.5% from out-of-pocket spending, and 0.5% from donor financing.[183] Why can we not provide universal health coverage when we are already spending eight times *more* than we need to fund it? There are two fundamental problems. The first is that the distribution of expenditure is unequal across countries, and the second is that the distribution of expenditure is inappropriate across disease categories.

Let's look at the healthcare expenditure across countries. Countries with fewer resources have less to spend on health. The 2016 estimates are that upper-middle income countries spent on average $130 per capita, while lower-middle income countries spend less than half that amount, at $58 dollars per capita.[179] Less than 10% of the spending of low-income countries is on surgical services.[181]

Although only $100 is needed to provide the essential package of 218 interventions, estimates are that of the 49 of lower-middle countries, only nine (18%) can afford this. If one uses the more affordable $50 basic package of highest priority interventions, a further 16 countries (33%) can afford the 108 interventions, but, disturbingly, 24 countries (49%) still cannot even afford the basic package. In low-income countries, the average government spend is $9 per head,[179] less than 20% of the amount required to provide a basic package of health for the highest priority interventions. The contributions to health funding outside of government spending are associated with a country's World Bank income group classification.[183] Development assistance for health (donor funding) is dominant in low-income countries (28% of 2017 health spending), out-of-pocket spending is dominant in lower-middle-income countries (55% in 2017), and prepaid private spending is dominant in high-income countries (86% in 2017).[33] In resource-poor environments, approximately 60% of funding is government health spending, and nearly the entire remainder (39%) is made up by personal expenditure through prepaid private spending, and out-of-pocket spending.[183] The remaining proportion of under 1% is donor-based funding.[33]

Although the donor contribution sounds small, the role and importance of donor funding cannot be underestimated. It contributed $40 billion in 2017,[62] or 4% of the pack needed to achieve universal health coverage at $1 trillion. Donors are crucial to ensuring that the most basic package for universal health coverage could theoretically be achieved, considering that 49% of middle-income countries, and all low-income countries currently cannot deliver this package. As personal financing of health is nearly impossible in low-income and lower-middle-income countries, the importance of donor funding can be seen in the estimated proportional donor contribution to total healthcare expenditure in 2018, which was 30% for low-income countries, and 10% for low- and middle-income countries.[182] The total global health spending per HDI category, which includes all sources of funding for health (e.g. government, out of pocket, donor etc.), is the following: approximately $40 for low-income countries, $115 for lower-middle-income countries, $446 for upper-middle-income countries and $3313 for high-income countries.[182] There are three important points. Firstly, in lower-middle income countries and low-income countries, donors are an important component to the delivery of healthcare. Secondly, despite donor contributions, low-income countries are currently unable to provide universal health coverage. Based on the current estimates, low-income countries need an additional $60 dollars per capita to provide universal health coverage. In 2019, the population of the 32 low-income countries was approximately 650 million people,[184] meaning that an additional $39 billion dollars will be needed to achieve universal health coverage, or $6.5 billion for the basic package. The third concerning observation is that, despite the theoretically sufficient combined funding for middle-income countries, these countries cannot provide universal healthcare coverage. This observation speaks to the fact that the total spend is not aligned with where the money should be spent to meet the health requirements of the population. That is, the allocation of funds for health are inappropriately distributed across disease categories.

Funding allocations by donors provides an insight into priorities according to disease categories. Global funding in 2017 in the 135 low- and middle-income countries was the following: HIV/AIDS, $20 billion; tuberculosis, approximately $11 billion; and malaria, $5 billion.[183] In 2019, donor global health financing was approximately $41 billion dollars, with the largest chunk going to Africa ($13 billion).[183] HIV ($9.5 billion), malaria ($2.3 billion), and tuberculosis ($1.7 billion) received a third of all the donor healthcare funding. It is not that these are unnecessary allocations, but that there are large disease gaps in financing health, and until these are addressed we will never achieve universal health coverage. Essentially, the funding of health is not appropriately allocated to disease categories, nor is it following the changing proportional disease burden of the population. The funding priority areas appear to be informed retrospectively, as opposed to prospectively. More people die within 30 days of surgery every year (over 4 million), than from HIV, malaria, and tuberculosis combined (approximately 3 million).[83] Only ischaemic heart disease and stroke have a higher burden of mortality than surgery.

Surgery is in a terrible position when being considered for funding. Its biggest problem is that it does not have a category (or silo) for funding. Surgery must siphon money from the small pots allocated to 'sector-wide approaches' and 'health systems strengthening' (total donor allocations of $5–6 billion), after scrapping with all other disease categories competing for a slice of the financial pie.[183]

Currently, there is zero signal that this trend in funding allocation is going to change any time soon to align with need. The trends in donor health expenditure are not heading towards future support to address the disease gaps for universal health coverage. Between 2010 and 2019, child and newborn health expenditure has increased by 77%, reproductive and maternal health by 26%, and other infectious diseases by 63%. Yet, sector-wide approaches and health system strengthening (the area from which surgery may get a little funding) has instead decreased by 2%.[183]

The recent history of mortality and funding

We need to change our thinking to 'all boats rise with the tide'. Strong health systems include financing all aspects of robust functioning medical systems with sufficient resources – it is not a zero-sum game.

Wayne Morriss, *Earth Cast* S3E35

Donor funding is important for improving health, especially in low-resource environments. Donors may provide a financial bridge to universal health coverage in low-income and lower-middle-income countries, but their priorities are inconsistent with need, so in the foreseeable future they will not help address this problem. It is possible to determine the value donors put on preventing mortality by tracking donor funding against global deaths using mortality data[62] and donor funding data.[183] Taking 1990 as a baseline, there were 43 million deaths, and donor funding was about $132 per death (Table 8).

Table 8 (right top). Deaths and donor expenditure per death in 1990[183]

Table 9 (right bottom). Deaths and donor expenditure per death in 2017 (and funding from 2019 reports)[183]

CAUSE OF DEATH	PROPORTION OF DEATHS	NUMBER OF DEATHS	BILLIONS OF DOLLARS	DOLLARS PER DEATH
Infectious diseases	15.45%	6 654 090	0.61	92
Maternal and child health	16.19%	6 969 692	2.58	370
Non-communicable	60.42%	26 016 982	0.13	5
Injuries	7.94%	3 418 364	2.4	702
Total		43 059 128	5.72	132

CAUSE OF DEATH	PROPORTION OF DEATHS	NUMBER OF DEATHS	BILLIONS OF DOLLARS	DOLLARS PER DEATH
Infectious diseases	10.67%	5 731 008	16.3	2844
Maternal and child health	7.54%	4 048 733	13.3	3285
Non-communicable	75.27%	40 417 218	0.73	18
Injuries	6.52%	3 501 115	5	1428
Total	1	53 698 074	35.33	658

By 2019, the deaths had risen to 56 million (although I can only account for 54 million deaths when trying to link these deaths to donor funding), and the donor funding had increased to $658 dollars per death, a fourfold increase from 1990 (Table 9). The CPI inflation index would suggest that $1 in 1990 is now equivalent to $2, so the relative donor contribution to health has more than doubled between 1990 and 2019.

However, the really distressing finding is the relative difference in the number of donor dollars spent per death between disease categories. Non-communicable deaths have received only $18 dollars per death in 2019, compared to infectious diseases and maternal and child health, which received approximately $3000 per death, or nearly 170 times more funding per death. Yet, in 1990, the proportional difference in funding per death was less than half that, at 74 times difference between donor funding for noncommunicable diseases compared to infectious diseases and maternal and child health. This is totally inconsistent with the changing proportional contribution to mortality: non-communicable diseases continue to contribute a bigger and bigger proportion to global mortality, while the proportional allocation of donor funding is becoming less and less (Table 10).

This is the current state of the donor financing of health. Firstly, funding is skewed towards specific disease categories, predominated by infectious diseases. Yet the trend associated with mortality is predominated by the rise of non-communicable disease deaths. The rise in non-communicable diseases is also reflected in surgical patients in low-resource environments. In Africa, 42% of patients have surgery for non-communicable disease, 27% for caesarean delivery, 18% for trauma, and then the

CAUSE OF DEATH	PROPORTIONAL INCREASE IN DEATHS	PROPORTIONAL INCREASE IN EXPENDITURE
Infectious diseases	-13.87%	2672.13%
Maternal and child health	-41.91%	515.50%
Non-communicable	55.35%	561.54%
Injuries	2.42%	208.33%

Table 10. Proportional change in mortality and donor funding between 1990 and 2019

remaining 13% for infection.[1] Secondly, the allocation of donor funding continues to increase in the disease areas where mortality is actually decreasing proportionately. Thirdly, surgery has a large role to play in global health equity. However, because funding is siloed and there is no surgical silo, surgical funding will remain under-represented in less-resourced environments.

What would be an equitable donor allocation for surgery? Well, if more deaths follow surgery than are caused by HIV, malaria, and tuberculosis combined[83] (which received more than $13.9 billion in donor funding in 2017, or 34% of global funding expenditure on health), then a reasonable starting point would be to give at least an equivalent amount for surgery. Surgical outcomes are not going to improve until there is an increase in funding allocation. This is borne out by the striking association between donor funding and mortality between 1990 and 2019. Increased funding was associated with a decrease in mortality, while lesser funding was associated with less impact on mortality. In fact, the inequity between disease categories and funding will continue to diverge if we do not act now. Based on the projected global burden of disease and mortality data for 2030, we see that mortality associated with infectious diseases and maternal and child health will continue to fall through to 2030, while deaths following injuries will remain constant, and deaths following non-communicable diseases will continue to increase (Table 11). [61,185,186]

DISEASE CATEGORIES	GBD 1990	WHO 2016	WHO 2030
INFECTIOUS DISEASES	15.45%	15.66%	12.10%
MATERNAL AND CHILD HEALTH	16.19%	4.52%	2.72%
NON-COMMUNICABLE	60.42%	71.22%	77.01%
INJURIES	7.94%	8.59%	8.17%

Table 11. Proportional contributions to global mortality
Source: Global Burden of Disease; World Health Organisation

What is important to note are the future trends in mortality. Importantly, non-communicable diseases will exceed the combined burden of communicable, maternal, neonatal, and nutritional diseases as the leading cause of mortality in sub-Saharan Africa by 2030.[187] There is a sombre warning related to these disease trends, as it is predicted that future expenditure in the management of non-communicable diseases will outstrip the budget allocations in African countries that are unprepared, as current resources are being directed away from the management of non-communicable diseases instead of towards them.[188] The upshot of this is that there is a lack of health systems preparedness to respond to the changing need of disease priorities. An appropriate response to these disease trends demands prioritisation of surgical health financing.

For the poorest billion people, non-communicable diseases and injuries (NCDI) account for more than a third of the burden of disease, and exceed HIV, tuberculosis and maternal mortality combined.[189] The need for surgical interventions are even more important in these low-resource environments, with the poor access to surgery, and the relative absence of some specialised surgical services in these environments further compromising health equity. In the poorest billion, deaths from non-communicable diseases and injuries exceed 800 000 per annum in those under 40. It is estimated that investing in cost-effective and equitable treatment for non-communicable diseases and injuries would save 4.6 million lives between 2020 and 2030.[189]

However, when you look at the interventions necessary for the poorest billion based on cost-effectiveness and health equity (defined by priority to the poor, women, those with the least lifetime health, and those with severely disabling conditions),[189] the role of surgical delivery is strikingly obvious, as surgical interventions are represented in over 50% of the necessary interventions. There are 27 interventions in the highest effectiveness category, and a further 19 either in the high or highest cost-effectiveness and equity categories.[189] Twenty-three of those 46 interventions (50%) are surgical interventions, and 14 of the 27 highest effectiveness interventions (52%) are surgical.[26] It appears that surgery may have a proportionally bigger role to play in low-resource environments than in high-resource environments, approaching 50%, compared to the global 30% proportional contribution.

In summary, surgery is not expensive, running at about 10% of the costs for essential health, but it provides about 30% of the healthcare that a population needs. This need may approach as much as 50% for the poorest billion. Furthermore, the ability to provide surgery strengthens healthcare systems by enabling other disciplines needed for healthcare. To manage the Covid-19 pandemic, we leveraged the resources of surgical systems: anaesthesiologists, ventilators, and the ability to provide safe airway management, for example. Strengthening surgery strengthens health systems.[190] Poor surgical systems, however, mean that the presentation and treatment of diseases comes late, and this compromises patient survival.[1,32] To provide access to safe surgery requires a systems and infrastructure change. Increasing access to emergency surgery also increases access to other emergency facilities,[190] such as maternal and paediatric emergency management. Similarly, improving access to elective surgery results in an increased network across disciplines, as managing a number of these surgical diseases requires multidisciplinary care.[190] Thus, health systems strengthening is key to determining access to universal healthcare, and the need for strengthening is proportionally larger in low-resource and vulnerable environments. The cost of strengthening health systems in low- and middle-income countries to achieve SDG 3 goals by 2030 amounts to an increase in the mean share of GDP expenditure from the current 5.6% to a projected 7.5% – a 33% increase in healthcare expenditure.[191]

The same can be said for critical care in low-resource environments. Critical care resources are limited in Africa, largely due to a lack of recognition of the value of critical care to the whole health system and inadequate funding for these services. Critical care services strengthen the whole hospital (and health) system, and there is value in money spent to deliver critical care. However, the perception is that critical care is an expensive service for low-resource health systems. This is not true, as basic critical care is a core component necessary for the provision of universal health coverage. At least 16 of the 46 essential interventions for universal health coverage are likely to require some critical care support to ensure safe provision (e.g.: repair of cleft lip and cleft palate; surgical treatment of early stage colorectal cancer; definitive surgical management of orthopaedic injuries; management of acute critical limb ischemia with amputation; percutaneous coronary intervention for acute myocardial infarction; medical management of acute, decompensated heart failure; bowel obstruction; bowel perforations; colostomy; hernia repairs, including emergency surgery; shunts for hydrocephalus; trauma thoracoscopy; trauma laparotomy; trauma-related amputations; and treatment of congenital endocrine or metabolic disorders).[189]

The cost of providing surgical health

Thirty per cent of global health requirements have a surgical component.[52,132] There are several approaches to reaching this conclusion. A simple approach is the frequency of operations per admission to hospital according to the global burden of disease categories.[33,132] Approximately one third of all hospital admissions are for surgery. Surgery is required for 23.9% of communicable diseases, maternal, neonatal, and nutritional disorder admissions combined, while 33.9% of non-communicable diseases require surgery and 34.6% of injuries require surgery.[132] Categories with a surgical need exceeding a third of all admissions include maternal disorders, transport injuries, unintentional injuries excluding transport, and conditions involving the digestive tract, neoplasm, and musculoskeletal system.[132] Of the surgical conditions requiring surgery in Africa, the commonest indication for surgery is non-communicable disease (42%), then caesarean section (27%), trauma (18%), and acute infection (13%).[1]

Funding should be aligned with the predicted burden of disease and the associated mortality. Siloing funding according to disease categories alone is inappropriate, as it leads to underfunding of cross-cutting care such as surgery, which does not have a silo. If one is to improve global health, then one either needs to break down these disease silos,[192] or ring-fence a surgical budget within each silo. If we moved away from silo budgeting, then here are two back-of-the-envelope suggestions for the re-allocation of funding. (Those with more financial skills can flesh out the real numbers, but this is a start.) Firstly, we could reallocate funding to burden of disease (which is not rocket science). Based on mortality, the budget for surgery should be 133% of that allocated to HIV, malaria, and tuberculosis, as there are four deaths following surgery compared to every three deaths from HIV, malaria, and tuberculosis combined.[83] An alternative approach is to base funding on surgery's contribution to health. If we assume that approximately 30% of hospital care requires surgery,[132] then approximately 30% of hospital budgets should be allocated to delivering surgery. Although some funding may be considered already allocated to surgery, as surgery is important for managing all categories of health, the reality is that little of this funding reaches surgical healthcare delivery – certainly not in the order of 30%. About 30% of population health is dependent on surgical care, and this rises in low-resource environments.[52] Therefore, a country's health budget should have 30% of the budget earmarked for surgical services.

If a universal health package costs about $100 per person per year,[179] and surgery contributes between 30%[132] and 50%[189] of this package, it then requires between $30 and $50 per capita per year, or 8 to 14 cents per person per day. Tanzania recently costed the increase in funding needed to provide safe and affordable surgery. This scale-up would only require an additional 0.5 cents per capita per day, or $2 per person per year.[137] At full coverage, the DCP3 essential universal health coverage package costs about $84 per capita annually in low-income countries and $120 per capita in lower-middle-income countries. The NCDI poverty package costs about 62% ($52 per capita) of the essential universal health coverage costs in low-income countries and 70% ($84 per capita) in low- and lower-middle-income countries.[189] Accepting that surgical conditions account for approximately 50% of interventions,[189] we can assume that surgical needs for NCDI cost about $28 per capita for low-income countries and about $42 per capita for low- and low-middle-income countries, which is 33% and 23% of the total package.

Therefore, an appropriate strategy may be to ensure a surgical silo with approximately 30% of the total health budget based on these assumptions, and within each disease category budget, there should be a ring-fenced proportion for surgical care. So, a third of the budget for non-communicable diseases and injuries should be ring-fenced for surgical treatment and surgical strengthening, and possibly less allocated to infections. There are tools now to customise a health package according to various surgical needs (https://dcp-uw.shinyapps.io/dcp-cm/)[193] and resource requirements.[181] We can literally design our own healthcare package. We can also calculate the cost of a establishing and running an operating theatre.[141]

To ensure that surgery is allocated the appropriate budget for population health, we need to do the following. Firstly, we need to explicitly track healthcare expenditure on surgical care for health provision. Thanks to the WHO, we can now track global health financing,[194] although we still cannot track surgical expenditure, as all the spending summaries remain within disease categories and surgery is not represented. This is the deal-breaker: 'In low-income countries, infectious diseases accounted for half of overall health spending, while in middle-income countries, they accounted for one third. Non-communicable diseases accounted for about 30% of health spending in middle-income countries and about 13% in low-income countries.'[182] Reproductive health had the same share of health spending in low-income countries and middle-income countries (12–13%), as did injuries, at 4%.[182] Until we track surgical expenditure, we will not be able to track the proportional expenditure on surgery in each of these categories.

However even if we can improve on the appropriate allocation of funds to support universal health coverage, we need to ensure accountability for financial spending for this to work. We also have to address the problem of Africa being the region with the least efficient health spending amongst low- and middle-income countries.[37] We have to institute mechanisms to ensure that the allocated funds are used as intended. Simple reallocation of an appropriate budget will not ensure surgical health for all until we address all the problems that have been identified as driving these inefficiencies: 'unused fiscal space for health across African countries, [the] disproportionate spending on tertiary care to the detriment of primary care, procurement, inappropriate workforce distribution and motivation (financial and non-financial), medical errors, and corruption.'[37]

We need various strategies to address this financial threat to health equity. This requires lobbying citizens, civil society, governments, and donors. First and foremost, our role as citizens is to ensure that our governments are accountable. This is important, as governments are spending less on health. 'Average government spending on health in low-income countries was only $9 per capita in 2018, about 1.2% of GDP, and the priority given to health has been declining between 2000 and 2018.'[182] So, priority one is to stop the decrease in government spending on health. Secondly, we must ensure that funding allocations are appropriate to disease areas of need. Thirdly, we must document and record the allocation to surgical care. We know people want this, especially following Richard Horton's call for safe and affordable surgery in his WHA opening address. It is appropriate to advocate for documentation of expenditure on the cross-cutting disciplines and categories contributing to population health, as the dialogue of health priorities is shifting from individual diseases to broad categories of health that encompass many different diseases: planetary health; women's rights and sexual and reproductive health and rights for all; and safe and affordable surgery. Health is a whole government issue and not just a department of health issue.

In demanding that our governments deliver safe surgery, we as citizens must also play our part in guaranteeing a better life for all. We must pay our taxes, and then hold our governments accountable for the appropriate spending of our money. This includes addressing corruption and the inappropriate allocation of funds. The role of citizens in high-income countries is to ensure that the priorities for donor healthcare spending are proportionately representative of need when money is allocated to global health. Those citizens should also demand that governments donate more money to foreign aid, as less than 1% of gross national income is currently allocated to foreign aid almost across the board.[195] The exception is Norway, which runs at about 8%. How is that possible?

The current push for tax cuts in high-income countries adversely affects life expectancy in both the home nation and in low-resource nations.[196] The UK is a sad example. Funds were squeezed due to BREXIT and Covid-19, which will decrease UK life expectancy because less funds will be available for health. Sadly, this has simultaneously led to a cut in international spending by the NIHR. Tax cuts in high-income countries have important negative implications for global health spending.

In low- and middle-income countries, the citizens who willingly pay taxes must trust that the government will spend their money appropriately. This is a challenge because corruption is rife in these countries, setting up a vicious cycle where corruption and siphoning of funds leads to less tax payment, resulting in less government funding for healthcare.

To improve the quality of surgical care, the workforce needs to be scaled up, training should reach a minimum standard of care, and adequate resources are required to practice care according to acceptable training standards. To this end, appropriate funding is needed to furnish resources and strengthen the healthcare system, so that it can provide the surgical care needed for the 30% coverage of population health.

We understand the problem of insufficient surgical health, the politics of delivering this care, and the global policies around surgical health. We now need to leverage the resolutions of WHA 68.15 and 76.2, and the global call that Richard Horton delivered at the WHA. Clinicians must work hand in hand with governments and policymakers to realise the ambition of safe surgery and anaesthesia for all in Africa. Clinicians need to help deliver improved health outcomes through quality surgical care, otherwise the politicians will never support the changes required to make surgery safer.

Political leverage

It is not enough to simply provide good health care; clinicians need to understand politics. Being aware of policies across different health systems ensures the best surgical outcomes and brings in development financing and resources.

Salome Maswime, *Earth Cast* S3E36

Holding politicians accountable

P oliticians work in voting cycles. As such, longer-term projects seem to always get relegated to the back-burner in favour of the short-term wins designed to lure voters at the next election. This popularity contest always trumps the more important requirements for creating a stable environment for the population. Longer-term projects will consume funds but are not easily visible to most of the voting public on the eve of an election. A classic example of this principle was when Cape Town seemed to be heading towards the infamy of becoming the first city in the world to run out of water, a catastrophe that became locally known as 'Day Zero'. The signs of Cape Town's potential water problem had been there for ages, and engineers had alerted the government to the problem decades in advance. However, in the world of politics it got relegated to a low priority for future leaders to address. There were always more immediate issues to leverage in the pursuit of votes.

This is the challenge facing the scaling up of resources needed for surgery. Achieving the scale-up needed requires finance and time, and the results are unlikely to be visible within the sort time span of a single political term. High-visibility projects such as building one big hospital are all the rage, while the more important responsibility of an NSOAP, which would provide the existing hospitals with equipment and human capital, are ignored. We know that we need this longer-term view of surgical scale-up,[33] and we know how to do it using the national NSOAP process and implementation plans to make surgery safe and affordable in a country. So how do we get politicians and policymakers to look further down the road, beyond the next election? We, as individuals and communities, must lobby governments to deliver universal healthcare that includes safe and affordable surgery, just as communities, advocates, and activists did in the early days of the HIV pandemic.

Citizens and civil society can exert enormous pressure for change in healthcare. One need look no further than HIV and the role that normal citizens played in transforming HIV care. The inability to access antiretroviral therapy led to funding through advocacy by the Treatment Action Campaign (TAC). The strength of this movement was that it was characterised by multiple small actions from many people. There are many stories. A colleague in the Western Cape was a provincial coordinator for the TAC, and later helped establish the Médecins Sans Frontières (MSF) antiretroviral distribution centre in Khayelitsha. He spent his Saturdays teaching the public about HIV in small workshops. There was a tremendous commitment to creating a public awareness about HIV, its treatment, and everyone's rights to accessing treatment. This educational foundation led to the success of the HIV movement. Similarly, it is only through education that citizens and civil society can rise up and demand the social accountability necessary from governments to deliver safer surgery for all. It is hoped that this book will provide some of the knowledge needed to do this.

Early HIV advocacy has shown us how a common social and human rights issue can create a passionate community with a common purpose. The TAC evolved from the injustice of a lack of access to treatment, a source of anger that many individuals felt. The evidence for antiretroviral efficacy was so strong that individuals were willing to give up their time to ensure everyone knew. This was a human rights issue to which they were all committed.

The outstanding success of the HIV campaign is evident in the funding that poured into HIV treatment, and 30 years later it continues to fund HIV research and care. The current disparity between the success of HIV advocacy and the limited advocacy for safe surgical care is well summarised in Figure 10 from the Global Surgery Foundation, illustrating the relationship between HIV and surgical funding, and the global deaths per year.

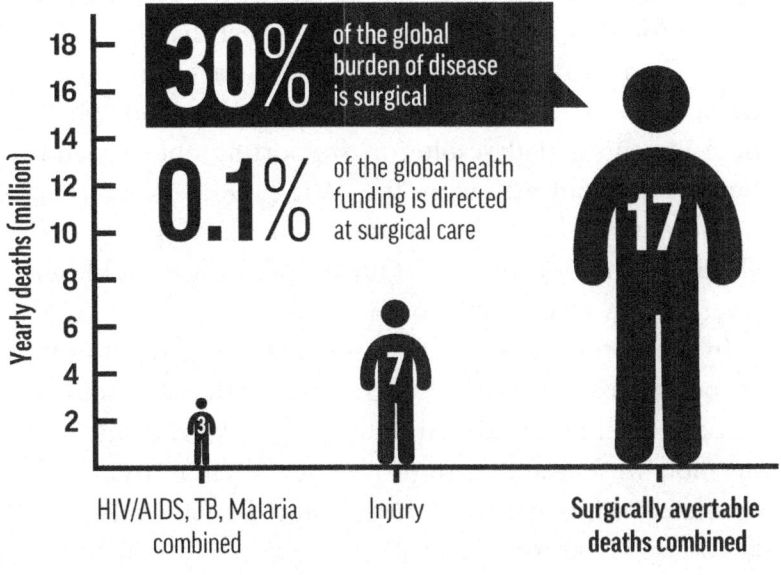

Figure 10. Deaths associated with HIV, TB, and malaria, injuries, and surgery. Source: Global Surgery Foundation, https://www.globalsurgeryfoundation.org/why

We should feel indignant that, in 2024, with the overwhelming evidence supporting the need for adequate surgical services to support global health, we still have the funding picture shown here. Although funding for HIV, TB, and malaria is important, the population health burden associated with insufficient and unsafe surgery should lead to an outcry. Clearly, a large proportion of the public does not understand the importance of surgery for population health. It is time for us as citizens to rise up and challenge the status quo and advocate for safer surgery and anaesthesia.

The challenge to ensure that governments provide safe surgery for all should theoretically be easier than it was for the TAC and other HIV advocates to ensure antiretroviral therapy for all. The TAC faced an environment where there was no global resolution supporting antiretroviral therapy. In contrast, with the WHA 68.15 resolution, most countries have already agreed to ensuring safe and affordable surgery for all.[130] Our challenge is to hold our governments accountable to this resolution.

In many countries in Africa, no amount of wealth can buy optimal care. This is only too evident in the behaviour of the political elite. Based on the fantastic work by Sir Michael Marmot, we know that improved social circumstance is associated with improved health and better healthcare outcomes.[10] However, in healthcare systems as challenged as those in Africa, even political elites, with all their social advantages, cannot always get adequate healthcare in their own countries. Due to limited resources, these countries have healthcare barriers that exist independent of social circumstance. If there is no hospital, no operating room, no surgeon, then it doesn't matter how wealthy you are – the right surgery just won't happen. In times of need, the only way to overcome these barriers is to flee to a country that can provide the necessary care. Many of Africa's leaders have done exactly that. It is not uncommon for African leaders to die in foreign hospitals, as leaders from Malawi, Gabon, Togo, Nigeria, and Tanzania all have. Sadly these heads of state would 'prefer to pour taxpayers' money into overseas medical facilities rather than spending it on improving healthcare at home'.[197] Their actions are an admission of the inadequacy of the medical resources and healthcare their own governments are providing for their populations at home. The impact of seeking care outside of Africa has a further negative impact on health at home. It was estimated that, in 2016, Africans spent $6 billion on medical tourism outside of Africa.[198] There will be little impetus to improve the quality of care at home if this behaviour of the political elite is tolerated. It was estimated in 2017 that the bill for treating Ugandan government officials overseas could have funded the building of 10 new hospitals per annum.[198]

Funding healthcare in any African country (and any low- or middle-income country) will be a challenge, particularly as the ratio of tax revenue to GDP is so low. While most European countries have a ratio in excess of 30%, most African countries are below 20%.[199] Low-resource countries therefore need to embrace the potential solutions offered in this book, and the public need to hold politicians accountable and ensure that public funds are not siphoned off through corruption and state capture, which has held South Africa ransom in recent years.

What we need is a public intolerance of the inability to provide safe surgical care for all. We need to honour WHA resolution 68.15. No one is safe until everyone is safe. As citizens, and civil society, we need to demand this. But this will not happen until everyone is educated about the surgery that they are entitled to, why they should receive it, and what they are currently offered. Only then will we drum up an intolerance for the current state of surgical care in Africa, and agitate for change.

The surgical community has previously failed in its advocacy campaign.[200] The power of leaders in the global surgery community was weak due to fragmented ideas, resulting in an inability to publicly position the problem of safe surgery and anaesthesia. Within the political contexts up to 2015, the surgical community did not capitalise on political opportunities such as health development goals. The data on the burden of surgical disease and the messaging to the public was poor.[200] This should no longer be the case. There is now a wealth of knowledge showing the position and place of surgery in health, and its impact on society. Research has shown it to be a necessary and cost-effective component of health.[33] Now is the time for us to realise the delivery of safe and affordable surgery for all, as it is clearly needed for global health priorities.

How to communicate surgical need to politicians

Politicians don't like us presenting problems, especially when we know that governments have many problems to deal with. What we need to do is present solutions. Rifat Atun, professor of Global Health Systems at Harvard University says, 'For every problem, bring three solutions.' This must be our strategy, and this book provides the kernels for these solutions.

So how do we communicate this strategy and these solutions effectively to influence politicians?[201] Jeremy Shiffman provides a structure for communicating priorities with politicians based on four categories: actor power (the strength of the individuals and organisations); ideas; political context; and the characteristics of the issue.[201] I will show you how to use this strategy to influence politicians to improve surgical care.

Actor power has provided surgical policy cohesion at a global level with the WHA 68.15 and WHA 76.2 resolutions. We have champions for the cause, such as John Meara from Harvard, Emmanuel Makasa from Zambia (who led the first NSOAP), Salome Maswime (head of global surgery in

Cape Town), and others. They are respected global voices. We have guiding institutions leading the initiative, such as the Global Surgery Foundation, Harvard's Program in Global Surgery and Social Change, the World Federation of the Societies of Anaesthesiologists (WFSA), the NIHR Global Health Research Unit on Global Surgery and the NIHR Global Group on Perioperative and Critical Care, amongst others. They pretty much speak with the same voice, and so the agreement on what is needed for safe surgery is consistent globally.

Although the global health community has flagged surgery as an international priority as presented by Richard Horton to the WHA, from an actor power perspective we are currently failing in civil society mobilisation. Citizens and communities must tell the story. We must speak and advocate just as communities stepped up to respond to HIV.

When we consider the ideas part of the strategy for communicating to politicians, the surgical community have agreed on the internal framework necessary to deliver safe surgery, as documented in the NSOAP process. Where we are currently failing is the presentation of the external framework underpinning the need for safe surgical provision. We need to provide a clear message of the proportional contribution of surgery to population health, and the unacceptable adverse outcomes and disparity in the quality of surgical care across low-resource environments. We need to communicate the cost-saving benefits of providing adequate surgical care.

There are reasons to believe that the political context is receptive to providing safe surgery. Governments signed WHA 68.15, providing the policy needed to support surgery. This resolution demands the reporting of national surgical indicators. These indicators provide the information necessary to document our response to surgical provision, and the quality of the surgical care. We must demand the delivery of these indicators.

Tracking the surgical indicators and, most importantly, the perioperative mortality rate, has the potential to influence politicians. Just like we tracked maternal mortality and shone a light on its successes and failures, we can do the same with surgery. We know that the burden of mortality associated with surgery is important, exceeding that of TB, HIV, and malaria combined.[83] We have data on effective surgical procedures, which will affect global health, from the poorest billion[189] to all health systems more broadly.[181] We are armed to present the case for safe surgery and anaesthesia.

You may retort that you are but one person; how can you possibly make a difference? It's simple. Immaterial of your station, if you believe in the message of this book, there will be an opportunity to contribute, even if it is only to share the message. If you have but one opportunity, make it count. This is my strategy to maximising a single opportunity. If you can present the problems and solutions as a simple pitch, I believe that you will be on the way to successfully advocating for change. This is my favourite framework for creating a simple pitch.[202] Practice this:

- 'We have a problem of …
- We have learnt that …
- We have a solution …
- which can achieve …
- This is intervention is cost-effective because …
- and it would give us the following benefit …
- There is plenty of data to back this up.'

How does this sound? 'We have a problem of too many deaths following surgery in Africa. We have learnt that it is because too few patients receive surgery, and there aren't enough surgical providers to care for all the patients. We have a pragmatic government solution to increase surgical support, which other countries have successfully implemented. This can achieve more and safer surgeries. It's a cost-effective intervention because, for a small increase in spend, we would have the benefit of a healthier and more economically active population. We have plenty of data to back this up.'

In conclusion, if we want to improve surgical health and thereby population health, we need to do three things:

1. Get patients who require surgery into the operating room. We are losing lots of lives, and the economic impact of untreated surgical disease is crippling.
2. Improve the quality of surgery in low-resource environments. This is multifactorial, and in several circumstances it is the current state of the health system which is a major contributor to this excess mortality.
3. Do everything possible to provide excellent care, even if a patient has surgery in a low-resource environment. There are local strategies that we can provide to support quality surgical care. We need to build these interventions and processes into care provided on the ground in the surgical environment.

Part 5

A manifesto for surgical health in Africa

Health system strengthening

We need to reimagine surgery as a solution for health system strengthening and supporting peoples' socioeconomic footing.

– Emmanuel Makasa, *Earth Cast* S3E34

It was a Sunday in mid-2015, and I was driving home from a weekend away at a nature reserve in Northern Kwazulu-Natal when I received a call: 'Hi, this is Salome. I would like to come to the meeting.' This is how Salome Maswime and I met. I was trying to establish a perioperative research network for South Africa, and Salome was adamant that obstetrics be represented. It was a fortuitous crossing of paths, and now, eight years later, we work closely in obstetric outcomes research in Africa. Salome is professor and head of the Division of Global Surgery at the University of Cape Town, and a leader in this space. She is amiable, thoughtful, and a great communicator across all levels. She has a tremendous capacity to bring leaders with diverse skills together for a common cause. She is leading change in surgery at the highest level in Africa.

I asked Salome what drew her to obstetrics. Just like Tinashe, it was a personal experience that shaped her career. As a young doctor completing her community service in 2008, she ran the labour ward of the hospital in a small rural town in KwaZulu-Natal. The maternal deaths she witnessed in that ward were to determine her future. This was in the same small town where, many years before, I did not have the courage to do a super GP weekend locum, and thus avoided having to perform a caesarean section without any previous experience. In that tiny hospital, with less than 150 beds, there were two maternity cases that really affected Salome. The first was a mother who needed a caesarean section. The patient complicated with a high spinal anaesthetic, requiring endotracheal intubation, general anaesthesia, and cardiovascular and respiratory support. Only one of the medical officers at the hospital could perform general anaesthesia, but this doctor was unavailable, so managing the high spinal was complicated and difficult. The mother died while awaiting transport to the regional centre for expert care.

The second case followed shortly afterwards. The mother presented acutely short of breath. While the working diagnosis had been pneumocystis carinii pneumonia (PCP) secondary to HIV, it was only when the pink froth of pulmonary oedema started to pour from her mouth that it became clear that her heart was failing, and the back pressure on her lungs was forcing fluid out of her vessels and into her lungs. Managing this condition required doctors who had had the cross-training of anaesthesia to provide the endotracheal intubation and cardiovascular support. This mother, too, died awaiting transfer to the regional centre for care. At this early stage in her career, Salome knew that she needed to learn more to provide holistic care for these mothers. It had been a traumatic time working in this distressing and disabling clinical environment.

The following year, Salome moved from that small hospital in rural KwaZulu-Natal to Chris Hani Baragwanath, the biggest hospital in Africa, to train in obstetrics and gynaecology. She moved quickly through the ranks, and by 2014, with her training complete, Salome embarked on her doctorate in caesarean section haemorrhage. When we spoke for the first time, about the meeting to launch a perioperative research group in South Africa, Salome was in the thick of it, reviewing patient files of obstetric haemorrhage from 15 South African hospitals. It felt like reliving the distressing labour ward of her community service. Even though her specialist training had since given her the clinical skills to manage obstetric haemorrhage, she still felt disempowered because she could see that her early experience of maternal deaths was playing out all over South Africa.

After the successful launch of the South African Perioperative Research Group (SAPORG) in 2015,[203] we created the African Perioperative Research Group (APORG) in 2016, and it was here that ASOS was launched. Salome was actively involved in the obstetric arm of the research, and so it felt like another blow to the stomach when the results came out. While doing her doctorate she'd learnt that frequent maternal deaths weren't an isolated phenomenon in rural KwaZulu-Natal or South Africa, and ASOS confirmed that it was a universal African travesty. Rolling forward to Salome's appointment as head of global surgery in 2019, and our early meetings on the vision and strategy for the division, I clearly remember her comment that access to and the delivery of quality surgical care should be centred on health system strengthening. She'd seen health system strengthening clearly from her experience with maternal haemorrhage. As a junior doctor in rural KwaZulu-Natal, she did not have all the clinical skills to manage maternal haemorrhage, and then when she did have all the clinical skills after training at Baragwanath, she could still not stop all the bleeding – mothers around South Africa and Africa were dying from haemorrhage. The health system was failing both the clinicians and the patients.

It is only by working through the narrative of this book that I really got to understand health system strengthening. Salome sees all the clinicians across Africa trying to deliver the best care they can for bleeding mothers, but the health system in which they work is literally killing the patients. 'Once you see it you cannot unsee it,' she says. 'Poor outcomes are not the result of a single person, but rather a system failure.' She was understandably nervous to walk away from her known clinical obstetric career. It felt like a massive risk, especially when moving to the unknown broader visionary work of global surgery. But she could not unsee what she had learnt from ASOS – that this problem was huge, pervasive, and extended across the continent. 'It felt too important not to take the step.'

The conversation is more positive now, as we have a clearer idea of the problems preventing the delivery of safe anaesthesia and surgery in Africa. What we need to do is to work on the solutions to those problems. Working in this environment as clinicians and researchers certainly provides an important perspective on how to achieve this goal. The journey of trying to articulate my thoughts in this book has led me to see that the need for health system strengthening had been there from the very beginning. It was everywhere when I read through the manuscript again.

The health systems in Africa are broken in so many ways. There was no antenatal care for the high-risk pregnancy mother who died in a pool of blood after delivering at home in Zimbabwe. It was inadequate human resources that forced Sue and a final year medical student to provide an emergency caesarean section to save a mother and child, and a lack of blood transfusion resources that meant the medical student had to donate her own blood for the mother. Sue's experience is similar to that of the non-physicians who are forced to deliver sedation in Africa to enable surgery, because the resources and expertise necessary to provide safe general anaesthesia do not exist in these environments. The emotional trauma for these non-physicians must be enormous, given the high complication rate following these surgeries. It must be similar to the emotional trauma that Salome experienced when she watched a young mother die after the high spinal anaesthetic complication, because there was inadequate anaesthesia experience to manage it.

What is health system strengthening? I would define it as creating a healthcare environment that enables the clinician to provide the best care possible for their patient. It includes the many components of the inside-out quality surgical model, and the outside-in surgical resources model. System strengthening also requires the supporting services necessary to ensure that everyone can access quality surgical services. Health system strengthening to ensure safe anaesthesia and surgery in Africa would probably improve public health by about 30%, a potentially massive contribution. It is likely that the impact on population health will be more than the 30% stated, due to cross-training. This would have helped Salome's patient who died with pulmonary oedema in rural KwaZulu-

Natal. Similarly, a surgeon's skill set also extends to other disciplines, and may have prevented Dolly's patient from having to take a six-hour trip to Kinshasa for a chest drain. The death of Agya's patient was aggravated by an environment lacking sufficient staff, patient monitors, and antibiotics. A sick patient cannot survive without these basic requirements.

We know from our work across Africa that clinicians care. Our responsibility must be to create an environment that enables and supports them at the coalface to provide the best care possible, to every patient. It is not right that Dr Azza Mashumba, the paediatrician from Parirenyatwa in Harare, has to say, 'I come to work, I do my very best, but my output are stillbirths, my output are disabled babies', leading her to conclude that 'we are not helping patients'. She, and all the clinicians in Africa, *are* helping their patients. But the health systems are failing them. We must support clinicians by creating an enabling and safe clinical working environment. The task may seem enormous, as the scope of the interventions needed is huge. It spans human resources, which includes, amongst other things, training and education, employing more healthcare providers, mentorship, and leadership. It requires physical resources, from disposable equipment such as PPE, to expensive equipment such as anaesthesia machines, monitors, and surgical instruments, as well as facilities like operating theatres and hospitals. It requires drugs and antibiotics. It requires policies, and budgets to create and maintain an environment capable of providing safe anaesthesia and surgery.

You may throw up your hands and walk away at this point, but please don't. When I floated the idea of this book on advocacy for safe anaesthesia and surgery in

Africa, Tinashe implored me to write a manifesto for the end. Writing this manifesto has made me reflect critically on what I now understand about the intersection between health, surgery, and society. It has also helped me understand how a declaration of intent is framed by the position from which it is made, whether as an individual, a community, a profession, a group, a political party, government, country, or region. If we can honour our place in these declarations, each of us, in our own small way, will contribute to immense health system strengthening in Africa. If we can each deliver on our intentions, as individuals we will collectively contribute either directly or indirectly to the provision of an environment capable of delivering quality, safe anaesthesia and surgery.

A manifesto for surgical health for all

We have a unique opportunity in Africa to reimagine a resilient system of sustainable surgical care.

Bruce Biccard, *Earth Cast* S3E34

As an individual I will reflect on the implications of any potentially negative demands on the community and the government that I make. I will commit to avoiding selfish demands, such as demanding lower taxes, which may negatively impact on the delivery of health for others. Instead, I will commit to my personal responsibility in ensuring my own good health.

As a community, we will articulate and demand appropriate healthcare for all. We will ensure that our representatives in government who fail to deliver on these demands or abuse their power to the detriment of the community, will not be tolerated and will be held accountable for their deeds.

As a healthcare worker, I will do my best to provide quality healthcare. I acknowledge that we are more likely to achieve this objective as a healthcare team than as individuals. I will value the contributions of my colleagues, and I will respect every team member, immaterial of their position. I understand that to provide quality healthcare we need to create a working environment that encourages speaking up. I therefore commit to listening and communicating in an open and respectful manner, devoid of any traditional or supposed workplace hierarchies. I understand that this will then ensure that the necessary healthcare interventions will be timeously communicated and initiated in the workplace. I will place the patient at the centre of care.

As healthcare workers and researchers, we will commit to increasing the quality of healthcare provision by embedding broadly applicable and generalisable evidence-based interventions into healthcare delivery. We will decrease amenable deaths by ensuring that these interventions are available to all, and decrease avertable deaths by ensuring that these interventions are appropriately and effectively implemented.

As a donor organisation, we will identify the areas of our health interests that have a surgical requirement. We understand that as much as 30% of the management of any disease may have a surgical component, and we will explicitly include a budget for the surgical systems and interventions needed for comprehensive disease management.

As a government, we will focus on strengthening our health system. This will include ensuring that approximately a third of healthcare financing is ring-fenced for safe anaesthesia, surgical provision, and surgical system strengthening. We will commit to providing quality healthcare for all, with the understanding that universal healthcare includes access to timely, appropriate, and affordable anaesthesia and surgery for all. To achieve this, we will ensure that surgery and anaesthesia is explicitly considered and financed within all healthcare sectors. As a government, we will honour our commitments to globally agreed health goals, including the implementation of a National Surgical, Obstetric and Anaesthesia Plan.[130]

As a government, we will not use simplistic financial political hooks to ensure voter support, such as diverting budget allocations from health system strengthening and impoverished communities to more visible but less effective short-term projects, both within and outside national borders. Rather, we will commit to intermediate and long-term healthcare system strengthening strategies that exceed the short-term political voting cycles.

Together, as a global community we will strive for health equity for all.

The challenge

Africa has a problem. Nearly a billion of the five billion people globally who do not have access to safe and affordable surgery live in Africa. This amounts to over 80% of the African population who do not have safe and affordable surgery. How do we rise to this challenge? I hope you are inspired to contribute to making a change. You do not need to be a clinician or in government to positively impact on surgical health in Africa. If you have skills or expertise in education, people, institutions, design, or sustainability, then there is an opportunity for you to make a positive difference to surgical health in Africa.

There are simple rules that we can follow to capacitate surgery. If you can contribute to the delivery of some of these principles, we will be able to scale up surgical and anaesthesia care as a collective.

- Rule no. 1: **Educate the community.** People need to understand what surgical disease is, and what their rights are regarding access to safe surgical care and treatment. Only then will they expect and demand access to the surgical care they need, by putting pressure on governments to deliver.
- Rule no. 2: **Invest in the correct people.** This is about human resources. Surgical teams need people who value teamwork. We need to focus on building surgical teams with flat hierarchies. To extend the reach of quality surgical care, we need surgical teams who embrace task shifting and task sharing. We need a supportive surgical structure, and not an authoritarian one. In the longer term, we need to be educating and employing towards

personalities that embrace collaborative teamwork.

- Rule no. 3: **Build the capacity of existing institutions.** We should resist the temptation to scale up the number of institutions before addressing the deficits within existing institutions. We should rather scale up the capacity to deliver better and safer surgical care at existing sites. This is epitomised by the assessment of critical care facilities in Ethiopia. Of 51 facilities, not one was equipped to provide the highest level of critical care, and almost all of them could only provide critical care at the most basic level.[204,205] I suspect that, just as the base infrastructure exists for increasing critical care capacity in these institutions, there is a massive opportunity to improve surgical capacity at many African surgical hospitals by focusing on equipping these facilities appropriately for the delivery of anaesthesia and surgery first.

- Rule no. 4: **Build capacity with physically close environments within a surgical institution.** If we are to realise the power of task shifting and task sharing to maximise care despite limited personnel, then operating theatres, high-care facilities, and surgical wards need to be physically close. If we develop theatres or high-care units in remote areas of the hospital, we diminish the ability to cross-cover and provide the support necessary for task shifting and sharing. The inability to cross-cover decreases efficiency, and the inability to provide clinician support for task sharing and shifting results in an unsafe clinical environment. Operating theatres become less functional, less safe, and less surgical care is delivered.

- Rule no. 5: **Build replication models when equipping operating theatres and, more broadly, in the recovery and postoperative wards.** A replication model similar to the principle of KidsOR will ensure that costs can be contained through bulk negotiation, and maintenance can be standardised. Replication is associated with improved patient safety because the same arrangement of equipment and drugs makes things easier to find. A classic example is emergency drug administration, where a standardised drug cart is the highest ranked intervention for patient safety according to operating theatre experts.[206] It is possible that a replication model will result in quicker clinical responses, despite an environment lacking surgical resources, and a safer clinical environment in general. While it works within institutions, on a bigger scale it could work across institutions and training facilities.

- Rule no. 6: **Go green in scaling quality surgical provision in Africa.** Climate change is adversely affecting population health, and in low-resource environments this will be further aggravated by an increase in infectious diseases such as malaria, cholera, and dengue fever, while decreased crop production will negatively affect nutritional health.[207] We must focus on strategies to reduce, reuse, and recycle to ensure that the most financially advantageous strategy does not contribute to other health challenges through a lack of sustainability and negative effects on the climate and environment. With such limited healthcare resources, we have an opportunity to build a green healthcare system from the roots up. We must not miss this opportunity, because once we have resourced the surgical and healthcare system that we intend to use for the next few decades, it will be difficult to change to a more environmentally friendly model.

- Rule no. 7: **Integrate data into surgical provision.** We need to report the Lancet Commission surgical indicators so that we can track our performance in delivering safe and affordable surgical care. Similarly, we need to ensure that surgical outcomes data, together with process data supporting clinical care, are regularly shared and discussed with the surgical team to enable improvements in quality of care.
- Finally, rule no. 8: **Work towards an organisational culture that stimulates internal motivation.** Only once this is embedded in the organisation will there be a sustained, meaningful change to patient care. Only then will an organisation have the hope of retaining people and thus retaining the skills necessary to ensure health for all.

Conclusion

Universal healthcare is a human right, but we will never achieve it unless we can provide safe and affordable surgery for all. The under-resourced and under-capacitated healthcare systems of Africa are resulting in a preventable loss of lives. We must provide more surgery of a better quality in Africa. We can do this, although it is going to need action on almost every front. It is going to need community education and health systems strengthening, so that the mother of five in Masvingo is identified as high-risk early in the pregnancy, and through an appropriate antenatal plan is regularly assessed during the pregnancy and in touching distance of a surgical facility that can identify peripartum haemorrhage early and manage it quickly should it occur.

We can capacitate hospitals to provide the type of surgical care that saves lives. A model for surgical teams was presented in the inside-out quality surgery model. We need to move away from accepting the provision of little to no anaesthesia when surgery is needed, to clear intervention implementation plans to ensure that we deliver the best quality care within the operating room and out into the postoperative ward. The clinicians on the ground will have to commit to walking the hard yards in ensuring that they build teams to implement evidence-based care that is monitored through appropriate processes and outcomes. I personally think this is the easier part of the task, as clinicians in low-resource environments have shown that they care in numerous ways.

However, we must remember that no matter how good a local surgical team may become, we cannot accept working environments with suboptimal surgical resources. We need to capacitate surgical sites with human and infrastructure resources as discussed in the outside-in surgical resources model to ensure that we can provide the appropriate surgical care commensurate with the level of the hospital. It cannot be accepted that essential surgical services are simply not available, and that a patient with an injury requiring a simple chest drain must drive six hours on a motorbike to receive lifesaving care elsewhere. We all have a role to play in advocating for good quality surgery and the implementation of NSOAPs. We must remember that money is not a barrier to ensuring surgical health. We must reimagine budget allocations that are more in line with our understanding of public health, where diseases do not exist in tiny silos but are components of many parts of a health system.

Finally, from small individual and community contributions to large charitable, corporate or governmental initiatives, there is a space for everyone to positively impact on surgical health and ultimately universal health in Africa. Although the continent's surgical mortality figures are distressing, it is possible to save many patients from a preventable surgical death and ensure more patients realise the tremendous benefits of modern surgery. This is not going to be easy. But it is not impossible either. As Mandela famously said, 'It always seems impossible until it's done.'

The biggest challenge is to ensure that people far from the coalface of surgical provision buy into the importance of getting surgical care right in Africa. It is not financially difficult. We are asking for the appropriate use of money already earmarked for health. We are also not asking for unreasonable or difficult advocacy. It exists. People have spoken and put it high on healthcare agendas. The hard work has been done. We know it is a key component to population and global health. We know that it accounts for the treatment of nearly a third of all diseases. The challenge is now for us as a global community to ensure that it is implemented by governments, non-governmental organisations, and civil society, right up to the WHO.

Only then, will it be 'done'.

Acknowledgements

Thank you to the African Perioperative Research Group (APORG) who have inspired me and led groundbreaking surgical research in Africa. APORG is a diverse group of frontline clinicians from over 40 African countries who are committed to improving perioperative outcomes in Africa. These are the people who deliver the research needed to improve outcomes in Africa, while providing care in the most trying of situations. They are too many to name – close on 2000 clinicians, literally from Cape to Cairo. They are all individually listed in APORG's many publications, with the most impactful research published in the Lancet journals. This is game-changing research for surgical health in Africa. Thank you to every one of you across Africa. You embody collaborative research. Thank you to the project-steering committees, and the continental and national leaders of these projects: Bareeq Abdallah, Meriem Abdoun, Adesoji Ademuyiwa, Simbo D Amanor-Boadu, Lalatiana Andriamanarivo, Ernest Aniteye, Akwasi Antwi-Kusi, Daniel Zemenfes Ashebir, Paulin Banguti, Venerand Barendegere, Apollo Basenero, Kélan Bertille Ki, Ronald Bisegerwa, Mustapha Lamin Bittaye, Souad Bouaoud, Greg Calligaro, Maman Sani Chaibou, Yacaria Coulibaly, Youssouf Coulibaly, Shukri Dahir, Hassan Ali Daoud, Leon du Toit, Hanel Duvenage, Hailu Tamiru Dhufera, Milliard Derbew, Ahmed Rhassane El Adib, Mohamed Elfagieh, Mahmoud Elfiky, Muhammed Elhadi, Abdulaziz M Elkhogia, Tonya Esterhuizen, Tarig Fadalla, Marvin Fanny, Maher Fawzy, David Fredericks, Patrice Forget, Meseret Gebre, Abebe Genetu Bayih, Veekash Gobin, Dean Gopalan, Christina Gordon, Anneli Hardy, Adam Hewitt-Smith, Donamou

Joseph, Ivan Joubert, Jean Jacques Kalango, Nahla Kechiche, Fitsum Kifle, Hyla-Louise Kluyts, Yannick Le Manach, Maia Lesosky, Heidi Meyer, Lygia Lopes, Cynthia Lule, Kieran Macleod, Farai Madzimbamuto, Lazaro Mboma, Bernard Mbwele, Ryad Mehyaoui, Zelalem Mekonnen, Mervyn Mer, Malcolm Miller, William Michell, Mubarak Mohamed, Hassen Mohammed, Atilio Morais, Vanessa Msosa, Wakisa Mulwafu, Dolly Munlemvo, Landon Myer, Mary Nabukenya, Pisirai Ndarukwa, Gabriel Ndayisaba, Henry Ndasi, Raymond Ndikontar, Andrew Ndonga, Kara Neil, Zipporah Ngumi, Mame Yaa Adobea Nyarko, Mohamed Abdinor Omar, Akinyinka Omigbodun, Babatunde Babasola Osinaike, Gilbert Fabrice Otiobanda, Nazinigouba Ouerdraogo, Fathima Paruk, Ushmah Patel, Jenna Piercy, Agya Prempeh, Arsitide Romain Raherison, Sylvia Rakotoarison, Christian Owoo, Kushal Ramkalawan, Mamy Richard Randriamizao, Vaonandianina Ravelojaona, Hamza Doles Sama, Ahmadou Samateh, Zimogo Sanogo, Yakob Seman, Juan Scribante, Sarah Shalongo, Isaac Smalle, Tim Stephens, Desalegn Bekele Taye, Elliott Taylor, Mikiyas Teferi, Mahlet Tesfaye, David Thomson, Emma Thomson, Alexandra Torborg, Mamadou Mour Traore, Janat Tumukunde, Mpoki Ulisubisya, Dawid van Straaten, Nicola Vickery, Mohyeddine Zarouf, Eugene Zoumenou.

I would like to thank the many colleagues across the APORG network who have educated me and helped me in my thoughts about surgical health in Africa. Thank you to those of you have patiently read, edited, and improved my writing. Thank you to those who made time to chat to correct me when I misunderstood some concepts. My understanding is clearer for your insights.

Rupert Pearse who, through his generosity, opened the door to pragmatic, collaborative work across Africa.

Rupert has shared generously from our first meeting, and is largely responsible for the success of APORG, sharing his work freely with us and providing incredible mentorship. Thank you, Rupert, for mentoring me in the art of telling a simple story. From mentee to colleague, it has been and is a privilege to work with you.

Professor Thandinkosi Madiba, who partnered with me to take the early work across Africa. I will always fondly remember your generous, warm personality. This would never have got off the ground without your humble leadership.

Reitze Rodseth, who walked the early road of research with me, and who educated me in research while I was supposed to be educating him.

To my colleagues who supported the development of the South African Perioperative Research Group (SAPORG) and its growth into APORG. There are many people who opened doors to allow us to work. Christella Alphonsus helped craft the early messaging for the launch of SAPORG. Rob Dyer almost literally dragged every perioperative researcher in South Africa to the first SAPORG meeting, and Christina Lundgren vigorously supported me when surgeons rolled their eyes at the thought of an anaesthetist delivering surgical outcomes research. If Chris had not stood her ground that day, the road we were to travel would have been so much harder. I am grateful to all my surgical colleagues who wholeheartedly supported and collaborated in this work. APORG is now truly multidisciplinary, exemplifying how surgery crosses and strengthens health across the disciplines. The APORG network now includes colleagues in public health, paediatrics, internal medicine, anaesthesia, surgery, obstetrics, critical care, family and rural medicine, quality improvement, government health departments, community activism, and statistics, amongst others. Thank you, all, for making APORG what it is.

Hyla Kluyts had the vision of a data network for surgery across South Africa. She will ultimately far surpass this, with a data network supporting safe surgery and anaesthesia across Africa. Hyla's vision for Safe Surgery SA has facilitated and supported most of our research. Thank you to the South African Society of Anaesthesiologists (SASA), who provided immense support to sustain Safe Surgery SA. Dawid van Straaten was there from the beginning of SSSA. He built all our research and data systems, and we patiently learnt together on how to manage data and communication across Africa. I appreciated your WhatsApps in the middle of the night as you provided another solution to an unexpected data challenge. And now I must thank Hanel Duvenage, who has taken over the reins and continues to drive this research engine forward, with unwavering support from Roz Prinsloo.

Natalie Zimmelman mentored me through my time on the SASA Council, providing invaluable learning in the intersection between medicine, governments, and regulators. Thank you for carving out time every week to chat to me.

Many colleagues walked selflessly with me down this road. Leon du Toit has been amazing and is quite literally a genius. He also gave so much of his time to help navigate the ASOS-2 trial from my office, with hundreds of WhatsApp groups to ensure that all the investigators were on the same page, and that all concerns were timeously and readily addressed. He was ably assisted by the immense work of Ayga Prempeh and Niki Vickery. Tim Stephens taught me about process evaluation and helped lead our understanding of processes and quality of care in Africa.

Kris Schwebler designed our media materials for ASOS-2.

My trial mentors (and virtual educationalists) include PJ Devereaux and Paul Myles. They are icons, selfless and knowledgeable. I am lucky to have had your mentorship, and continued support.

Tinashe Chandauka is always an inspiration to talk to, and has given willingly to our efforts. His work and understanding of patient safety factors is a core component of this book.

The researchers who have supported our perioperative research work locally include Margot Flint, Simphiwe Gumede, Mbale Mbuyisa, Thuli Biyase, and the numerous clinicians who have been the stalwarts of our original research offices in Durban and Cape Town: Christella Alphonsus, Larissa Cronje, Leanne Drummond, Jenna Taylor, Alex Torborg, Kobus Bergh, Estie Cloete, Ettienne Coetzee, Matthew Gibbs, and Marcin Nejthardt. Thank you for the selfless support in the many trials we have participated in.

An amazing group of obstetric legends educated and supported me in obstetric outcomes and strategies to improve maternal outcomes in Africa: Dave Bishop, Rob Dyer, Sue Fawcus, Salome Maswime and Dominque van Dyk. It is a pleasure of working with you every day.

Thank you, Rob Dyer, for your unwavering support, and mentorship from day one in Cape Town. To Salome Maswime, thank you for entrusting me with the research directorate of the Division of Global Surgery at UCT. You are an inspirational leader, and I have learnt a tremendous amount from your ability to lead leaders across multiple disciplines when trying to solve complex problems.

To the friends and colleagues who have willingly supported the APORG vision. Monty Mythen and Mike

Grocott led fundraising from EBPOM to support our work. Thank you to Monty and to John Myburgh for making their way to Cape Town on their own steam to spend a week listening to and discussing our vision for APORG and helping us understand strategies for continental perioperative research in Africa. Monty, and Desiree Chappell of TopMedTalk, have spread the message of APORG's work through their podcasts. Michael Avidan gave us an opportunity to share our research in the United States, and Angela Enright helped us share our message. Zoë Boshoff has mentored me patiently in strategy and organisational growth, which has been so important for APORG.

Thank you, Genevieve Goulding, Rob Packer, and the ANZCA Foundation for supporting APORG's work.

To those in the NIHR Global Health Research Unit on Global Surgery – Dion Morton, Aneel Bhangu, Ewen Harrison, Dmitri Nepogodiev, James Glaseby, Pollyanna Hardy, Matt Soden, Sohini Chakrabortee, Rachel Lillywhite, Divya Kapoor – and the broader network including Adesoji Ademuyiwa, Antonio Ramos, and Dhruv Ghosh, and others: thank you for your support, leadership, education, and inspiration. Your work is heavily cited in this book.

Janet Martin has always had time to listen and advise and support our efforts. To the WFSA and in particular Adrian Gelb, Jannicke Mellin-Olsen, Bisola Obembe, and Wayne Morriss: your advocacy for safe anaesthesia is inspirational. Our Lifebox colleagues Kris Torgeson, Remy Turc, Tito Negussie, Gauri Singh, and Tom Weiser, have always looked out for APORG.

John Meara led the Harvard team in the Program in Global Surgery and Social Change. John is the most humble individual I have ever met, and he graciously shares his knowledge and time. Most of the work in this book is based on the foundational work led by John and his team. I cannot think of a better advocate for safe surgery. Thank you John for always having time to advise and educate me.

Emmanuel Makasa is a force of nature and an inspiration. *Safer Surgery for Africa* is in a better place because of your advocacy. Thank you for always being available to share your knowledge and experience, especially in interacting with governments. If you, the reader, would like to feel the inspiration of Emmanuel, please listen to the fourth podcast in *Earth Cast* season three. Emmanuel really set the NSOAP ball rolling.

Pierre Barker spent countless hours teaching me about quality improvement. His experience and understanding of quality improvement is unparalleled. Thank you for your patience, especially considering how naïve I was, and how much ground you had to cover to get me up to speed. Thank you, too, to the Institute for Health Improvement and the many colleagues I met, learnt from, and have had the privilege to work with as a result.

The team at *The Lancet* stood in our corner and fought bravely to bring our African research work to the international stage: Jocalyn Clark, Zoe Mullin, Naomi Lee, Jessamy Belamy, and Rebekka Park. It is your conviction in our work that has made the world stand up and acknowledge the problems surrounding surgical, anaesthesia, and critical care in Africa. Your advocacy for surgical health in Africa has emboldened us all to dream big and speak up. Thank you.

To our NIHR Global Group on Perioperative and Critical Care, it is exciting to have the opportunity work with all of you and learn from your varying fields of expertise.

Thanks for tolerating my ignorance. It is an honour to be part of this team: Rupert Pearse, Priya Dias, Tim Stephens, Niki Vickery, Fitsum Kifle, Kokeb Desta, Fred Bulamba, Adam Hewitt-Smith, Tim Baker, Karima Khalid, Arthur Kwizera, Hyla Kluyts, Busie Mrara, Gill Bedwell, Rowan Duys, Marian Kinnes, Nowhi Mdayi, Salome Maswime, Marcelle Crowther, Dave Bishop, Rob Dyer, Gill Bedwell, amongst our many other colleagues in the group.

There are numerous other colleagues who have educated me, shaped my thoughts and shared their knowledge across a range of the topics in this book: Lydia Cairncross, Kat Chu, Tim Cook, Larissa Cronje, Gareth Davies, Silke Dyer, Zane Farina, Lionel Green-Thompson, Carl Hillermann, Ivan Joubert, Maia Lesosky, Yannick le Manach, Malcolm Miller, Ramani Moonesinghe, Landon Myer, Ntobeko Ntusi, Ravi Oodit, Romy Parker, Vinicius Caldeira Quintao, Ant Reed, Chris Rout, Karen Sliwa-Hahnle, Martin Smith, Ted Somerville, Richard Spence, and Luciana Stefani. Thank you. I have tried to acknowledge everyone who played a role in my education and understanding necessary for this book, but please forgive me if I have inadvertently not listed your name.

Thank you to my work colleagues who gave me space for research while you were at the coalface saving lives in the operating theatre. Thank you to Dean Gopalan and Justiaan Swanevelder for believing in me and creating an environment that has enabled this work.

Thank you to all my colleagues and family who read early drafts of this book, and had the courage to give me honest feedback. This work is so much better because of you.

Alex Torborg has always been a quiet, honest colleague who kept pushing me when I doubted myself. I am proud to be associated with the amazing work she led in the ASOS-Paeds study. This book would not have seen the light of day had Alex not pushed me and introduced me to Olivia Taylor (@olivia_earth) of *Earth Cast*. Olivia, along with Jeremy Bishop, opened up podcasting to me and helped spread the message of this book. Thank you for selflessly supporting the cause for safe surgery and anaesthesia in Africa. Your podcast work is beautiful. Not one of my colleagues refused the invitation to participate in the episodes, and I thank you all: Sue Fawcus, Agya Prempeh, Nicky Kalafatis, Rupert Pearse, Emmanuel Makasa, John Meara, Lydia Cairncross, Wayne Morriss, Tinashe Chandauka, and Salome Maswime.

Thank you to Professors Pierre Foëx and John Sear, who were my first true academic mentors. Despite my youthful exuberance, you never told me I was wrong. Instead, you opened corridors of knowledge with subtle suggestions of 'maybe you should read this'. To my own readers, thank you for getting this far. I hope I have opened some corridors for you to explore further.

Thank you Lauren Smith, for the wonderful editing that made my messaging concise and clear. Gaelen Pinnock, thank you for taking my words and presenting them beautifully with your design. It has been a pleasure to work with both of you.

Finally, to my family: Penny, Duncan, and Robyn, my mom and dad, and Pete and Lu. Thank you for allowing me to dream. I love you guys.

References

1. Biccard, B.M., Madiba, T.E., Kluyts, H.L., et al. 'Perioperative patient outcomes in the African Surgical Outcomes Study: A 7-day prospective observational cohort study' *The Lancet*, 2018; 391(10130): 1589-98.
2. Bishop, D., Dyer, R.A., Maswime, S., et al. 'Maternal and neonatal outcomes after caesarean delivery in the African Surgical Outcomes Study: A 7-day prospective observational cohort study'. *The Lancet. Global Health* 2019; 7(4): e513-e22.
3. Torborg, A., Meyer, H., Elfiky, M., et al. 'Outcomes after Surgery for Children in Africa: A fourteen-day prospective observational cohort study (ASOS-Paeds)'. *The Lancet* 2023: in press.
4. Fawcus, S., Mbizvo, M.T., Lindmark, G., and Nystrom, L. 'A community based investigation of causes of maternal mortality in rural and urban Zimbabwe. Maternal Mortality Study Group. *The Central African Journal of Medicine* 1995; 41(4): 105-13.
5. Chandauka, T. 'Patient safety culture in South African obstetric theatres'. DPhil thesis,Trinity College, University of Oxford, 2020.
6. 'Ebola virus disease'. WHO, 2020. www.who.int/news-room/fact-sheets/detail/ebola-virus-disease (accessed 11 July 2020).
7. Maternal mortality. Levels and trends 2000 to 2017. 2020. mmr2017.srhr.org/ (accessed 11 July 2020).
8. Hanson, C. 'Data on maternal mortality. Historical information compiled for 14 countries (up to 200 years)'. www.gapminder.org/documentation/documentation/gapdoc010.pdf (accessed 5 April 2020).
9. Högberg, U. and Wall, S. 'Secular trends in maternal mortality in Sweden from 1750 to 1980'. *Bull World Health Organ* 1986; 64(1): 79-84.
10. Marmot, M. 'The health gap: the challenge of an unequal world'. *The Lancet* 2015; 386(10011): 2442-4.
11. Lewis, J. '"Tis a misfortune to be a great ladie": Maternal mortality in the British aristocracy, 1558-1959'. *Journal of British Studies* 1998; 37(1): 26-53.
12. Loudon, I. 'Maternal mortality in the past and its relevance to developing countries today'. *American Journal of Clinical Nutrition* 2000; 72(1 Suppl): 241s-6s.
13. Kerr, R.S. and Weeks, A.D. 'Lessons from 150 years of UK maternal hemorrhage deaths'. *Acta Obstetricia et Gynecologica Scandinavica*, 2015; 94(6): 664-8.

14. Loudon, I. 'Obstetric care, social class, and maternal mortality'. *British Medical Journal (Clinical Research Edition)* 1986; 293(6547): 606–8.
15. 'Effect of early tranexamic acid administration on mortality, hysterectomy, and other morbidities in women with post-partum haemorrhage (WOMAN): An international, randomised, double-blind, placebo-controlled trial'. *The Lancet* 2017; 389(10084): 2105–16.
16. Young, P., Hortis De Smith, V., Chambi, M.C., and Finn, B.C. 'Florence Nightingale (1820-1910), a 101 años de su fallecimiento [Florence Nightingale (1820-1910), 101 years after her death]'. *Revista medica de Chile* 2011; 139(6): 807–13.
17. Neuhauser, D. 'Florence Nightingale gets no respect: As a statistician that is'. *Quality and Safety in Health Care* 2003; 12(4): 317.
18. Fawcus, S.R., Van Coeverden de Groot, H.A., and Isaacs, S. 'A 50-year audit of maternal mortality in the Peninsula Maternal and Neonatal Service, Cape Town (1953-2002). *BJOG: An International Journal of Obstetrics and Gynaecology* 2005; 112(9): 1257–63.
19. Hagberg, C.J. 'The Cape Town Obstetric Flying Squad; its inception, organization and operation'. *South African Medical Journal* 1956; 30(47): 1140–4.
20. Van Coeverden de Groot, H.A. 'Trends in maternal mortality in Cape Town, 1953-1977'. *South African Medical Journal* 1979; 56(14): 547–52.
21. Alkema, L., Chou, D., Hogan, D., et al. 'Global, regional, and national levels and trends in maternal mortality between 1990 and 2015, with scenario-based projections to 2030: A systematic analysis by the UN Maternal Mortality Estimation Inter-Agency Group'. *The Lancet* 2016; 387(10017): 462–74.
22. Pattinson, R.C. 'Safety versus accessibility in maternal and perinatal care'. *South African Medical Journal* 2015; 105(4): 261–5.
23. Hart, J.T. 'The inverse care law'. *The Lancet* 1971; 1(7696): 405–12.
24. 'The L. 50 years of the inverse care law'. *The Lancet* 2021; 397(10276): 767.
25. Kassebaum, N.J., Bertozzi-Villa, A., Coggeshall, M.S., et al. 'Global, regional, and national levels and causes of maternal mortality during 1990-2013: A systematic analysis for the Global Burden of Disease Study 2013'. *The Lancet* 2014; 384(9947): 980–1004.
26. Fawcus, S. and Moodley, J. 'Postpartum haemorhage associated with caesarean section and caesarean hysterectomy'. *Best Practice and Research. Clinical Obstetrics and Gynaecology* 2013; 27(2): 233–49.

27. Molina, G., Weiser, T.G., Lipsitz, S.R., et al. 'Relationship between cesarean delivery rate and maternal and neonatal mortality'. *JAMA* 2015; 314(21): 2263–70.

28. Betran, A.P., Ye, J., Moller, A.B., Zhang, J., Gulmezoglu, A.M. and Torloni, M.R. 'The increasing trend in caesarean section rates: Global, regional and national estimates: 1990–2014. *PLoS One* 2016; 11(2): e0148343.

29. Miller, S. and Belizán, J.M. 'The true cost of maternal death: Individual tragedy impacts family, community and nations. *Reproductive Health* 2015; 12: 56.

30. Mets, B. *Waking Up Safer? An Anesthesiologist's Record.* Bristol, UK: SilverWood Books; 2018.

31. Pearse, R.M., Moreno, R.P., Bauer, P., et al. 'Mortality after surgery in Europe: A 7-day cohort study'. *The Lancet* 2012; 380(9847): 1059–65.

32. Biccard, B.M. and Madiba, T.E., 'South African Surgical Outcomes Study I. The South African Surgical Outcomes Study: A 7-day prospective observational cohort study'. *South African Medical Journal* 2015; 105(6): 465–75.

33. Meara, J.G., Leather, A.J., Hagander, L., et al. 'Global Surgery 2030: Evidence and solutions for achieving health, welfare, and economic development'. *The Lancet* 2015; 386(9993): 569–624.

34. International Surgical Outcomes Study group. Global patient outcomes after elective surgery: prospective cohort study in 27 low-, middle- and high-income countries. *British Journal of Anaesthesia* 2016; 117(5): 601–9.

35. Pinker, S. *Enlightenment Now.* Harlow, England: Penguin Books; 2019.

36. 'Equity vs. equality: What's the difference?' Milken Institute School of Public Health; 2020. https://onlinepublichealth.gwu.edu/resources/equity-vs-equality/ (accessed 1 September 2021).

37. Agyepong, I.A., Sewankambo, N., Binagwaho, A., et al. 'The path to longer and healthier lives for all Africans by 2030: The Lancet Commission on the future of health in sub-Saharan Africa'. *TheLancet* 2017; 390(10114): 2803–59.

38. 38. Nepogodiev, D., Abbott, T.E.F., Ademuyiwa, A.O., et al. 'Projecting COVID-19 disruption to elective surgery'. *The Lancet* 2022; 399(10321): 233–4.

39. GlobalSurg Collaborative. 'Mortality of emergency abdominal surgery in high-, middle- and low-income countries'. *British Journal of Surgery* 2016; 103(8): 971–88.

40. GlobalSurg Collaborative. 'Surgical site infection after gastrointestinal surgery in high-income, middle-income, and low-income countries: a prospective, international, multicentre cohort study. *The Lancet. Infectious Diseases* 2018; 18(5): 516-25.

41. COVIDSurg Collaborative. 'Elective surgery cancellations due to the COVID-19 pandemic: global predictive modelling to inform surgical recovery plans'. *British Journal of Surgery* 2020; 107(11): 1440-9.

42. Reuter, A., Rogge, L., Monahan, M., et al. 'Global economic burden of unmet surgical need for appendicitis'. *British Journal of Surgery* 2022; 109(10): 995-1003.

43. Bedwell, G.J., Dias, P., Hahnle, L., et al. 'Barriers to quality perioperative care delivery in low- and middle-income countries: A qualitative rapid appraisal study'. *Anesthesia and Analgesia* 2022; 135(6): 1217-32.

44. Patel, J., Tolppa, T., Biccard, B.M., et al. 'Perioperative care pathways in low- and lower-middle-income countries: Systematic review and narrative synthesis'. *World Journal of Surgery* 2022; 46(9): 2102-2113.

45. Personal communication with Adam Boutall, colorectal surgeon at Groote Schuur Hospital, Cape Town, South Africa.

46. Ng'ang'a, M. 'Delays in provision of breast cancer care in patients seen at a district hospital diagnostic breast unit in South Africa'. University of Cape Town: University of Cape Town; 2017. https://open.uct.ac.za/items/34bb845e-2bbc-4df9-beab-e8f6b0b59ce4

47. Dickens, C., Joffe, M., Jacobson, J., et al. 'Stage at breast cancer diagnosis and distance from diagnostic hospital in a periurban setting: A South African public hospital case series of over 1,000 women'. *International Journal of Cancer* 2014; 135(9): 2173-82.

48. Hanna, T.P., King, W.D., Thibodeau, S., et al. 'Mortality due to cancer treatment delay: Systematic review and meta-analysis'. *BMJ (Clinical Research Edition)* 2020; 371: m4087.

49. Ouma, P.O., Maina, J., Thuranira, P.N., et al. 'Access to emergency hospital care provided by the public sector in sub-Saharan Africa in 2015: A geocoded inventory and spatial analysis. *The Lancet. Global Health* 2018; 6(3): e342-e50.

50. Unpublished work by Paul Ouma, Emelda Okiro and Bruce Biccard.

51. Adde, H.A., Van Duinen, A.J., Oghogho, M.D., et al. 'Impact of surgical infrastructure and personnel on volume and availability of essential surgical procedures in Liberia'. *BJS Open* 2020; 4(6): 1246-55.

52. Shrime, M.G., Bickler, S.W., Alkire, B.C. and Mock, C. 'Global burden of surgical disease: An estimation from the provider perspective'. *The Lancet. Global Health* 2015; 3 Suppl 2: S8–9.

53. Geleto, A., Chojenta, C., Musa, A. and Loxton, D. 'Barriers to access and utilization of emergency obstetric care at health facilities in sub-Saharan Africa: A systematic review of literature'. *Systematic Reviews* 2018; 7(1): 183.

54. Wariri, O., Onuwabuchi, E., Alhassan, J.A.K., et al. 'The influence of travel time to health facilities on stillbirths: A geospatial case-control analysis of facility-based data in Gombe, Nigeria'. *PLoS One* 2021; 16(1): e0245297.

55. Bishop, D.G., Le Roux, S. 'Anaesthesia for ruptured ectopic pregnancy at district level'. *South African Family Practice: Official Journal of the South African Academy of Family Practice/Primary Care* 2021; 63(1): e1–e5.

56. Personal communication with Desalegn Bekele, Addis Ababa, Ethiopia, 1 May 2022.

57. Debas, H.T., Donkor, P., Gawande, A., Jamison, D.T., Kruk, M.E. and Mock, C.N. (eds). *Essential Surgery: Disease Control Priorities, Third Edition: Volume 1.* Washington, DC: The World Bank; 2015.

58. Mock, C.N., Donkor, P., Gawande, A., Jamison, D.T., Kruk, M.E., and Debas, H.T. 'Essential surgery: Key messages from Disease Control Priorities, 3rd edition'. *The Lancet* 2015; 385(9983): 2209–19.

59. Abbott, T.E.F., Fowler, A.J., Dobbs, T.D., Harrison, E.M., Gillies, M.A. and Pearse, R.M. 'Frequency of surgical treatment and related hospital procedures in the UK: A national ecological study using hospital episode statistics'. *British Journal of Anaesthesia* 2017; 119(2): 249–57.

60. Tefera, A., Lutge, E., Sartorius, B. and Clarke, D. 'The operative output of district hospitals in KwaZulu-Natal Province is heavily skewed toward obstetrical care'. *World Journal of Surgery* 2019; 43(7): 1653–60.

61. 'Projections of mortality and causes of death, 2016 to 2060'. WHO, 22 July 2020. www.who.int/healthinfo/global_burden_disease/projections/en/. (accessed 22 July 2020).

62. Ritchie, H., Roser, M. 'Causes of death'. Our World in Data, 2018. ourworldindata.org/causes-of-death (accessed 21 July 2020).

63. Betran, A.P., Ye, J., Moller, A-B., Souza, J.P. and Zhang, J. 'Trends and projections of caesarean section rates: Global and regional estimates'. *BMJ Global Health* 2021; 6(6): e005671.

64. 'Population data, population ages 0–14 (% of total population) – Sub-Saharan Africa', World Bank, 2019. data.worldbank.org/indicator/SP.POP.0014.TO?locations=ZG (accessed 22 January 2024).

65. Torborg, A., Cronje, L., Thomas, J., et al. 'South African Paediatric Surgical Outcomes Study: A 14-day prospective, observational cohort study of paediatric surgical patients'. *British Journal of Anaesthesia* 2019; 122(2): 224–32.

66. Mullapudi, B., Grabski, D., Ameh, E., et al. 'Estimates of number of children and adolescents without access to surgical care'. *Bulletin of the World Health Organization* 2019; 97(4): 254–8.

67. Harrison, G.G. 'Death due to anaesthesia at Groote Schuur Hospital, Cape Town--1956–1987. Part I. Incidence'. *South African Medical Journal* 1990; 77(8): 412–5.

68. Bainbridge, D., Martin, J., Arango, M. and Cheng, D. 'Perioperative and anaesthetic-related mortality in developed and developing countries: A systematic review and meta-analysis'. *The Lancet* 2012; 380(9847): 1075–81.

69. 'Randomised trial of intravenous atenolol among 16 027 cases of suspected acute myocardial infarction: ISIS-1. First International Study of Infarct Survival Collaborative Group'. *The Lancet* 1986; 2(8498): 57–66.

70. VISION Study investigators. 'Association between complications and death within 30 days after noncardiac surgery'. *Canadian Medical Association Journal* 2019; 191(30): E830–E7.

71. Knight, S.R., Shaw, C.A., Pius, R., et al. 'Global variation in postoperative mortality and complications after cancer surgery: A multicentre, prospective cohort study in 82 countries'. *The Lancet* 2021; 397(10272): 387–97.

72. Paterson, A., Maswime, S., Hardy, A., Pearse, R.M. and Biccard, B.M. 'Postoperative outcomes associated with surgical care for women in Africa: An international risk-adjusted analysis of prospective observational cohorts. *BJA Open* 2022; 4.

73. Langer, A., Meleis, A., Knaul, F.M., et al. 'Women and health: The key for sustainable development'. *The Lancet* 2015; 386(9999): 1165–210.

74. Devereaux, P.J., Chan, M.T., Alonso-Coello, P., et al. 'Association between postoperative troponin levels and 30-day mortality among patients undergoing noncardiac surgery'. *Jama* 2012; 307(21): 2295–304.

75. Habre, W., Disma, N., Virag, K., et al. 'Incidence of severe critical events in paediatric anaesthesia (APRICOT): A prospective multicentre observational study in 261 hospitals in Europe'. *The Lancet. Respiratory Medicine* 2017; 5(5): 412-25.

76. Moroz, L.A., Wright, J.D., Ananth, C.V. and Friedman, A.M. 'Hospital variation in maternal complications following caesarean delivery in the United States: 2006-2012'. *BJOG: An International Journal of Obstetrics and Gynaecology* 2016; 123(7): 1115-20.

77. Botto, F., Alonso-Coello, P., Chan, M.T., et al. 'Myocardial injury after noncardiac surgery: A large, international, prospective cohort study establishing diagnostic criteria, characteristics, predictors, and 30-day outcomes'. *Anesthesiology* 2014; 120(3): 564-78.

78. Donabedian, A. 'The quality of care. How can it be assessed?' *Jama* 1988; 260(12): 1743-8.

79. Cookson, R., Doran, T., Asaria, M., Gupta, I. and Mujica, F.P. 'The inverse care law re-examined: A global perspective'. *The Lancet* 2021; 397(10276): 828-38.

80. Rout, C.C. and Farina, Z. 'Anaesthesia-related maternal deaths in South Africa Chapter Seven of the 5th Saving Mothers Report 2008-2010'. *South African Journal of Anaesthesia and Analgesia* 2012; 18(6): 281-301.

81. Kruk, M.E., Gage, A.D., Arsenault, C., et al. 'High-quality health systems in the Sustainable Development Goals era: Time for a revolution'. *The Lancet. Global Health* 2018; 6(11): e1196-e252.

82. Biccard, B.M. and APORG working group. 'Priorities for peri-operative research in Africa'. *Anaesthesia* 2020; 75(Suppl 1): e28-e33.

83. Nepogodiev, D., Martin, J., Biccard, B., Makupe, A. and Bhangu, A., and the National Institute for Health Research Global Health Research Unit on Global Surgery. 'Global burden of postoperative death'. *The Lancet* 2019; 393(10170): 401.

84. Roa, L., Jumbam, D.T., Makasa, E. and Meara, J.G. 'Global surgery and the sustainable development goals'. *British Journal of Surgery* 2019; 106(2): e44-e52.

85. Alkire, B.C., Raykar, N.P., Shrime, M.G., et al. 'Global access to surgical care: a modelling study'. *The Lancet. Global Health* 2015; 3(6): e316-23.

86. Kluyts, H.L., Le Manach, Y., Munlemvo, D.M., et al. 'The ASOS Surgical Risk Calculator: Development and validation of a tool for identifying African surgical patients at risk of severe postoperative complications'. *British Journal of Anaesthesia* 2018; 121(6): 1357-63.

87. Biccard, B.M., Du Toit, L., Lesosky, M., et al. 'Enhanced postoperative surveillance versus standard of care to reduce mortality among adult surgical patients in Africa (ASOS-2): A cluster-randomised controlled trial'. *The Lance., Global Health* 2021; 9(10): e1391–e401.

88. Peden, C.J., Stephens, T., Martin, G., et al. 'Effectiveness of a national quality improvement programme to improve survival after emergency abdominal surgery (EPOCH): A stepped-wedge cluster-randomised trial'. *The Lancet* 2019; 393(10187): 2213–21.

89. Vickery, N., Stephens, T., Du Toit, L., et al. 'Understanding the performance of a pan-African intervention to reduce postoperative mortality: A mixed-methods process evaluation of the ASOS-2 trial'. *British Journal of Anaesthesia* 2021; 127(5): 778–88.

90. Bate, P., Mendel, P. and Robert, G. *Organizing for Quality: The Improvement Journeys of Leading Hospitals in Europe and the United States*. Oxford, UK: Radcliffe Publishing; 2008.

91. Vincent, C. 'How to improve patient safety in surgery'. *Journal of Health Services Research and Policy* 2010; 15(Suppl 1): 40–3.

92. Schein, E.H. 'Organization culture: A dynamic model'. Sloan School of Management, MIT, 1983. dspace.mit.edu/bitstream/handle/1721.1/48689/organizationalcu00sche.pdf?seq (accessed 14 December 2021).

93. Perlo, J., Balik, B., Swensen, S., Kabcenell, A., Landsman, J. and Feeley, D. *IHI framework for improving joy in work. IHI White Paper*, 2017. ihi.org/resources/white-papers/ihi-framework-improving-joy-work (accessed 22 January 2024).

94. Conradie, A., Duys, R., Forget, P. and Biccard, B.M. 'Barriers to clinical research in Africa: A quantitative and qualitative survey of clinical researchers in 27 African countries'. *British Journal of Anaesthesia* 2018; 121(4): 813–21.

95. COVIDSurg Collaborative and GlobalSurg Collaborative. 'Timing of surgery following SARS-CoV-2 infection: An international prospective cohort study'. *Anaesthesia* 2021; 76(6): 748–58.

96. Biccard, B.M., Duys, R.A., Nejhardt M.B. and Kluyts, H.L. 'It is time for Africa to lead the way in pragmatic clinical trials' *South African Journal of Anaesthesia and Analgesia* 2018; 24(1): 3.

97. Kalafatis, N.A. 'Fitness for purpose of South African anaesthesiologists'. PhD thesis, University of KwaZulu-Natal; 2021.

98. Kalafatis, N.A., Somerville, T. and Gopalan, P.D. 'Defining fitness for purpose in South African anaesthesiologists using a Delphi technique to assess the CanMEDS framework'. *South African Journal of Anaesthesia and Analgesia* 2019; 25(2): 14-23.

99. Pérezts, M., Russon, J-A. and Painter, M. 'This time from Africa: Developing a relational approach to values-driven leadership'. *Journal of Business Ethics* 2020; 161(4): 731-48.

100. Johnston, M.J., Arora, S., King, D., et al. 'A systematic review to identify the factors that affect failure to rescue and escalation of care in surgery'. *Surgery* 2015; 157(4): 752-63.

101. APORG Caesarean Delivery Haemorrhage Group. 'Identifying interventions to reduce peripartum haemorrhage associated with caesarean delivery in Africa: A Delphi consensus study'. *PLOS Global Public Health* 2022; 2(8): e0000455.

102. Gladwell, M. *Outliers: The Story of Success.* New York: Little, Brown and Company; 2008.

103. Zampieri, F.G., Salluh, J.I.F., Azevedo, L.C.P., et al. 'ICU staffing feature phenotypes and their relationship with patients' outcomes: An unsupervised machine learning analysis'. *Intensive Care Medicine* 2019; 45(11): 1599-607.

104. Gawande, A. *The Checklist Manifesto: How to Get Things Right.* New York: Metropolitan Books; 2010.

105. Haynes, A.B., Weiser, T.G., Berry, W.R., et al. 'A surgical safety checklist to reduce morbidity and mortality in a global population'. *New England Journal of Medicine* 2009; 360(5): 491-9.

106. Abbott, T.E.F., Ahmad, T., Phull, M.K., et al. 'The surgical safety checklist and patient outcomes after surgery: A prospective observational cohort study, systematic review and meta-analysis'. *British Journal of Anaesthesia* 2018; 120(1): 146-55.

107. Biccard, B.M., Rodseth, R., Cronje, L., et al. 'A meta-analysis of the efficacy of preoperative surgical safety checklists to improve perioperative outcomes'. *South African Medical Journal* 2016; 106(6): 592-7.

108. Stephens, T.J., Peden, C.J., Pearse, R.M., et al. 'Improving care at scale: Process evaluation of a multi-component quality improvement intervention to reduce mortality after emergency abdominal surgery (EPOCH trial)'. *Implementation Science* 2018; 13(1): 142.

109. Heath, K., Levi, J. and Hill, A. 'The Joint United Nations Programme on HIV/AIDS 95-95-95 targets: Worldwide clinical and cost benefits of generic manufacture'. *AIDS* 2021; 35(Supplement 2): S197-S203.

110. Rowe, A.K., Rowe, S.Y., Peters, D.H., Holloway, K.A., Chalker, J. and Ross-Degnan, D. 'Effectiveness of strategies to improve health-care provider practices in low-income and middle-income countries: A systematic review'. *The Lancet. Global Health* 2018; 6(11): e1163–e75.

111. Ljungqvist, O., De Boer, H.D., Balfour, A., et al. 'Opportunities and challenges for the next phase of enhanced recovery after surgery: A review'. *JAMA Surgery* 2021; 156(8): 775–84.

112. Gustafsson, U.O., Hausel, J., Thorell, A., Ljungqvist, O., Soop, M. and Nygren, J. 'Adherence to the enhanced recovery after surgery protocol and outcomes after colorectal cancer surgery'. *Archives of Surgery* 2011; 146(5): 571–7.

113. Alidina, S., Menon, G., Staffa, S.J., et al. 'Outcomes of a multicomponent safe surgery intervention in Tanzania's Lake Zone: A prospective, longitudinal study'. *International Journal for Quality in Health Care* 2021; 33(2).

114. Alidina, S., Kuchukhidze, S., Menon, G., et al. 'Effectiveness of a multicomponent safe surgery intervention on improving surgical quality in Tanzania's Lake Zone: Protocol for a quasi-experimental study'. *BMJ Open* 2019; 9(10): e031800.

115. Wurdeman, T., Staffa, S.J., Barash, D., et al. 'Surgical safety checklist use and post-caesarean sepsis in the Lake Zone of Tanzania: Results from Safe Surgery 2020'. *World Journal of Surgery* 2021.

116. Forrester, J.A., Starr, N., Negussie, T., et al. 'Clean Cut (adaptive, multimodal surgical infection prevention programme) for low-resource settings: A prospective quality improvement study'. *British Journal of Surgery* 2021; 108(6): 727–34.

117. Allegranzi, B., Aiken, A.M., Zeynep Kubilay, N., et al. 'A multimodal infection control and patient safety intervention to reduce surgical site infections in Africa: A multicentre, before-after, cohort study'. *The Lancet. Infectious Diseases* 2018; 18(5): 507–15.

118. Abate, S.M., Chekole, Y.A., Minaye, S.Y. and Basu, B. 'Global prevalence and reasons for case cancellation on the intended day of surgery: A systematic review and meta-analysis'. *International Journal of Surgery Open* 2020; 26: 55–63.

119. Komashie, A., Ward, J., Bashford, T., et al. 'Systems approach to health service design, delivery and improvement: A systematic review and meta-analysis'. *BMJ Open* 2021; 11(1): e037667.

120. Epiu, I., Tindimwebwa, J.V., Mijumbi, C., et al. 'Challenges of anesthesia in low- and middle-income countries: A cross-sectional survey of access to safe obstetric anesthesia in East Africa'. *Anesthesia and Analgesia* 2017; 124(1): 290–9.
121. Burke, T.F., Suarez, S., Sessler, D.I., et al. 'Safety and feasibility of a ketamine package to support emergency and essential surgery in Kenya when no anesthetist is available: An analysis of 1216 consecutive operative procedures'. *World Journal of Surgery* 2017; 41(12): 2990–7.
122. Phelan, H. and Johnson, T. 'Acute pain management and perioperative drugs used in low-resource settings'. *Anaesthesia and Intensive Care Medicine* 2019; 20(9): 522–5.
123. Craven, R. 'Ketamine'. *Anaesthesia* 2007; 62(Suppl 1): 48–53.
124. Litswa, L. 'Safety and feasibility of a ketamine package to support emergency and essential surgery in Kenya when no anaesthetist is available'. *World Journal of Surgery* 2018; 42(9): 3044–5.
125. WHO, UNFPA and UNICEF (eds). *Managing Complications in Pregnancy and Childbirth: A Guide for Midwives and Doctors*, Second Edition. WHO; 2017.
126. Van der Merwe, F., Vickery, N.J., Kluyts, H.L., et al. 'Postoperative outcomes associated with procedural sedation conducted by physician and nonphysician anesthesia providers: Findings from the prospective, observational African Surgical Outcomes Study'. *Anesthesia and Analgesia* 2022; 135(2): 250–63.
127. Personal communication with Isabeau Walker, British anaesthetist, London, United Kingdom, May 2020.
128. Delisle, M., Pradarelli, J.C., Panda, N., et al. 'Variation in global uptake of the Surgical Safety Checklist'. *The British Journal of Surgery* 2020; 107(2): e151–e60.
129. Lilaonitkul, M., Kwikiriza, A., Ttendo, S., et al. 'Implementation of the WHO Surgical Safety Checklist and surgical swab and instrument counts at a regional referral hospital in Uganda – a quality improvement project'. *Anaesthesia* 2015; 70(12): 1345–55.
130. 'Strengthening emergency and essential surgical care and anaesthesia as a component of universal health coverage'. World Health Assembly; 2015.
131. *National Surgical, Obstetric and Anaesthesia Planning Manual: 2020 Edition*. Geneva: United Nations Institute for Training and Research; 2020.

132. Rose, J., Chang, D.C., Weiser, T.G., Kassebaum, N.J. and Bickler, S.W. 'The role of surgery in global health: Analysis of United States inpatient procedure frequency by condition using the Global Burden of Disease 2010 framework'. *PLoS One* 2014; 9(2): e89693.

133. Sonderman, K.A., Citron, I., Mukhopadhyay, S., et al. 'Framework for developing a national surgical, obstetric and anaesthesia plan'. *BJS Open* 2019; 3(5): 722-32.

134. Truché, P., Shoman, H., Reddy, C.L., et al. 'Globalization of national surgical, obstetric and anesthesia plans: The critical link between health policy and action in global surgery'. *Global Health* 2020; 16(1): 1.

135. Personal communication with Dr Bezaye Zemed, Addis Ababa, Ethiopia, January 2022.

136. Davies, J.I., Gelb, A.W., Gore-Booth, J., et al. 'Global surgery, obstetric, and anaesthesia indicator definitions and reporting: An Utstein consensus report'. *PLoS Med* 2021; 18(8): e1003749.

137. Citron, I., Jumbam, D., Dahm, J., et al. 'Towards equitable surgical systems: Development and outcomes of a national surgical, obstetric and anaesthesia plan in Tanzania'. *BMJ Global Health* 2019; 4(2): e001282.

138. Kifle, F., Belihu, K.D., Beljege, B.Z., et al. 'Perioperative care capacity in East Africa: Results of an Ethiopian national cross-sectional survey'. *IJS Global Health* 2021; 4(3).

139. 'Integrated emergency, critical and operative care for universal health coverage and protection from health emergencies'. WHO; 2023. apps.who.int/gb/ebwha/pdf_files/EB152/B152(3)-en.pdf (accessed 22 January 2024).

140. Leslie, H.H., Sun, Z. and Kruk, M.E. 'Association between infrastructure and observed quality of care in 4 healthcare services: A cross-sectional study of 4,300 facilities in 8 countries'. *PLoS Medicine* 2017; 14(12): e1002464.

141. Samuel, J.P. and Reed, A. 'The costing of operating theatre time in a secondary-level state sector hospital: A quantitative observational study'. *South African Medical Journal* 2021; 111(6): 595-600.

142. Childers, C.P. and Maggard-Gibbons, M. 'Understanding costs of care in the operating room. *JAMA Surgery* 2018; 153(4): e176233-e.

143. 'A review of maternal deaths in South Africa during 1998. National Committee on Confidential Enquiries into Maternal Deaths'. *South African Medical Journal* 2000; 90(4): 367-73.

144. Moodley, J., Fawcus, S. and Pattinson, R. '21 years of confidential enquiries into maternal deaths in South Africa: Reflections on maternal death assessments'. *Obstetrics and Gynaecology Forum* 2020; 30(4): 4–7.

145. Jayakody, H. and Knight, M. 'Implementation assessment in confidential enquiry programmes: A scoping review'. *Paediatric and Perinatal Epidemiology* 2020; 34(4): 399–407.

146. Leslie, H.H., Gage, A., Nsona, H., Hirschhorn, L.R. and Kruk, M.E. 'Training and supervision did not meaningfully improve quality of care for pregnant women or sick children in sub-Saharan Africa'. *Health Affairs (Millwood)* 2016; 35(9): 1716–24.

147. Pattinson, R.C., Bergh, A.M., Ameh, C., et al. 'Reducing maternal deaths by skills-and-drills training in managing obstetric emergencies: A before-and-after observational study'. *South African Medical Journal* 2019; 109(4): 241–5.

148. 'Population by age group, World'. Our World in Data; 2021. ourworldindata.org/grapher/world-population-and-projected-growth-to-2100-by-age-group-young-vs-working-age?country=~OWID_WRL (accessed 22 January 2024)

149. Kempthorne, P., Morriss, W.W., Mellin-Olsen, J. and Gore-Booth, J. 'The WFSA Global Anesthesia Workforce Survey'. *Anesthesia and Analgesia* 2017; 125(3): 981–90.

150. World Anaesthesiology Workforce Map. WFSA; 2021. wfsahq.org/resources/workforce-map/ (accessed 5 March 2021).

151. Davies, J.I., Vreede, E., Onajin-Obembe, B. and Morriss, W.W. 'What is the minimum number of specialist anaesthetists needed in low-income and middle-income countries?' *BMJ Global Health* 2018; 3(6): e001005.

152. Morriss W, Ottaway A, Milenovic M, et al. 'A global anesthesia training framework'. *Anesthesia and Analgesia* 2019; 128(2): 383–7.

153. LeBrun, D.G., Chackungal, S., Chao, T.E., et al. 'Prioritizing essential surgery and safe anesthesia for the Post-2015 Development Agenda: Operative capacities of 78 district hospitals in 7 low- and middle-income countries'. *Surgery* 2014; 155(3): 365–73.

154. Gelb, A.W., Morriss, W.W., Johnson, W., et al. 'World Health Organization–World Federation of Societies of Anaesthesiologists (WHO–WFSA) International Standards for a Safe Practice of Anesthesia'. *Anesthesia and Analgesia* 2018; 126(6): 2047–55.

155. Biccard, B.M., Gopalan, P.D., Miller, M., et al. 'Patient care and clinical outcomes for patients with COVID-19 infection admitted to African high-care or intensive care units (ACCCOS): A multicentre, prospective, observational cohort study'. *The Lancet* 2021; 397(10288): 1885-94.

156. Boyd, N., Sharkey, E., Nabukenya, M., et al. 'The Safer Anaesthesia from Education (SAFE)® paediatric anaesthesia course: Educational impact in five countries in East and Central Africa'. *Anaesthesia* 2019; 74(10): 1290-7.

157. Fagan, J.J., Otiti, J., Aswani, J., et al. 'African head and neck fellowships: A model for a sustainable impact on head and neck cancer care in developing countries'. *Head and Neck* 2019; 41(6): 1824-9.

158. Personal communication with Melesse Geneyehu, Addis Ababa, Ethiopia, 1 May 2022.

159. Fagan, J.J. 'Open access publishing of textbooks and guidelines for otolaryngologists in developing countries'. *OTO Open* 2019; 3(3): 2473974x19861567.

160. Larsson, J. 'Monitoring the anaesthetist in the operating theatre – professional competence and patient safety'. *Anaesthesia* 2017; 72(Suppl 1): 76-83.

161. Dony, P., Seidel, L., Pirson, M. and Forget, P. 'Anaesthesia care team improves outcomes in surgical patients compared with solo anaesthesiologist: An observational study'. *European Journal of Anaesthesiology* 2019; 36(1): 64-9.

162. Hodges, S.C., Mijumbi, C., Okello, M., McCormick, B.A., Walker, I.A. and Wilson, I.H. 'Anaesthesia services in developing countries: Defining the problems'. *Anaesthesia* 2007; 62(1): 4-11.

163. Naidu, P. and Chu, K.M. 'District hospital surgical capacity in Western Cape Province, South Africa: A cross-sectional survey'. *South African Medical Journal* 2021; 111(4): 343-9.

164. Personal communication with Professor Steve Reid, professor of Primary Health Care, University of Cape Town, South Africa, 4 May 2021.

165. Fagan, J.J., Zafereo, M., Aswani, J., Netterville, J.L. and Koch, W. 'Head and neck surgical subspecialty training in Africa: Sustainable models to improve cancer care in developing countries. *Head and Neck* 2017; 39(3): 605-11.

166. Chu, K., Naidu, P., Reid, S., et al. 'The role of family physicians in emergency and essential surgical care in the district health system in South Africa'. *South African Family Practice: Official Journal of the South African Academy of Family Practice/Primary Care* 2020; 62(1), e1-e3.

167. Chu, K. and Weiser, T.G. 'Cold steel might cure, but it takes a village to prevent surgical infections'. *The Lancet. Infectious diseases* 2018; 18(5): 476–7.

168. 'Utstein Abbey'. Wikipedia. en.wikipedia.org/wiki/Utstein_Abbey. (accessed 9 October 2021).

169. Tjomsland, N., Baskett, P. and Asmund, S. 'Laerdal'. *Resuscitation* 2002; 53(2): 115–9.

170. Cheng, A., Lockey, A., Bhanji, F., Lin, Y., Hunt, E.A., and Lang, E. 'The use of high-fidelity manikins for advanced life support training – A systematic review and meta-analysis. *Resuscitation* 2015; 93: 142–9.

171. Finan, E., Bismilla, Z., Whyte, H.E., LeBlanc, V. and McNamara, P.J. 'High-fidelity simulator technology may not be superior to traditional low-fidelity equipment for neonatal resuscitation training'. *Journal of Perinatology* 2012; 32(4): 287–92.

172. Nimbalkar, A., Patel, D., Kungwani, A., Phatak, A., Vasa, R. and Nimbalkar, S. 'Randomized control trial of high fidelity vs low fidelity simulation for training undergraduate students in neonatal resuscitation'. *BMC Research Notes* 2015; 8: 636.

173. Craig, P., Dieppe, P., Macintyre, S., Michie, S., Nazareth, I. and Petticrew, M. 'Developing and evaluating complex interventions: The new Medical Research Council guidance'. *BMJ* 2008; 337: a1655.

174. Blencowe, N.S., Brown, J.M., Cook, J.A., et al. 'Interventions in randomised controlled trials in surgery: Issues to consider during trial design'. *Trials* 2015; 16: 392.

175. 'Global reference list of 100 core health indicators, 2015'. WHO; 2015. www.who.int/healthinfo/indicators/2015/metadata/en/. accessed 22 July 2020).

176. Personal communication with Emi Suzuki, demographer at The World Bank, Norway, June 2019.

177. Kamali, P., Marks, I., Sama, G., Vervoort, D. and Davies, J. 'Measuring surgical systems worldwide: An update'. The World Bank; 2018 blogsworldbankorg/opendata/measuring-surgical-systems-worldwide-update (accessed 22 July 2020).

178. 'Universal Health Coverage'. WHO; 2021. www.who.int/healthsystems/universal_health_coverage/en/ (accessed 4 May 2021).

179. Schäferhoff, M., Martinez, S., Ogbuoji, O., Sabin, M.L. and Yamey, G. 'Trends in global health financing'. *BMJ* 2019; 365: l2185.

180. Watkins, D.A., Yamey, G., Schäferhoff, M., et al. 'Alma-Ata at 40 years: Reflections from the Lancet Commission on Investing in Health'. *The Lancet* 2018; 392(10156): 1434–60.

181. Watkins, D.A., Qi, J., Kawakatsu, Y., Pickersgill, S.J., Horton, S.E. and Jamison, D.T. 'Resource requirements for essential universal health coverage: A modelling study based on findings from *Disease Control Priorities*, 3rd edition'. *The Lancet. Global Health* 2020; 8(6): e829–e39.

182. 'Global spending on health: Weathering the storm'. WHO; 2020.

183. 'Financing global health'. Institute for Health Metrics and Evaluations; 2020. vizhub.healthdata.org/fgh/ (accessed 13 July 2020).

184. The World Bank Data. data.worldbank.org/country/XM (accessed 15 August 2021).

185. Vollset, S.E., Goren, E., Yuan, C.W., et al. 'Fertility, mortality, migration, and population scenarios for 195 countries and territories from 2017 to 2100: A forecasting analysis for the Global Burden of Disease Study'. *The Lancet* 2020; 396(10258): 1285–306.

186. Mathers, C.D. and Loncar, D. 'Projections of global mortality and burden of disease from 2002 to 2030'. *PLoS Medicine* 2006; 3(11): e442.

187. Gouda, H.N., Charlson, F., Sorsdahl, K., et al. 'Burden of non-communicable diseases in sub-Saharan Africa, 1990–2017: Results from the Global Burden of Disease Study 2017'. *The Lancet. Global Health* 2019; 7(10): e1375–e87.

188. Bollyky, T.J., Templin, T., Cohen, M. and Dieleman, J.L. 'Lower-income countries that face the most rapid shift in noncommunicable disease burden are also the least prepared'. *Health Affairs (Millwood)* 2017; 36(11): 1866–75.

189. Bukhman, G., Mocumbi, A.O., Atun, R., et al. 'The Lancet NCDI Poverty Commission: Bridging a gap in universal health coverage for the poorest billion'. *The Lancet* 2020; 396(10256): 991–1044.

190. Christie, S.A., Nwomeh, B.C., Krishnaswami, S., et al. 'Strengthening surgery strengthens health systems: A new paradigm and potential pathway for horizontal development in low- and middle-income countries'. *World Journal of Surgery* 2019; 43(3): 736–43.

191. Stenberg, K., Hanssen, O., Edejer, T.T., et al. 'Financing transformative health systems towards achievement of the health Sustainable Development Goals: A model for projected resource needs in 67 low-income and middle-income countries'. *The Lancet Global Health* 2017; 5(9): e875–e87.

192. Wasserman, I., Peters, A.W., Roa, L., Amanullah, F. and Samad, L. 'Breaking specialty silos: Improving global child health through essential surgical care'. *Global Health, Science and Practice* 2020; 8(2): 183–9.

193. 'Disease control priorities cost model'. dcp-uw.shinyapps.io/dcp-cm/ (accessed 15 September 2021).

194. 'Global health expenditure database'. WHO. apps.who.int/nha/database (accessed 4 March 2021).

195. 'List of development aid country donors'. Wikipedia. en.wikipedia.org/wiki/List_of_development_aid_country_donors (accessed 15 September 2021).

196. Marmot, M. 'Lower taxes or greater health equity'. *The Lancet* 2022; 400(10349): 352–3.

197. Brinkley, J. 'National leaders go abroad when they get sick'. *Newsday* 2012. www.newsday.com/opinion/commentary/national-leaders-go-abroad-when-they-get-sick-joel-brinkleyh-y24424.

198. Liedong, T.A. 'African politicians seeking medical help abroad is shameful, and harms health care'. *The Conversation*, 24 August 2017. theconversation.com/african-politicians-seeking-medical-help-abroad-is-shameful-and-harms-health-care-82771.

199. 'List of countries by tax revenue to GDP ratio'. Wikipedia. en.wikipedia.org/wiki/List_of_countries_by_tax_revenue_to_GDP_ratio (accessed 22 January 2024).

200. Shawar, Y.R., Shiffman, J. and Spiegel, D.A. 'Generation of political priority for global surgery: A qualitative policy analysis'. *The Lancet. Global Health* 2015; 3(8): e487–e95.

201. Shiffman, J. and Smith, S. 'Generation of political priority for global health initiatives: A framework and case study of maternal mortality'. *The Lancet* 2007; 370(9595): 1370–9.

202. Greenhalgh, T. *How to Implement Evidence-Based Healthcare.* Oxford, UK: Wiley Blackwell; 2017.

203. Biccard, B.M., Alphonsus, C.S., Bishop, D.G., et al. 'National priorities for perioperative research in South Africa'. *South African Medical Journal* 2016; (5): 485–8.

204. Kifle, F., Boru, Y., Tamiru, H.D., et al. 'Intensive care in sub-Saharan Africa: A national review of the service status in Ethiopia. *Anesthesia and Analgesia* 2022; 134(5): 930–7.

205. Biccard, B.M., Baker, T., Mabedi, D. and Waweru-Siika, W. 'The state of critical care provision in low-resource environments'. *Anesthesia and Analgesia* 2022; 134(5): 926–9.

206. McCreedy, A., Wacker, J., Ffrench-O'Carroll, R., Berthelsen, K.G., Kremeňova Tatičová, Z. and Smith, A.F. 'Patient safety practices in European anaesthesiology: Expert evaluation and ranking'. *European Journal of Anaesthesiology* 2023; 40(2): 113–20.

207. Romanello, M., McGushin, A., Di Napoli, C., et al. 'The 2021 report of *The Lancet* Countdown on health and climate change: Code red for a healthy future'. *The Lancet* 2021; 398(10311): 1619–62.

Index

A

actor power 240

advocacy 99, 153, 189, 209, 210, 211, 235, 239, 253, 262

Africa 09, 11, 17, 20, 23, 34, 38, 39, 40, 42, 43, 44, 45, 46, 47, 48, 49, 50, 53, 54, 55, 57, 61, 62, 64, 65, 66, 67, 69, 70, 73, 75, 76, 79, 81, 82, 83, 86, 87, 88, 89, 90, 93, 94, 97, 98, 104, 110, 112, 115, 119, 120, 125, 136, 137, 138, 146, 147, 154, 156, 157, 159, 161, 165, 167, 168, 173, 178, 180, 181, 182, 183, 189, 192, 193, 200, 205, 206, 207, 214, 218, 222, 225, 227, 228, 231, 238, 239, 245, 247, 253, 257, 262

African Perioperative Research Group
– APORG 88, 114, 249

APRICOT study 76

ASOS
– African Surgical Outcomes Study 43, 44, 55, 62, 76, 87, 88, 89, 97, 104, 110, 111, 114, 162, 207, 249, 250

ASOS-2 87, 88, 90, 92, 93, 97, 100, 103, 104, 106, 107, 108, 110, 114, 115, 116, 118, 121, 125, 126, 128, 130, 131, 136, 142, 185

ASOS-Paeds 76, 160, 175

ASOS Surgical Risk Calculator 89, 90

Association of Anaesthetists of Great Britain and Ireland 178

Atun, Rifat 240

autonomy 102, 119, 121, 122, 123

B

Barker, Pierre 97, 130

Barton, Clara 32, 33

beliefs and values 101, 104, 107, 108, 109, 113, 115, 116, 117, 118, 124

bellwether procedures 62, 64, 186, 188, 194

Botswana 208

budget 137, 138, 139, 154, 156, 189, 207, 225, 228, 230, 231, 262

C

caesarean delivery 09, 24, 29, 35, 36, 37, 38, 39, 40, 41, 42, 44, 46, 48, 52, 57, 62, 64, 73, 74, 75, 79, 81, 82, 86, 87, 88, 104, 119, 120, 134, 166, 171, 181, 184, 187, 205, 206, 222, 228, 248, 249, 251

cancer 42, 53, 54, 56, 62, 63, 64, 65, 67, 72, 151, 206, 227

ceiling effect 103, 137, 141, 163

CEMD
– Confidential Enquiry into Maternal Deaths 15, 32, 34, 60, 164, 212

Chandauka, Tinashe 20, 114, 139, 248, 253

China 156

Chu, Kat 189, 194

Clean Cut 135

co-design 119, 120, 137

collective competency 119, 121, 185, 194, 199

communication 52, 100, 103, 115, 126, 134, 142, 192

context-specific 181, 191, 193

COVID-19 46, 47, 139, 207, 226

Coxcomb charts 32

Crimean War 30

D

Davies, Justine 51
deliverable intervention 102, 131, 137
Democratic Republic of the Congo 61, 62, 65, 91, 174, 189
Devereaux, PJ 68, 69, 106, 126
disease
  – Global Burden of Disease 224
diseases
  – communicable 45, 206, 225, 228
  – non-communicable 206, 222, 224, 225, 228, 230
Donabedian 80, 82, 199
donors 146, 216, 217, 218, 219, 220, 222, 223, 224, 232
Duys, Rowan 97, 104, 197, 198

E

ectopic pregnancy 58, 59, 60
Edendale hospital 78, 79, 80, 170, 171, 184
education 80, 99, 101, 103, 112, 115, 116, 118, 119, 127, 133, 148, 150, 165, 166, 167, 172, 173, 176, 179, 181, 190, 191, 192, 193, 194, 197, 199, 207, 252, 257
enhanced recovery after surgery 132
Epiu, Isabella 146
EPOCH 125, 126, 128, 130, 142
ESM-Ketamine 147, 149
ESMOE
  – Essential Steps in Managing Obstetric Emergencies 166, 180
Ethiopia 61, 135, 155, 157, 178, 258
European Society of Breast Specialists 53
EuSOS
  – European Surgical Outcomes Study 42
evidence-based practice 68, 101, 106, 114, 123, 134, 158, 165, 200, 261

F

Fagan, Johan 182, 183, 192, 193
failure-to-rescue 73, 74, 77, 87, 89, 90, 93, 118, 131, 148
Farina, Zane 80, 85, 186, 187, 188, 190
Fawcus, Sue 15, 16, 35, 36, 40, 52, 139, 164, 168, 251
fidelity 102, 126, 127, 128, 129, 130, 131, 132, 134, 135, 136, 142, 178, 197, 198, 199, 201
funding 10, 51, 110, 177, 214, 215, 217, 218, 219, 220, 222, 223, 227, 229, 231, 233, 235, 236, 237

G

Gabon 238
Ghana 71
Gladwell, Malcolm 122
Global Surgery Foundation 236, 241
golden hour 102, 123
Groote Schuur Hospital 53, 68, 139, 163, 168
gross domestic product 50, 227, 231, 239
guidelines 61, 120, 146, 181, 183, 191, 193
Guyatt, Gordon 68

H

haemorrhage 18, 21, 23, 33, 38, 58, 74, 75, 119, 120, 166, 167, 181, 187, 249
Harrison, Gaisford 68, 69
Hart, Tudor 36
health equity 10, 11, 43, 44, 46, 94, 154, 223, 225, 231
health system strengthening 219, 247, 249, 250, 253
hepatitis B 206
hierarchy 115, 121, 194, 257
HIV

Photo © Llewellyn Lloyd

Bruce Biccard is professor and second chair in the Department of Anaesthesia and Perioperative Medicine at Groote Schuur Hospital and the University of Cape Town, South Africa. His research is focused on making surgery safer for all, through an understanding of surgical complications and what can be done to manage them. He conducts large international collaborative research, particularly on the African continent, working with the African Perioperative Research Group (APORG). This research network has over 2000 clinician researchers and spans more than 40 African countries. They have conducted acclaimed research, including the African Surgical Outcomes Study (ASOS), the ASOS-2 Trial, the African Covid-19 Critical Care Outcomes Study (ACCCOS) and the African Paediatric Surgical Outcomes Study (ASOS-Paeds). He is the co-lead, with Professor Rupert Pearse of Queen Mary University of London, for the UK's National Institute for Health Research (NIHR) Global Health Group on Perioperative and Critical Care. He delivered the eponymous John Snow Lecture for the Royal College of Anaesthetists in 2021. Bruce lives in Cape Town with his wife, Penny, and two children, Duncan and Robyn. He is an avid endurance cyclist.

Made in the USA
Las Vegas, NV
17 April 2024